THE NEW POLITICS OF FINANCING THE UN

The New Politics of Financing the UN

Anthony McDermott
Senior Researcher
International Peace Research Institute
Oslo

First published in Great Britain 2000 by
MACMILLAN PRESS LTD
Houndmills, Basingstoke, Hampshire RG21 6XS and London
Companies and representatives throughout the world

A catalogue record for this book is available from the British Library.

ISBN 0–333–63209–5

First published in the United States of America 2000 by
ST. MARTIN'S PRESS, INC.,
Scholarly and Reference Division,
175 Fifth Avenue, New York, N.Y. 10010

ISBN 0–312–22224–6

Library of Congress Cataloging-in-Publication Data
McDermott, Anthony.
The new politics of financing the UN / Anthony McDermott.
p.   cm.
Includes bibliographical references and index.
ISBN 0–312–22224–6 (cloth)
1. United Nations—Finance.   I. Title.
JZ4976.M39   1999
352.4'2113—dc21   99–23353
                                                                                CIP

This book is printed on paper suitable for recycling and made from fully managed and sustained forest sources.

10   9   8   7   6   5   4   3   2   1
09   08   07   06   05   04   03   02   01   00

Printed and bound in Great Britain by
Antony Rowe Ltd, Chippenham, Wiltshire

Contents

List of Figures

List of Acronyms

ACABQ	Advisory Committee on Administrative and Budgetary Questions
ACC	Administrative Committee on Co-ordination
ASEAN	Association of South East Asian Nations
BAMB	Bureau of Administrative Management and Budget
CIS	Commonwealth of Independent States
CPC	Committee for Programme and Co-ordination
EBF	Extrabudgetary funds
EC	European Community
ECOSOC	Economic and Social Council
ECOWAS	Economic Community of West African States
EU	European Union
FAO	Food and Agriculture Organization
GAO	General Accounting Office
GATT	General Agreement on Tariffs and Trade
GDP	Gross Domestic Product
GNP	Gross National Product
HDI	Human Development Index
IAEA	International Atomic Energy Agency
IBRD	International Bank for Reconstruction and Development (World Bank)
ICAO	International Civil Aviation Organization
ICC	International Chamber of Commerce
ICJ	International Court of Justice
ICRC	International Committee of the Red Cross
IDA	International Development Association
IFAD	International Fund for Agriculture Development
IFC	International Finance Corporation
ILO	International Labour Organization
IMF	International Monetary Fund
IMO	International Maritime Organization
INSTRAW	International Research and Training Institute for the Advancement of Women
ITC	International Trade Centre
ITU	International Telecommunication Union
JIU	Joint Inspection Unit
MFO	Multinational Force and Observers

MIGA	Multilateral Investment Guarantee Agency
MINURCA	UN Mission in the Central African Republic
MINURSO	UN Mission for the Referendum in Western Sahara
MIPONUH	UN Civilian Police Mission in Haiti
MNF	Multinational Force
MONUA	UN Observer Mission in Angola
NATO	North Atlantic Treaty Organization
NGO	Nongovernmental organization
NPT	Non-Proliferation Treaty
OAS	Organization of American States
OAU	Organization of African Unity
OIOS	Office of Internal Oversight Services
ONUC	UN Operation in Congo
OSCE	Organization for Security and Co-operation in Europe
PDD	Presidential Decision Directive
PLO	Palestine Liberation Organization
RCF	Revolving Credit Fund
SWAPO	South-West Africa People's Organization
UN	United Nations
UNAVEM	UN Angola Verification Mission
UNCHS	UN Centre for Human Settlements (Habitat)
UNCTAD	UN Conference on Trade and Development
UNDCP	UN International Drug Control Programme
UNDOF	UN Disengagement Observer Force
UNDP	UN Development Programme
UNEF	UN Emergency Force
UNEP	UN Environment Programme
UNESCO	UN Educational, Scientific and Cultural Organization
UNFICYP	UN Peace-keeping Force in Cyprus
UNFPA	UN Population Fund
UNHCR	Office of the UN High Commissioner for Refugees
UNICEF	UN Children's Fund
UNIDO	UN Industrial Development Organization
UNIFEM	UN Development Fund for Women
UNIFIL	UN Interim Force in Lebanon
UNIKOM	UN Iraq-Kuwait Observation Mission
UNITAR	UN Institute for Training and Research
UNMIBH	UN Mission in Bosnia and Herzegovina
UNMIH	UN Mission in Haiti
UNMOGIP	UN Military Observer Group in India and Pakistan
UNMOP	UN Mission of Observers in Prevlaka

UNMOT	UN Mission of Observers in Tajikistan
UNOMIG	UN Observer Mission in Georgia
UNOMSIL	UN Mission of Observers in Sierra Leone
UNPREDEP	UN Preventive Deployment Force
UNRWA	UN Relief and Works Agency for Palestine Refugees in the Near East
UNSCOB	UN Sub-commission on the Balkans
UNSF	UN Security Force in West New Guinea (West Irian)
UNTAG	UN Transition Assistance Group
UNTSO	UN Truce Supervision Organization
UNU	UN University
UPU	Universal Postal Union
UNYOM	UN Yemen Observation Mission
WCF	Working Capital Fund
WEU	Western European Union
WFP	World Food Programme
WHO	World Health Organization
WIPO	World Intellectual Property Organization
WMO	World Meteorological Organization
WTO	World Trade Organization

Introduction

Any exploration behind the facts and figures of the financing of the United Nations system reveals more about this complex organization than the documented statistics by themselves might suggest. For a start, they can be deceptive in more senses than one. Almost four decades ago, David Singer lamented the lack of detailed and thorough accounts of budgetary questions of the League of Nations, the UN, and their affiliated agencies. He was a forerunner in just such missing studies and wrote: 'It is unfortunate that this is so'. He added the wry thought: 'Not that the fate of the world rides on the United Nations budget, or that matters of peace and war will be determined by the dollars and cents of the Secretary-General's estimates'.[1] How the member states, which number 185 today, help the UN's chief administrator, the secretary-general, through formal and informal meetings and, more often than not, sheer politicking, to reach these estimates is one story that an examination of the UN's finances helps reveal. How the variety of the UN's different budgets arrive at their final public forms is almost always yet another tale.

There is a further complicating factor. It may appear to be comforting to have the UN's operations quantified through figures, graphs and illustrations. But these indicators are often notional at best and, not infrequently, 'economical with the truth' to use the phrase of Sir Robert Armstrong, the then British Cabinet Secretary, before the Supreme Court of New South Wales, Australia. The context of that utterance was very different but its elegant turn has condemned it to frequent usage. More than 30 years after Singer, Klaus Hüfner, a leading statistician and analyst of the UN system, observed of his own writing that:

> To sum up, it might be once more emphasised that there is no 'correct' series of figures; and that this author has not succeeded in preparing the whole material in such a way that it, at the very least, has become a consistent attempt at a reflection of reality. The consolation, though, resides in the fact that every attempt at statistical analysis depends on numerous definitional limitations which are made only partly transparent. The collected series of figures qualify therefore only as 'proxies' for describing reality. They serve as a better orientation for the description of the developments of the UN system and must be always interpreted with the appropriate caution.[2]

This book has been written with these distinguished warnings in mind. They color the broad conclusion that, seen from a historical perspective, the UN's financial system has perforce changed over the years. But this must be heavily qualified because the UN, as a whole, would not have survived for more than half a century if one of its most characteristic features had not been the ability to adapt rather than to innovate. The organization has obviously always had to be aware of the global politics of the day. In addition, partly because of the accident of the headquarters being in New York, it has had to be especially mindful, too, of the US, its major contributor of funds and godfather. At the same time, its room for independent maneuver and reform is as bounded as it always has been – by the diversity of its membership. It means, too, that the process of reforms which the Secretary-General, Kofi Annan, announced in July 1997 has proved so far to be less than radical, particularly in the financing sector. In this broader context of UN change through the pressure of circumstances rather than choice, a study of the UN's finances is justified if it sheds light on the policies and often selfish methods used by its member states to enable the system to continue functioning.

My intention behind the chapter headings was to awaken the curiosity of the reader. Chapter 1 gives a broad presentation of the ways in which the UN system has over the years raised its money and of the range of crises it has had to face in this process. In the period after the Cold War, the UN has come under particular scrutiny, and Annan has faced special challenges with the Clinton administration. Chapter 2 reviews the principles of universality and collective responsibility governing the running of a financial system, in which there was neither political nor economic equality. Peace-keeping operations in Sinai and the Congo raise familiar problems. Chapter 3 looks at the history of the whole budgetary system comprising the General Assembly and Security Council, through the Economic and Social Council (ECOSOC) to the largely autonomous specialized agencies, organizations, programs and organs dealing with a wide range of economic, social, development, infrastructural and humanitarian affairs. The main concentration is on the regular budget and the peace-keeping budgets, which incidentally account for only a small portion of the whole UN system's expenditures.

These budgets are examined in detail in Chapter 4 and Chapter 5, with particular emphasis on the complicated and changing system of raising money from the member states through assessed percentage contributions. The sizes of the budgets have been consistently under criticism for being too large. The assessment process has always been a source of controversy.

Chapter 6 is devoted to the crucial role of the US. Washington has been central to the UN from its formulation during the Second World War until today in the post-Cold War era. As the organization's most important provider of funds and simultaneously its largest debtor, the US has had greater influence on the organization's finances than any other country. Despite Washington's disdainful official attitude towards the UN, there continues to be a lively domestic debate about the place of the UN in US foreign policy.

Chapter 7 examines the medley of proposals for alternative methods of raising money to finance the UN. Most suggestions and devices have been around for a long time. They range from international taxes to greater involvement with the private sector. Few have been adopted. In Chapter 8, attention moves to the ways through which the persistent problems with the regular and peace-keeping budgets might be tackled. Reform of the UN system has been proposed and tried at regular intervals since the earliest days – largely without bringing about fundamental changes. The difficult financial situation in 1998 seems to have changed little from previous years.

Chapter 9 traces the developments since the beginning of the decade leading to the latest round of reform initiated in 1997. This had its roots in the changed global political circumstances that followed the ending of the Cold War. The first stages were set in motion during Boutros-Ghali's period in office as secretary-general and promulgated by Kofi Annan, his successor. Chapter 10 concludes that those running the UN's financial system have been remarkably resistant to change despite the challenges of globalization. This is largely a function of the nature of the UN system as an intergovernmental organization representing theoretically the diverse interests of its 185 member states. Above all, no single state would want the UN to develop, even if it were possible, a strength and influence independent of its components. A five-year plan is proposed to stimulate greater interest on the part of the US. Further reforms might make it possible for the UN to break free from its persistent budgetary weaknesses and apparent near-bankruptcy to move with rather than merely react to the changing times.

My active interest in the financing of the UN started during a sabbatical leave at Brown University, Providence, Rhode Island in 1992 and has taken some time to reach this present form. It would not have come to fruition had it not been for assistance and encouragement from many directions and people, notably, in the most recent period from Kim Garval, the Deputy Director of the Information Centre for the Nordic Countries in Copenhagen, and the International Peace Research Institute, Oslo. Anne

C. Kjelling, Head Librarian at the Norwegian Nobel Institute, gave matchless and sustained support and affectionate encouragement way beyond the provision of books, documents, information and advice. The most valuable observations, criticisms and suggestions came, late in the proceedings, from Professor Klaus Hüfner of the Freie Universität Berlin who generously set aside time from a busy schedule for me. T. M. Farmiloe, Macmillan's Publishing Director, was unfailingly patient and understanding. Together they all contributed to the merits this book may contain. Responsibility for errors and deficiencies lies solely and squarely with the author who should have heeded wise counsel and guidance.

Anthony McDermott
Oslo, September 1998

1 The Business of Making Ends Meet

The finances of the United Nations have always been under regular official and popular scrutiny. The tendency has been to judge them in terms of the habits of a skilled but unreformed bankrupt. The recurrent theme in periodic announcements is that the world organization is threatened by bankruptcy, is operating in the red or is switching money between budget accounts to keep itself afloat. In some senses, these terms are not unrealistic. They can be easily associated with the everyday hazards of most people who have to deal with stern bank managers. This constant financial plight of the UN receives little sympathy. To grasp some idea of the complexity of the UN's budgetary systems requires delving into the reports from a myriad of committees, which set figures first and then adjust them later. Finally, after considerable debate, agreement is reached. For the record, there follows a so-called final auditing. These procedures and the figures they produce do not evoke as much popular interest as, say, peace-keeping operations or humanitarian intervention. But those latter activities could hardly take place without the financial calculations behind them. Furthermore, the way these calculations are arrived at and tracing the flow of UN money through the veins of the complicated system is a revealing way of exposing and exploring how the system works.

The system – and here the concentration is on the regular (or program) budget, the peace-keeping budgets and, to a somewhat lesser extent, the budgets of the related specialized and affiliated agencies – has survived with and in spite of its chronic imperfections. If the new era is taken to be from the ending of the Cold War, it has been characterized by two secretaries-general, Boutros Boutros-Ghali and Kofi Annan, undertaking a two-stage exercise in reform to cope with a period, under the former, in which resources were seriously overstretched and then followed by retrenchment. It is and was a period during which the US in its role of the sole super-power was a constantly overbearing factor. It was a period, too, in which globalization became paramount and forced on the UN an awareness that its role had to take account of the fact that a measure of its independence, and perhaps some of its universality, had diminished, particularly where financial resources were concerned. In this it mirrored the experience of most of its component parts – 185 member states.

If there is interest, it often comes in the form of suspicion and doubt. The suspicion stems from the impression that the UN is a vastly opulent concern, operating as it does from a spectacular, sprawling headquarters site in New York on the East River waterfront in Turtle Bay, with other architecturally striking centers in Geneva and Vienna. And were the UN finally in response to countless calls over the years to relocate its headquarters elsewhere, the land, which it was given and occupies would revert to the federal government and not to New York city. It is both home to 185 nations and ultimately homeless. For it should be remembered that the UN is hampered in the end by having no net worth, almost no assets and no capital of its own beyond the political will of its members. Joseph E. Connor, the UN Undersecretary-General for Administration and Management told the High-Level Open-ended Working Group on the Financial Situation of the United Nations on 21 February 1995:

> A last word on our overall financial situation. Some Member States question whether there is indeed a financial crisis. Some Member States and others say that the United Nations has never run out of cash. And that is true. We have not run out of cash. And the way we manage to do so is simply by not paying our bills.[1]

And on the way, the UN seems always to have avoided coming to a complete halt.

Over the fifty or so years of its existence, the constant complaints about impecuniousness and the major contributing countries not paying their dues have taken on the sounds of the shepherd boy in Aesop's fable who would drive his flock some distance from the village and then shout to the villagers for help, saying that wolves were attacking – which they were not. The villagers came to his rescue but came to tire of this joke after a couple of times. His scare mongering finally cost him his flock when the wolves attacked for real, even though he survived. But his credibility had disappeared long before. The UN runs the risk of suffering a similar misfortune. Persistent cries of pennilessness and pecuniary crisis have raised doubts about whether its administration is competent and honest and whether there are not some deeper motives behind its apparent resistance to change and modernization.

The 50th anniversary of the UN's existence predictably stirred up much concerted analysis of its workings, not least about its financial stability. The soul-searching went especially deep as it coincided with another drive at reform and restructuring, the departure of Boutros-Ghali as secretary-general and his replacement, from the beginning of 1997, by Kofi Annan. It was a succession forced through by the US and on the understanding that with Annan would, almost officially, come a new era of reform. The US, as the largest contributor to the UN's assessed and voluntary funds, saw reform in the financial system as a crucial part of a whole program of change.

Finance has been a topic of note and concern from the earliest days – and before. It was during a private meeting at Lake Success on Long Island – one of the temporary homes of the UN before its present headquarters was finally established – in the office of Trygve Lie, the first secretary-general, on the morning of 12 September 1946, that 13 people were gathered to discuss the UN budget.[2] Lie was, according to the record, 'most anxious to make a full estimate of our expenses and at the same time provide a fair estimate for the budget'. At the same meeting it was agreed that 500 cuff links should be ordered, presumably for gifts, at $2 a pair and The Committee of Experts advised that no special cars with chauffeurs should be provided after 15 September. Thereafter, they would have to make use of pool cars. Objections were raised by some of those present. At other meetings, of course, loftier matters, such as the UN's overall costs in the context of the budget were discussed.

But these recorded incidents do raise a substantial perennial issue as to the extent to which core and substantial considerations are discussed. The UN has passed through several cycles of crises, most of which have had as their starting-point political issues. For several decades, they reflected the rivalry between the two superpowers, the United States and the Soviet Union. But Third World disputes, notably in the Middle East, and more recently in Africa and former Yugoslavia have also commanded attention and caused tensions. Since the ending of the Cold War, political crises have been characterized by more local issues, and civil and intrastate wars have become more the norm than cross-border wars between established states. At almost every stage, but in different ways, the UN's financial systems have been severely tested. It has been an established pattern that the UN system has reacted to and changed under the impact of crises, and this is, almost inevitably, built into the nature of the organization. The UN has been consistently criticized for not anticipating or having procedures available to deal with crises. This is most apparent in financial crises and, in the end, for the simple reason that the member states of the UN have always been reluctant to put money aside for theoretical possibilities and this has put the UN's money mechanisms almost always on the defensive.

These mechanisms have suffered from being overloaded. In a memorandum in 1947 from Adrian Pelt, Assistant Secretary-General for Conference and General Services, to Byron Price, Assistant Secretary-General for Administrative and Financial Services,[3] entitled 'Policy Underlying

1948 Budget', Pelt complained that the General Assembly had failed to put ceilings on various programs it had been asked to approve. 'The consequence of this lack of balance between workload and budget are serious,' he wrote. Part could have been put down to inexperience, but this could not be the excuse for the 1948 budget, he argued. Those were the days 'of the present budget practice of quarterly allotments'. It was amazingly cumbersome and though long since dropped, bears some of the lasting traits which persist today in the different procedures for the present biennial budgets. Pelt wrote:

> You should realize the steps necessary to carry through the present procedure and the time of the operating officials which it requires. Budget forms (necessarily quite complicated and difficult to prepare) are completed in pencil or rough form by the section chiefs. Meetings are then held by the division director and a division estimate agreed upon. These division estimates, together with rough draft justifications, are then forwarded to the departmental Executive Officer, and he and his staff assemble them into a rough composite budget estimate for the Department. The Assistant Secretary-General and his top-ranking director must then review carefully and discuss with each division the individual estimates and their justifications. This process must necessarily be thorough and time-consuming. After the general budget and the form of justifications have been agreed upon, the divisions then re-work the forms, have them typed in final form and finalize the justifications. These in turn are forwarded to the Executive Officer for final assembly and preparation of the general budget letter. After final review by the top-ranking director and Assistant Secretary-General, they are forwarded to BAMB [Bureau of Administrative Management and Budget]. The budgets are then analyzed by your staff, which in turn sends investigators to the various divisions and sectors of the organization and holds frequent meetings with division directors and section chiefs. Generally, after this analysis the top-ranking director or the Assistant Secretary-General meets with the Director of BAMB and discusses the budget estimates in detail. After this discussion it is frequently necessary to revise estimates and change the general preparation. When finally ready, the material is submitted to the Advisory Committee, and the Assistant Secretary-General, top-ranking director, and members of their staff appear before the Advisory Committee for several days in defense of the estimates.
>
> After the hearings are completed, the Assistant Secretary-General and/or top-ranking director may in turn appear again before the Fifth Committee. After the budget has been approved by the Fifth Committee

and in turn the General Assembly, the BAMB does *not* allot automatically funds for operation, whether on a proportionate basis or otherwise, but then asks the department to prepare a detailed estimate and justification for the *first* quarterly allotment. The process is then repeated with personal surveys and inquiries by members of the BAMB staff, and generally a month to six weeks expires before the actual money for the first quarter is made available. In the meantime memoranda are continually being written back and forth between the Bureau of the Comptroller and the departments and between the departments and BAMB asking for emergency allotments to pay current bills. After the first quarterly allotments are received it is time to start immediately preparation for the second quarterly allotments, and the process continues throughout the four quarters of the year.

Pelt adds: 'I do not think this is an exaggeration of the actual steps which are now required, and it is certainly, I know, your intention to reduce them and shorten the time required.' He made a plea for '*annual* allotments'.

These days in both crises and day-to-day procedures, the member states and the UN Secretariat – and the UN runs budgets and accounts of several different natures simultaneously – have on the whole been found wanting and tied to the sort of laborious cross-referencing reminiscent of Pelt's account. Time and again, demands have gone forward for reforms to make the different parts of the UN more efficient and less wasteful in its spending methods. There have been changes as the historical narrative intends to show. But the overall impression remains that change and reform in the UN have come about chiefly in reaction to a crisis or changing circumstances. On the whole, it has been chasing to catch up on the events of new political eras. The control and running of its finances have suffered as a result.

There were new hopes at the beginning of 1997. There was the unique confluence of a new secretary-general in Annan and Bill Clinton, the US President, embarking on a second term. As a result, the way might have been open to an unprecedented opportunity to embark on a radical reform of key political and bureaucratic structures. At the same time, this would reopen the issue of the reform of the UN's financial procedures so as to put them on a more durable and secure footing than before. Changes in attitudes towards the role of the UN in the world and all the fields its agencies and organizations work in, together with greater emphasis on efficiency and co-ordination, raised the level of discussion and hopes that the chances of change – at the expense of the more conservative trends which had tended to prevail hitherto – might win the day, not immediately but eventually.

Boutros-Ghali had earlier grasped, not long after he became secretary-general in 1992, that there were new opportunities for the UN in the wake of the Cold War and the emergence of the US as the sole superpower. In his *An Agenda for Peace*, Boutros-Ghali wrote:

> In these past months a conviction has grown, among nations large and small, that an opportunity has been regained to achieve the great objectives of the [UN] Charter – a United Nations capable of maintaining international peace and security, of securing justice and human rights and of promoting, in the words of the Charter, 'social progress and better standards of life in larger freedom'. This opportunity must not be squandered. The Organization must never again be crippled as it was in the era that has now passed.[4]

In other words, the UN might be ripe for reform and change because global perceptions of its position and role were changing. The massive rise in the number of peace-keeping missions undertaken was one reaction. This not only severely overstretched the UN's financial system – amongst other impositions – it also exposed the UN as having a limited capacity to resolve conflicts and cope with the social disruptions caused by wars and fighting. In fairness, Boutros-Ghali was aware of this risk. On 13 May 1992, he said at a National Press Club luncheon in Washington: 'If there is a last difficulty, it is that the United Nations has almost too much credibility now. So the problem is how we can maintain this credibility and not disappoint the Member States and public opinion when they discover that may be we cannot cope with all the problems on which they ask our help.'

In part accurately and in part unfairly, the operations in Bosnia, Somalia and Rwanda were thrown at the UN as examples of its inherent inability to cope and its lack of coherent organization. The reaction was often twofold. On the one hand there was severe questioning of the nature of UN bureaucracy and effectiveness. The stereotypes were painted – bureaucratic wastage, duplication and competition not only between member states and ideologies, which had been a leading characteristic of the past, but also between different agencies and committees within the UN. In many cases these stereotypes were misleading. On financial issues the tensions were often more over issues between the developed, industrialized world of the North and the developing countries of the South than they were directly between the West and East. On internal UN financial matters, the US and the Soviet Union often found common ground and a shared reluctance to contribute unquestioningly to costly programs proposed by the South.

On the other, and linked to the first, there rose a strong body of views which argued that, in keeping with the globalization revolution of communications, financial power and information, the UN, for all its achievements of the previous fifty years, might perhaps not be the most important repository of wisdom, political influence and controller of funds and agencies connected with humanitarian, development and social improvement.

One conclusion from this coming together of factors is questioning of the UN's role as a global association with democratic aspirations towards equal representation of its members. It is an issue which translates itself easily into the troubled area of the funding of the UN, for the methods by which assessed contributions from individual member states are calculated have never been out of controversy. The percentage assessments, which convey both political and financial power but not in equal measure, have been constantly disputed by both the large and the small donors. The continued debate over representation within the UN Security Council that reached a new peak during the 1996–8 period was one indicator that the UN's claims to be a democratic institution were limited. And the debate continued vehemently, in spite of and probably because of the mood of reform set in train by Annan's reforms presented in July 1997.

But within this debate arises also the issue of sovereignty. The argument runs that the UN, through the Charter and its actions, exists to preserve sovereignty. But while Article 2.1 may proclaim that: 'The Organization is based on the principle of the sovereign equality of all its Members', the inviolability of sovereignty has become blurred and almost redefined. Annan put it bluntly in June 1998: 'The Charter protects the sovereignty of peoples. It was never meant as a license for governments to trample on human rights and human dignity. Sovereignty implies responsibility, not just power.'[5] If this has become eroded, and there are many instances where states, as is the case with former Yugoslavia, have dissolved into autonomous components, then also, to some extent, the special nature of the UN has become diminished and changed. This development in the nature of sovereignty spills over into the domain of the financial system with poorer member states complaining that they have to pay a disproportionate size in dues, and, at the other end of the scale, the US passing domestic legislation to reduce the size of the assessments set by the UN.

In addition, the standards with which the UN governs its modes and methods of governance have had to be re-examined and measured against the demands and results of another form of an assault on sovereignty – that of globalization, greater efficiency and professionalism. The criteria set up may have been derided by some as being too dominated by the philosophy of business rather than diplomacy, but there has perhaps been a greater appetite for change – whetted not just by the US, which holds the UN in its thrall through being both the largest contributor of funds and its largest debtor, but also by others such as the European Union and the G-7 group of industrialized states.

There have been financial crises since the earliest days. In the 1980s, during Pérez de Cuéllar's term of office (1982–91), an attempt to put the UN's house in order was made,[6] but it foundered in the end because there was too much established resistance to the business management approach to reforming systems which would have had a direct impact on financial decision-making. This did not mean that all enthusiasm for reform or a sense that it was needed had evaporated thereafter. The US has been reluctant to acknowledge it, but Boutros-Ghali did take measures to set in motion another round of reform. Annan has always acknowledged this. The US falling out with Boutros-Ghali was such that when Annan, with a professional background steeped in more than three decades of service within the UN, paid his first visit as secretary-general to Washington in January 1997, he was hailed as the great would-be reformer. This was, in large part, to celebrate the success of the US campaign to stymie Boutros-Ghali's second term of office. It was unfairly implied that he had been resistant to reform, whereas he had not only started cutting down the UN's complement but had also launched the Efficiency Board in November 1995 and begun executing, under pressure for spending restraints from the US, the first 'zero-growth' (in real terms) regular budget, set by the General Assembly for the biennium 1996–7 at $2.608 billion. Thus the vehicle of reform was already on the move when Annan took over at the beginning of 1997.

It is a truism that the balance of power globally has changed considerably as has the nature of wars and social and economic concerns. They continue to change as reaction builds against the hubris of the US in its predominant position in world affairs. Nevertheless, the size of the challenge facing the UN in the earlier part of 1997 can be outlined simply at this stage by taking the overall main components of the regular budget, the peace-keeping budgets and other regular expenditures outside those chapters and looking at the figures. Some elements of the story had clearly not changed over the years. The budgeted expenditures[7] of the UN in 1994 reached $8.3 billion, of which $1.3 billion went to the regular budget; $3.3 billion to peace-keeping operations; and the remaining $3.7 billion went on operational activities and programs supported by voluntary contributions. But assessed contributions unpaid at the end of that year amounted to $1.8 billion. For 1995, the regular budget was again put at $1.3 billion and for peace-keeping operations $3.1 billion. The finance for these UN activities is raised through assessments made on the capacity to pay of member states. Receiving these funds on a regular basis has been a chronic problem. Unpaid assessed contributions had risen by that date to $2.3 billion.

It is over peace-keeping operations, which will be examined in detail later, that the UN financial system has had to face its greatest challenge and most criticism. But costs incurred have risen sharply. For example, between 1945 and 1991, the UN Security Council authorized the use of force only twice on major occasions for any purpose other than self-defense (in Korea and the Congo). Between 1991 and mid-1994, the use of force under Chapter VII of the Charter – peace enforcement as opposed to peace-keeping – was authorized five times: in the Gulf, Somalia, former Yugoslavia, Rwanda and Haiti. This over-extension of its mandate from peace-keeping to peace enforcement came to grief in Bosnia and Somalia.

Expenditure has risen similarly. In more recent times, to give an idea of how this has grown, the annual peace-keeping budget increased from $230.4 million in 1988 to over $2.7 billion in 1992. A familiar specter lurked, for, at the end of August of the same year, all unpaid bills for peace-keeping amounted to $735.2 million (with another $831.2 million owed for the regular budget, making a total of $1.57 billion owed to UN budgets – among the top ten overall defaulters at the time were the US with $723 million, Russia $420 million, and South Africa $71 million). Between 1988 and 1994 the UN launched 21 peace-keeping operations, compared with 13 in the previous forty years. This was a turning point, which was to have intense repercussions for the UN, its standing, particularly with the US, and its finances.

In reaction, there were efforts to rein back expenditure which fell below $1 billion in 1998, lower than the figure for the regular budget. But before that, it had become apparent that, in the clear move away from the interpositional exercises of classical peace-keeping into peace enforcement and into operations closely involved in supporting humanitarian interventions, expenditures and the number of operations would have to fall. At the end of 1995 there were 17 missions falling roughly under the heading of peace-keeping. In 1998, the number of mission was still 17, having briefly fallen in the meanwhile. But the significant change was in the size of UN operations and expenditure. The peak number of UN personnel in various guises of peace-keeping was 78 744 in July 1993, but this had dropped considerably to 14 537 at the end of July 1998. There are two striking features about these developments which impinge directly on finances. The first is the sheer drop in the amount falling directly on the UN for peace-keeping missions. Connected with this was the realization brought home starkly by events in former Yugoslavia, Somalia and central Africa, that the UN could not expand its operations of peace-keeping in its broadest sense of intervention through a mandate from the UN Security Council, to fill a hole left by the ending of the Cold War. Missions were found to be wanting because of the complexities of the political situations into which they were pitched. Materially and in terms of training, the troops sent in were often under-equipped. The decision-making processes in New York were painfully slow. Above all, peace-keeping costs would have to be shared with and, in some cases, handed over in their entirety to other organizations.

Thus it was that the costs of keeping the peace fell, lessening the burden on troop-contributing countries and the member states of the UN which have to pay their assessed dues to peace-keeping budgets. In *An Agenda for Peace*, Boutros-Ghali foreshadowed a trend in advocating closer co-operation with regional organizations and bodies.[8] This, too, could lessen the direct financial burden on the UN. But it would also require that it changes its administrative role in participating in and ordering such operations. It would mean, too, a certain lessening of its authority and role on the ground. But this could make for the more efficient running of missions. In his *Supplement to an Agenda for Peace* Boutros-Ghali acknowledged their role and identified co-operation through consultation, diplomatic support, operational support (here he cited the example of NATO in former Yugoslavia), co-deployment (with ECOWAS in Liberia and the CIS in Georgia) and joint operations (UNMIH in Haiti, where staffing, direction and financing was shared with the OAS). He reaffirmed the possibility of the capacity of regional organizations for peace-making and peace-keeping but acknowledged that this 'varies considerably'. The UN was prepared to help develop this capacity, but: 'The primacy of the United Nations, as set out in the Charter, must be respected.'[9] In addition, there has been under active consideration and discussion the establishment of a stand-by, rapid deployment force – either on the basis of a created communal force or units earmarked in the armed forces of states with a proven pedigree of involvement in peace-keeping. Boutros-Ghali relaunched an associated idea – that of preventive diplomacy[10] – to identify, confront and head off conflicts in advance. Both would require some reorganization of the UN, but could, in theory, reduce costs.

There was a sense of inevitability in the progression of these developments, and the causes do not stem solely from the UN's unwieldiness. Globalization has perforce eroded the concept of the sovereignty of both states and regions. It has perversely also undermined to a certain extent the concept of universality, whereby, in theory at least, even the smallest members of the UN were permitted and entitled to an equal hearing of their views and plights. While much attention has focused on the regular and peace-keeping budgets, it should not be forgotten that the UN has varying degrees of responsibility for the disbursement of several billions of dollars of funds connected with humanitarian, social, and economic sectors, and development. Its whole system makes it the largest disburser of funds for development and relief in the world. In the areas of humanitarian aid and economic development in particular, the changing nature of modern wars has put on an equal footing many of the operations to conduct the support and aid of people suffering from civil wars into the hands of NGOs. These are, to a certain degree, not dependent on the UN for funding. The slow way in which the UN has patronisingly come to recognize the importance of this partnership has been chronicled ably elsewhere. It is enough to say that the involvement of the contemporary equivalents of NGOs in missions connected with peace and war has a pedigree in the shape of military participation in humanitarian operations which predated the UN's existence by several centuries.

The important point, which has a bearing on the conduct in the future of the UN's finances, is that the trend under way is patently towards devolving the running of a wide range of activities away from New York towards other centers and regions. It has already made more than possible that certain aspects of peace-keeping could be passed increasingly into private hands – and this has been advocated. But it does provoke a new context in which the proposition that the reform of the UN – and leading amongst these would be changes affecting its finances – has become more pressing than ever. Whether there are optimistic prospects will depend largely on how matters develop, mainly in New York and Washington.

In the interplay between reform of the UN and its finances, politics will perforce be the leading factor. Over the years there has never been a lack of proposals for improving the financial system, although they have tended to be enacted or proposed seriously only after a crisis is in full flow. One feature this time, which might have augured well for a proactive approach to gain the upper hand, is of course the feature which has already been noted that both Clinton and Annan were at the beginning of their terms of office. Two political events, both involving the US deeply, have had a profound effect: Clinton's battle with Congress over the payment of its arrears to the UN and the confrontations with Iraq in 1997–8 which Annan's diplomatic intervention stopped in the first instance from escalating into a heavy US attack. Here the value of the UN Security Council and the standing of the UN as a whole in US foreign policy were at stake. The net result of these factors was that the UN slipped further down the list of Clinton's foreign policy priorities during 1998 and with it urgent concern for UN reform and its budgetary solvency.

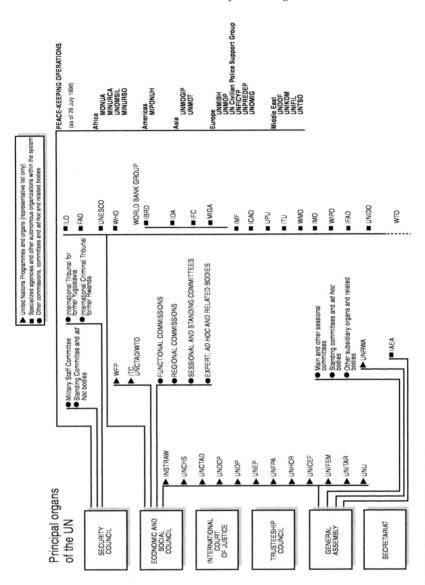

Figure 1.1   The United Nations System
Source: United Nations Department of Public Information, February 1997.

The second is a broader sense than has previously been the case that within the UN, if it is to remain in the forefront of organizations with a say in the running of foreign affairs and the main forum for international discussion, reform has to come about throughout the organization. The issue of reform has been over the years under constant discussion and debate. Since the beginning of 1997 it has been accelerating. As a result the General Assembly had been for several months in extended discussions about trimming back programs and reviewing the membership content and role of the Security Council among many items. There appeared to be an overall context of the will to reform and streamline within which the US and the UN Secretariat, in particular, could work out their roles. Eventually, it has to amount to more than improving the working of the Secretariat by modifying its structure, eliminating waste, reducing the number of posts and reorganization through interdepartmental and interorganizational change. There have to be signs of a broader reformist vision. Annan had grasped the main point from the start. He told the staff of the UN on 9 January 1997 that: 'We must heal the financial crisis of the Organization, which cannot be expected to move forwards if it is dragged down by the burden of unpaid dues ... [A]t bottom the financial crisis is a political crisis – a crisis of faith in the Organization.'

On reform, the first point that the main parties to this had to recognize, at least tacitly, was, as Annan has said, that 'reform is a process and not an event'. Clinton was always under much visible pressure from a Republican-dominated Congress to come up with signs from the UN that reform was indeed under way and that the US, the major contributor, was receiving value for its money. Furthermore, it is an era in which US government foreign assistance (and it is under that category that US payments to the UN come) is, as a percentage of its GDP, way below that of other wealthy nations. From the UN side some improvements were able to come about relatively swiftly in terms of jobs, and by streamlining agencies and avoiding duplication in the running of missions and projects. These could be seen as a statement of intent by Kofi Annan. But it does not yet seem to have gone much further than open discussion of new attitudes towards the involvement, say, of private business.

At the start of 1997 and at a more immediate level, there was already a divergence in approaches towards reform, which started to become as crucial as either side wanted to make it. For coincidental with his first visit to Washington as secretary-general, Annan was saying that the UN was committed to reform, but that this reform could only come about if outstanding debts were paid. The Clinton administration, with its eye on Congress, dominated by the Republicans and a long-standing hostile critic of the UN, retorted that money would only become available if reforms were effected. At the same time, Annan made initially a commitment to deliver a package of reforms within six months. There was a slight slip in the delivery date, in part because of disputes within the UN Secretariat, but Annan did deliver on 17 July 1997. Among the measures were some for the financial sector, involving the budget and a fund to provide a cushion against the perennial problem of unpaid dues. In line with strategies to make current spending more streamlined, the figures for the regular biennial budgets have been kept level and then reduced for the 1998–9 biennial budget. From the beginning there were signs of the shape the package might take. The four main targets were: the acceleration and expansion of managerial reform; a reduction in non-program costs of the organization; the modernization and enhancement of services and information provided to member states; and an increase in the accountability and responsibility of program managers.

In more detail, this 'first track' as it was called falling under the remit of the secretary-general as chief administrative officer of the organization, would involve: the cutting of the 1998–9 regular budget by $123 million; the reduction of 1000 posts; administrative costs would be reduced from current levels of 38 per cent of UN resources to 25 per cent; strengthening an integrated UN presence in countries to co-ordinate and implement plans; the consolidation of three economic and social departments into one; the streamlining of technical support for intergovernmental bodies; the reorganization of the Department of Public Information (to become the Office for Communications and Media Services); the consolidation of administrative, financial, personnel and procurement services; the creation of a UN Code of Conduct; and a reduction in documentation by 25 per cent. The 'second track' would involve Annan working with member states to make the structural changes in the organization which would require their approval.

The unseemly electioneering process in the autumn of 1996 produced Annan's acceptance as the seventh secretary-general after the US, despite a 1–14 minority vote in the Security Council, blocked through its veto Boutros-Ghali's reappointment. At the same time, it made a point relevant to the second track approach that reform, if it is to have respect and be meaningful to UN members would have to start from the top. The whole confused process of selecting or re-selecting a secretary-general raised the question as to whether a formal second position should be created of deputy secretary-general. It was, but, as a sad symbol of the extent to which Annan had carried out genuine reforms, the powers of this post, which went to a Canadian, Louise Fréchette, were slighter than had been hoped for. The general reaction to Annan's reforms was that they lacked any real vision of what the UN's role should be in the future. It certainly was far from extensive in the areas affecting the regular and peace-keeping budgets.

With the UN's membership having risen to 185 and the role of UN activities becoming more varied, expanded in number and increasingly shared with other non-UN agencies, both NGOs and in the private sector, its administration needs greater attention than ever before. Globalization has made the running of the UN easier in one sense because technology has facilitated communications and the transfer of goods and services. But at the same time, this revolution has facilitated the possibility of bypassing the UN. At present, in bureaucratic and financial terms, the UN lags behind. The broad range of reforms, as outlined above, was debated seriously and has been to some extent enacted. It will take some time before they enhance the image of the UN. They might have convinced the US administration that the organization was serious. But the US has been distracted by external events and Clinton by his struggle with Congress and other domestic diversions including impeachment. But, as set out so far, they appear to have overlooked a fundamental part of the UN's existence – one indeed, which has dogged it from its earliest days and surfaced as a severe crisis on a cyclical pattern ever since.

Attention to improving the financial system of the UN – in all its budgetary and extrabudgetary forms – has not been given the priority it deserves. The official statements and briefings have concentrated on savings and improving efficiency, but have paid less attention to explaining how this could be underpinned by better techniques for raising money to supplement the method of assessments on member states, or by longer-term strategies to sustain the administrative improvements. Adjustments to the number of base years on which assessments are calculated and to alternative methods of raising money are not subjects that draw public attention as stirringly as drives to eliminate corruption and waste in bureaucracy. But, it should be argued, the areas of administrative and financial reform are equally important, and need to be tackled hand-in-hand. It bears repetition that this issue is of relevance. For, where finances are concerned, it is crucial that the secretary-general from the beginning of 1997 commanded authority and the backing of the US, for without that there was a genuine fear that the US could bypass the UN, leaving it to remain inertly on the sidelines. These recurrent bouts of US isolationism as expressed in its attitudes towards the UN rise and fall and seemed during the second half of 1997 to have receded, but some of the onus continues to lie with the UN to stimulate and sustain the interest of Clinton's second administration in its activities.

The finances of the UN have in recent decades not been neglected but, as a topic, it has rarely had the stage to itself amongst examination of the organization's activities and administration. Much was written about the state and structure of the UN. The 50th anniversary of its founding stimulated a veritable industry of books and articles which fell roughly into three categories. The first was historical, and traced the organization's highs and lows, with the concentration largely on political, peace-keeping activity, dwelling especially on such crises as those in the Congo, over Suez in the 1950s and 1960s, and latterly involving Cambodia, Somalia and the aftermath of Yugoslavia's disintegration. Less attention was paid to the operations of the UN's non-political developmental, social and humanitarian programs and agencies, although this trend has been heavily reversed. In particular, some of the associated and specialized agencies, both in their financing and the execution of their projects, contained kernels of experience about operations, from which the mother organization has often given the impression of being slow to learn. Had it done so, and had it co-ordinated these activities more closely, the pressure for reform today might have been less and the overall standing and reputation of the organization higher.

The second category of books and articles, often following the pattern of the first, passed judgment on the UN at middle age and made predictions about the future – if it had one, the pessimists wondered. The balance seemed to imply that, against the political and organizational odds and given the inadequacies of running such a disparate association of interests and member-states, the UN had performed as well as could be expected. The anniversary also prompted a large number of books and articles centering on proposals for reform and improvement of the organization in all its aspects. Boutros-Ghali's demise concentrated attention on this, and, before his demonization is completed to justify Washington's pushing him aside in favor of Annan, the point should be repeated that he did initiate reforms. The reform issue was reflected in the vehemence which had for some time been evident, but which strengthened at the time of the anniversary, for its reform. Predictably, much of what was written assesses the UN's achievements and failures against the background of the universality of its membership and the end of the superpower rivalry between the US and the Soviet Union during the years of the Cold War and its replacement by the domination of the US as the sole superpower. The universality of membership has been a crucial theme, together with the concept of sovereignty, which in the end has a bearing on financing. It is both a bonus as an ideal, but also a problem, since it creates inevitable inefficiency. For, under the latter guise, the fact that it should be pursued as an ideal can be used as an excuse for not tampering with an existing system that may appear more often than not to be in worn but still working order.

In a third category has come a massive increase in the number of books and articles, prompted not just by the anniversary, but also by the expansion of peace-keeping operations in their broadest sense after Boutros-Ghali became the UN's chief.[11] As wars and their sorry aftermaths proliferated affecting both states and regions which had slipped messily out of the control of central governments, the full range of services – whether military operations, policing, election-monitoring, or providing humanitarian aid – came under greater and more detailed scrutiny than before. In addition, attention was increasingly paid to the operations of agencies and organizations outside the UN – personified mainly by the NGOs but also by the activities and internal politicking of the larger UN specialized and affiliated agencies. Initially, a curious and common phenomenon in the growing output of books, articles and records was the issue of the UN's finances. It is not as if nothing has been written.[12] There have been several worthy volumes written and almost every comprehensive guide to or analysis of the UN contains at least one chapter or section, devoted, usually either in over-dramatic terms or in gloomy prognostications, to the management or mismanagement of the UN's finances. Elusive, until recently, has been the advocating of any comprehensive list of reforms or refinements. Under the impact of this latest round of enthusiasm for reform, this may be changing. But, the UN is likely to find that, leaving aside its domestic difficulties in running its regular and peace-keeping budgets, there is ever-increasing competition for funds to run projects and missions – within or without the UN.

It would seem that few effective measures have been taken to bring the UN's funding processes under control, even though it has long been a topic of argument and debate. In the early days, at meetings for discussions of the budget, at a level loftier than the costs of cuff links and pool cars, complaints were made about UN overall costs. Indeed, the UN inherited problems from before it officially came into existence, for the League of Nations before it had suffered from a familiar difficulty: that of not receiving assessed contributions from its members. Familiar too was the argument that the UN was far too expensive, even though the target for the 1946 regular budget at that stage was a mere $21.5 million.[13] But during the discussions on how expensive the brand new organization was turning out to be, the point was made that 'the total budget constituted only a small fraction of wartime expenditures, being roughly equivalent to one hour's war expenditure of the United States Government'.[14] In the later years of the 1990s, there were efforts to save $200 000 by no longer issuing free pencils and notepads to delegates. At the same time, it should be noted, as it frequently is, that the budget for the UN's core functions – the Secretariat operations in New York, Geneva, Nairobi, Vienna and five regional commissions – is $1.3 billion a year. This is about 4 per cent of New York's annual budget, and nearly $1 billion less than the yearly cost of Tokyo's fire department. It is $3.7 billion less than the annual budget of the New York State University system.[15] Put another way, broadly and comparatively speaking, the UN has been able to meet and carry out successfully its political, humanitarian, economic and social commitments at a cheap price. One further example should suffice. The daily costs of Operation Desert Storm, which was carried out under the cover of a Security Council resolution, were virtually equal to the UN regular budget for the whole year (in 1991 $2.1 billion, compared with $1 billion for peace-keeping). This comparative cheapness is a point which is often overlooked or submerged beneath the complaints about the waste of resources and inefficiency.

Furthermore, these comparisons in expenditures are not as trivial as they may seem for they make the point that, whatever the criticisms of the running of the UN and its agencies and related operations and missions, when compared, almost at any time in its history, with both global and local expenditures, the UN services come inexpensively. One seasoned critical writer on UN affairs has observed that:

> The entire budget of the UN and its specialized agencies and technical agencies for the world of 5.7 billion people, including funds for development, peacekeeping, and humanitarian relief is about $11 billion a year. That is about what Americans spend in a year in beauty parlors and health clubs. It represents just under $2.00 per human being alive on Planet Earth, while governments are spending about $150.00 per capita of humankind on military establishments. The U.S *makes* over a billion dollars a year out of hosting the UN and out of UN procurement awards to U.S. companies.[16]

This particular juxtaposition of statistics may not be matching like with like, but they reinforce the broad issue of how much the UN costs and to whom. In 1997, the total operating expenses for the entire UN system came to $18.2 billion a year.[17]

But the concentration here is on the less costly items of the regular and peace-keeping budgets. There is little doubt that during the 1995–6 period, there were signs that the UN's financial circumstances had deteriorated on a greater scale than before. Even allowing for inflation, arrears and non-payments, the situation had threatened to get out of control to the extent that there appeared to be a serious risk that the organization would be unable to carry out the full range of its commitments. In addition, the picture was dire because financial reforms and alternative methods of raising funds would go only so far towards providing a solution without the support of political will from the leading contributors – in particular, the US. This aspect has become worse not better. Alternative means of raising funds – in other words those not paid by voluntary contributions and assessments on national governments out of national treasuries – have been suggested many times over the years and will be considered again. But while every avenue should be explored, equal consideration will have to be given as to how practical they are to implement and whether member states should permit the UN a measure of autonomy and independence in raising funds, at the expense of its member states.

In that context, it is noticeable that all specialized programs and organs are financed primarily outside the regular budget and depend on voluntary funds from governments, international organizations and other sources. The UN will have to face the fact that there is increased competition for funds globally which seem to be on the decline in size, even if this competition is muted to some extent by the system of assessments on governments. Against this background, it is clear that this topic is one which has been crucial in the past and underplayed. It will continue to be central. It needs to be confronted systematically.

What has to be faced and explored is the reality that the UN must answer two separate but related questions. On the one hand there is what can be loosely called the budgetary crisis. On the other is the issue of financing the UN system. To some extent, the accusation that UN officials have cried 'wolf' too often is justified. The UN's budgets – both the regular and peace-keeping versions – are not spiraling out of control. The 1995–6 period was bad and looked at one stage to be on the edge of the vortex. That the UN was not sucked in was ironically due to Russia, which, despite its severe economic problems, saved the day by paying up on the regular budget and settling some arrears. But the alarms were strong enough to strengthen moves towards austerity and reform. Thus in 1995, for the first time, the General Assembly appropriated an amount less than the total of estimated expenditures and instructed the secretary-general to propose savings to make up the difference. The original appropriation for the 1996–7 regular budget was $2.608 billion – less than the final appropriation for the previous biennium. The revised appropriation has reduced this figure to $2.603 billion. The appropriation for 1998–9 was $2.532 billion – a further projected reduction. By the time of the execution of that budget, after a protracted review, a new scale of assessments on member states had been proposed and enacted, amid much controversy and opposition from the US.

Simultaneously, peace-keeping costs have fallen sharply. The assessments amounted to $3.175 billion in 1995, to $1.407 billion in 1996 and, because certain major operations were due to be wound down and concluded, fell further in 1997 and again in 1998.[18] In short, the financial crisis is due, in the main, to lack of funds for budgeted activities. Collections are not equal to assessments, and member states do not fulfill what they have agreed should be done and paid for. This is not to paint the UN organization in a pure, innocent light, but its member states have been guilty for decades of failing to pay in full for obligations which they have freely assumed. On the voluntary contributions, through which the bulk of development and humanitarian activity is financed, pledges are many but, unfortunately, payments often fall far short. A third source of funds often under discussion are alternative methods, involving levies on a variety of sectors such as global travel and communications and tourism, and even an international lottery. The practical implications are formidable, the chances of enforcement remote and the enhancing of the UN's standing and global role questionable in the eyes of its member states. Nevertheless, these alternative methods should not be dismissed out of hand.

Bringing about the changes needed to stabilize and ultimately work towards an easement of the UN's financial problems will depend on four ideal and unattainable factors: political will, financial and administrative reform, efficiency and a program, combining all those features, with a framework of five years at the outside. The weight of these individual factors will differ from issue to issue, though political determination and commitment will consistently have to be the dominant driving forces. Otherwise, the reform process which showed some encouraging signs at an early stage of being taken seriously, will slip away as others have in the past. It would then run the risk of being written off as yet another cry of 'wolf' and evidence that the UN can continue to exist, with diminished authority, as it has done for years in a state of almost permanent financial difficulty or crisis.

2 Changes in Problems and Principles

A fundamental question to be addressed is whether the nature of the UN's financing and funding problem has changed; or indeed whether this is a new phenomenon for an international body such as the UN. On the face of it, the crisis has been around as long as the UN itself. The auditors of UN budgets have passed consistently gloomy views: 'During 1957, the cash position the United Nations in respect of its regular budget operations again reached very unsatisfactory levels during the recurrently difficult months of May and June ... '; 'The cash position ... continues to be a matter of deep concern ... ' in 1958; the situation was 'increasingly critical' the following year; 'remained precarious ... ' in 1970 and so on. For 1992–3, the auditors' talk was of the 'extremely high levels of outstanding assessed contributions' for peace-keeping operations. Each secretary-general has had his own excoriating say.

The framers of the UN Charter in 1945 sought to fashion a workable provision against delinquency to ensure financial solvency in their anxiety to avoid a repetition of the experience of the League of Nations. The Covenant of the League had simply assumed that member states would pay their assessed dues in full and on time, and it had no provision for dealing with delinquents. Its financial lack of success was one contributory reason for its failure.[1] At the core of the UN's problem – the provision of insufficient funds to meet obligations – is the fact that the criteria for assessing who owes what has become out of touch with current economic realities and the capacity to pay, and that there has been developed no realistic mechanism to force defaulters to pay. At the same time, the compilers of these complex criteria have had always to feed into their calculations non-fiscal, sensitive data imposed by political necessity. Above all, this situation is complicated by the fact that the main defaulter – the US – is also the main contributor of funds and therefore has always been able to use its special position to keep the organization on a short leash.

At the League of Nations there were areas of ill-defined financial responsibilities which became problems of their own and which were often unrelated to the political problems facing the League. Indeed, there have been issues in the life of the UN which have the ring of familiarity such as whether decisions affecting financing should be reached through the weight of the size of individual contributions, consensus or agreement.

The US, not a member of the League, has always had strong views on this. Drawing up and monitoring budgets were then as now the bane of economists, political planners and policy-makers. Achieving consensus and agreement on financial matters was a problem for the members of the League of Nations, which had a mere 58 members at its height. The UN has a membership more than three times larger, but its financial difficulties have turned out to be exponentially more complicated.

If there are obviously long-standing difficulties which have existed since the UN came into being after the Second World War, why do they persist? In the long run, it may be that they can only be confronted by modifying the ways and means of payment and disbursement of contributions. The UN can become more of an organization which commands widespread respect and responsibility, if its members pay their way. This suggests that, on one level, the weaknesses in the system can be largely defined as mechanical and technical. On another, more telling level, the reasons may lie with the organization itself illustrated by its slowness to adapt to the changing international political circumstances which have been outlined above.

In one sense, thus, the housekeeping should have been tidied up long ago. But it never was because the UN's role in the world evolved, and the methods for financing it never kept pace. Money came in through a variety of methods – initially through the regular budget and voluntary contributions. In many senses, peace-keeping operations have been both the making and near breaking of the organization. They gave the UN a global profile and also an indifferently earned reputation for inefficiency and only rare successes. But payment for the missions ranged from formal and systematic assessments tied to the regular budget, to separate accounts and budgets for each mission to the *ad hoc* and voluntary arrangements, and to a mixture of all different methods. The outcome has been that many of the operations have suffered badly from arrears in contributors' payments. Countries which have provided troops and *matériel* have not been reimbursed. Yet, other peace-keeping accounts have been, curiously, in surplus at certain times of the year. They have provided funds for bailing out the regular budget. But a basic imbalance remains and this shows itself particularly in compensation payments to contributors to peace-keeping. There should not have been the situation, at the end of 1995, where countries providing troops were owed about $1 billion in reimbursement – the level at which it has persisted since. This interplay between the regular and peace-keeping budgets is a microcosm of the UN's financing and administration at its most eccentric and often wasteful. The continuing existence of these kinds of arrangements makes it clear that, although the organization is acknowledged to be conservative and slow-moving when it comes to change or improvement, it has a certain instinct for survival through improvisation. The more serious side of this is that this kind of improvisation, in the form of swapping funds between budgets, has become an established habit.

At the same time, the changing nature of peace-keeping, from traditional, interpositional peace-*keeping* to peace *enforcement* and peace *consolidation* (involving such exercises as economic development and election-monitoring) has meant that costs have had to be shared with NGOs and the whole UN system, including specialized agencies and programs. Boutros-Ghali intimated as much in his *Supplement to an Agenda for Peace*.[2] It has meant that the lines between the older and more clearly defined methods of financing and extrabudgetary funds have become blurred. The UN has been forced to adapt and consider new methods.

Some change has been forced upon the UN system as the numbers have grown from the 51 that signed the Charter in 1945 to the 185 member states today. Other changes may be forced by circumstances. As the number of peace-keeping operations fall and with it the size of their budgets, so the comptrollers of the regular budget will have to find new sources to draw on to cover their seasonal deficits.

There are certain abstract concepts which have to be taken into consideration when formulating changes and reforms to the financial system and, above all, for these to work as effectively as the complex nature of the United Nations could permit. As constraints, they may have been in existence as long as the UN itself, indeed nearly all were deliberately intended to be there. They may not always be quantifiably visible, but they are invoked, consciously in debates or unconsciously in government policies when the issue of reform arises. But in essence, the solution to financial reform remains, as it always has been, political – first and foremost.

Most of these abstract and conceptual features are inter-related and have deep bearing on each other. Universality, equality and regionalism are all to some extent part of the same family of emotive concepts. The UN, as has been observed many times, is not a world government but an organization comprised of sovereign states, which in theory, as the Charter stipulates, have equal rights of expression and, equally, a responsibility, but in practice not an equal one, of providing funds towards the UN. The role of the five permanent members of the UN Security Council illustrate starkly when it comes to authorizing peace-keeping operations or the selection of the secretary-general that voting rights are not equally weighty. It is the richer countries which are in effect underwriting operations ranging from peace-keeping to humanitarian and development activities in poorer countries. On another level of inequality, in financial terms more often than not, the UN has not always matched up to expectations as a universal power policing emergencies or administering aid. Should, therefore, there be greater devolution of its powers – and financing – on to regional organizations and authorities? The latter's knowledge of local problems is often undervalued, but what is not clear yet is whether there is sufficient stability in, for example, Africa or the Far East, to make any genuine devolution of power possible. Nevertheless, in the last few years this form of sharing power and responsibility has become the subject of more active consideration as a viable alternative.

This must create some resentment and tension not only amongst the recipients but other potential donors whose say in how these operations could be carried out may be muted. Can a balance be struck? Should the larger contributing states be governed by the wishes of smaller, poorer states? In other words, should voting and therefore political power be proportional to the size of a financial contribution? They are, in effect, not equal at every level, so it is not quite a 'one state, one vote' system. But, overall, universality is a notion linked strongly with sovereignty and results very often in a conservative reaction to the more unconventional suggestions for alternative means of payment. It has resulted in a variation on the divide between the states of the industrialized North and the less developed countries of the South. Both sides are perceived to have pre-set intentions and motives in debates about practical issues such as the assessment of contributions and representation on the vital financial committees connected with budgets and finance.

Sovereignty has been often invoked as a barrier for the weak against the more powerful nations. But on a different level security is now involved increasingly with civil strife and wars within countries, rather than wars between countries. That coupled with an increasing trend towards intervention even if a host government rejects it, probably means that the inviolability of sovereignty has become more blurred. Is sovereignty violated when international UN action involves the provenance of civilian assistance such as aid, as much as military/civilian services, ranging from peace-keeping to monitoring elections or providing police? This in turn has an effect on the provision of funds. Would they come from the regular budget, peace-keeping budgets or voluntary funds? These days the answer probably comes from the involvement of all three. At the same time, governments still want very much to hang on to this notion of being their own masters for as long as they can, even when it is patently clear that they are not in complete control of their own countries, as the example of President Mobutu in the then-Zaire showed in 1997. On the other side, the

EU is perhaps the most blatant example of a situation where sovereignty has either been eroded or is being perceived as undergoing that process. On another level, any active attempt to enforce punishments for non-payment of assessed contributions can be interpreted, to some degree, as a potential infringement of this concept of sovereignty. The UN has never aspired to supranationality – even though some US politicians, usually with re-election to office have invoked this threat – and this hampers further any realistic notion of being able to enforce, on a regular basis, penalties for the failure to pay dues on time.

The question of authority, usually that of a government or organization, is closely tied with sovereignty. What happens, for example, when a civil war or collapse of civilian authority and government means that there is no authority capable of exercising its powers? Is this where the UN – almost always through the Security Council – or another agency steps in? There follows then the question as to who gives the mandate to intervene and in what form, and again how is such an authorized mission paid for? The authority of the UN could, for example, be undermined through its authority being theoretically diminished by being only *primus inter pares* in an undertaking involving others, even though this might mean that the financial burden would be shared by organizations outside the UN.

The Charter and its inviolability now enter the equation. Its wording, although largely regarded as immutable, was formulated in an earlier era. It is procedurally complicated to change, as amendments require ratification by two-thirds of the member states, including approval by all five permanent members of the Security Council. There have been three changes in 50 years, including one affecting the enlargement of the non-permanent membership of the Security Council. This change, once again the subject of extended topical debate, has some potentially important implications for the sharing of some aspects of the financing of the UN system, in particular in peace-keeping operations. Further changes in the Charter would be needed to encompass any profound reforms influencing the financing sector. But, in reality, the Charter, through Article 17 (affecting the General Assembly's approval of the budget; the responsibility of the member states' paying the organization's expenses as apportioned by the assembly and financial arrangements with the affiliated specialized agencies), is not, in effect, restrictive about the practical means of overall funding.[3]

Power introduces a further factor through which concepts of equity and legitimacy begin to disintegrate. Against the background of theoretical equality of membership, power, whether in terms of financial or global political standing, counts disproportionately. In purely financial terms, the political power of the US, Japan and Germany is not exactly commensurate with their ranking as the top three contributors to the UN (see chart for contributions, page 106). The US, over the years, leads by a margin – but Japan and Germany have been catching up rapidly and for some years have been the largest both *de facto* and in assessed terms. As a result, they have for some years been pressing for a permanent seat on the Security Council. And for different reasons, so have such countries as India, Egypt, Nigeria and Brazil. If political power were measured by the increasingly disfavored yardstick of GDP per head, some of the oil-rich countries of the Middle East and Far Eastern 'tigers', as a result of their financial disasters starting in 1997–8, would no longer qualify for increased influence in the UN through larger assessed contributions.

To this picture should be added an increasingly important element: the NGOs. On issues from humanitarian aid to human rights, the environment and future non-military political roles they have often become an important channel of communication, action and information between the UN, states and other participants in such activities. This is not the forum for debate about their political affiliation to the UN, but there is little doubt that their roles will need increasing acknowledgment. It is certain that their roles will become even more relevant to both activities on the ground and finances. When it comes to decisions on spending, it is probably right that they should be given a greater hearing, but in return for this they would probably have to contribute more money. Already they share responsibility for carrying out joint projects and receive money directly from UN specialized agencies. This impinges on the question – and has done for many years – of there being a direct, finite boundary, in terms of receiving and raising finance, between the UN and non-UN organizations and associations. It makes the argument of the inviolability and, as a consequence, inflexibility of the UN financing system as a separate entity harder to sustain.

Reform, efficiency and effectiveness run closely together, with the second lending strength to the third. It is indisputable that the UN can be run more efficiently. Cost-cutting as a goal may be entirely laudable, but it can often be at the expense of efficiency in specific areas of expertise and, above all, of representational equality, which, by the very differing nature of the resources it draws on, must lead to inefficiency. A series of reports coming out at about the time of the 50th anniversary of the UN all tended towards putting greater emphasis on efficiency and the role of the genuinely international civil servant than the idea that global representation should be adhered to. (When it comes to the highest posts in the UN, the apportionment is done on a balance between having certain offices the fiefdoms of particular nationalities and regional representation. In the latter case, the position of secretary-general has often been discussed in terms of regions. On that score, it is fairly questionable the extent to which Boutros-Ghali of Egypt qualified to fulfill Africa's turn in office,[4] any more than Annan of Ghana and a lifelong employee of the UN might!) The dilemma between regional representation has become an increasingly discussed issue as the UN addresses itself towards reforms and improvements. It is taken up frequently by outside study groups, which have increasingly tended towards sacrificing the notion of universality in this area in favor of streamlining and efficiency.

What powers of enforcement of its rules and regulations pertaining to finances does the UN have? There is the often-quoted Article 19 which says that a member 'in arrears in the payment of its financial contributions ... shall have no vote in the General Assembly if the amounts equals or exceeds the amount of the contributions due from it for the preceding two full years'. The let-out comes in the following sentence for, 'the Assembly may, nevertheless, permit such a Member to vote if it is satisfied that the failure to pay is due to conditions beyond the control of the Member'. The suspension of voting power has arisen in theory for smaller states but with no notable effect or enforcement of punishment.[5] In 1964, the device of the General Assembly not going to the vote permitted the Soviet Union to elude the embarrassment of punishment when it refused to make contributions for political reasons caused by the Congo operation. It is an interesting point that the US reacted at the time by giving grudging assent to the deal. US representative Arthur Goldberg warned that, if others could assert a right not to pay assessments for activities they opposed, the US might do the same.[6] And it has. More recently, efforts to bring pressure on the US to pay off its enormous arrears to both the regular and peace-keeping budgets have had little effect. There was, indeed, a time during 1998 when it looked as if the US would have fallen two years behind by the beginning of 1999. In short, it is apparent that the UN has neither the force nor the authority to press its members into paying their dues on time.

But despite the breakdown of the more formal interpretations of sovereignty, there remains the residual notion that no mandate should be able to be enforced without the approval of the host state. Translated into the economic sphere this means that, without approval from the organization, finance might be withheld at will. Since that appears in reality to be the case, it has been seen that punitive measures – such as the removal of voting rights in the General Assembly – have not been effective or they have simply been avoided. This certainly applies to larger powers, and, in the case of smaller countries, whether they default on their payments, or indeed have a real say in any mission on their territory, is almost irrelevant. This would not necessarily apply to the less formal methods of raising funds for the UN and its agencies. Since these often involve more easily defined objectives, such as transport and refugees, there tends to be greater commitment to paying contributions and accepting both penalties and rewards for arrears and promptness. But as a broad rule, it has proved impossible for the UN to meet their Charter-bound commitments to funding their own organization.

There has to be consideration given to the question of practicality where suggestions for alternative methods of raising money come up. There are problems with suggestions endowed with both vision and gimmicks. It raises, in terms of enforcement of payments, the question of how much international authority, besides that of moral suasion, the UN possesses. (The answer when it comes down to a confrontation over cash is probably very little.) Putting practicality into action inevitably means the spending of money and possibly additional bureaucracy, but when, for example, the case came up of a $1 billion offer over ten years from Ted Turner, the boss of CNN, ways of administering this through a fund, called the United Nations Foundation, were organized quickly. Alternative methods of raising money have been under discussion from the earliest days since any additional use of existing methods (beyond making payments more regular and efficiently disbursed), on the surface and through the literal interpretation of the Charter, appear to be out of the question. A UN working group has talked of some sort of global tax on a variety of sectors, from tourism to defense, but these all run into problems of the UN's implied assumption of international governmental authority – not to mention the issue of enforcement. There has been discussion of forming a new social and economic council, to bolster ECOSOC's existing functions. This council has been notably wayward in its achievements and execution of its potentially far-reaching authority and even in its reformed shape – as promised in 1997 – would look incapable of carrying out such a role. Furthermore, in the debate about alternative sources of funds, officials and diplomats of member states argue that, although alternative methods of finance are attractive and, in theory, feasible, they might lessen the obligation of others to pay their dues. Furthermore, they add inevitably that any sources which involve deadlines, punitive payments or incentives are inherently difficult to administer, even though, as has been noted, there are exceptions in some UN organizations.

An accusation thrown regularly at the UN has been and will continue to be that it is not only a waste of money but also of breath, theories and arguments. Almost any debate throws up a profusion of carefully thought-out theory, selfish thinking and practical suggestions, which provide the front-stage performances for the protracted negotiations, wheeling-dealing and drafting in committees. There has to be, in the end, progression from the conceptual and abstract to the practical. Some of these, which will be examined later, are feasible. For instance missions of long standing, such as those in south Lebanon and Cyprus, could be assessed financially on a maintenance level and on an annual basis. This could provide for a more even expenditure for peace-keeping, although a single, annual peace-keeping budget could never be possible as the nature of the tasks of peace-keeping has changed radically over the years.

To some extent the UN's monolithic New York-based format has evolved. The development side of its activities meant that regional offices had to be opened to channel aid and have personnel on the ground. There was a sense too that as it was a global organization, there should be regional headquarters in such major cities as Geneva, Vienna and Nairobi as well as a network of offices with specific regional rather than global responsibilities. The trend had been growing apace that regions should be bearing an increasing share in the costs and action of the full range of UN activities, but was blunted in 1998 by the worldwide economic and financial crisis and wars in Africa. But the UN's regional bodies have a network in place which has underlined the need for less duplication and more sharing of costs. To this regional trend could be added another practicality. Not only could funds be shared through more collaboration with regional organizations and but also with the NGOs which often benefit, controversially, from the presence of peace-keepers. This emphasizes the now-established view that governments, either individually, in groups or through international associations need not be the only sources of activities and action. The private sector has its growing role, having recognized that there is money to be made too in humanitarian aid and development projects. Thus looser co-ordination with those organizations involved in humanitarian actions will need to be further developed.

The potential partners of the UN are many – NATO, OSCE, WEU, OAU, CIS, OAS, ASEAN and ECOWAS are the immediate examples which come to mind. Already in almost each of these regions some measure of devolution of power and authority and sharing the burdens of the tasks they have set out to perform has taken place. It would be a mistake to describe these experiments as having been wholly successful. There have been notable shortages in skilled manpower, infrastructure and organization. Political stability has frequently undermined the effectiveness of regional organizations in developing continents. Even in military terms, the success of peace-keeping operations has been limited, and the fulfillment of potential a long way off. But, even at this stage, these mixed under-takings that involve some of the burden being devolved from the shoulders of the UN have a longer-term bearing through indications that there could be a financial burden-sharing aspect. This might be one more way, if managed properly, of relieving the UN of some of its perpetual financial struggles.

A detailed review of the running of the UN's management of finances shows that, although the idealism which inspired the foundation of the UN and its activities was never lost and the concepts accompanying this remain, the practical side of running this vast, varied organization has gradually imposed itself. It has not been a gentle progression. Historically, until the ending of the Cold War a regular pattern has displayed itself – almost without exception politically driven, but simultaneously with severe financial (and organizational) effects and implications.

There have been in the 1960s, 1970s and 1980s a series of crises in which the basic aspects have hardly changed, although each was in detail different from the previous one. Missions in peace and war under a series of secretaries-general with varying levels of charisma and understanding of the UN's standing and role often exceeded the organization's capabilities. Nevertheless, the regular budget in the earliest decades, which was spent largely on administration, remained mainly in balance even though its comparatively modest numbers were often under criticism. It was involvement in peace-keeping which caused the difficulties. And this has remained the case ever since. The first was a function of the political factors and of the fact that the UN system had not yet evolved sufficiently to produce a specific peace-keeping financing procedure. The one fell foul of the other. These were more often than not the result of political problems rather than a genuine inability to pay. They included the establishment of UNEF after the Suez crisis in 1956, involvement in the Congo, through ONUC, in the early 1960s, followed by war in the Middle East again, the interposition of a force in Cyprus and other cases in Africa, Latin America and the Far East. The methods of payments for these operations were uneven both in time and amounts. They were inconsistent as UNEF, for example, was financed at first through the regular budget, and the Congo operation through other means including the exceptional recourse to rais-ing money through a bonds issue. The irony in the 1970s and 1980s and thereafter has been that, while the peace-keeping operations have from a financial point of view been regarded publicly as the more obviously erratic, wasteful and impotent side, in extremes, when apparent bank-ruptcy loomed in the regular budget, it was through short-term transfers from the peace-keeping budgets that the wolf was kept from the door.

In the 1970s, the UN bureaucratic system was again showing signs of wearing out and Cold War political tensions made the political running of the organization difficult. Allied to this was the fact that the growing number of Third World and developing countries among the new members were being drawn into disputes between the Communist and non-Communist blocs. This held back both discussion of reform and the running of finances and their practical application. Significantly, the US felt particularly aggrieved in this competition as the largest contributor to UN funding, and as the host country to the organization. It must be added that the sectors of particular concern here – financing and related reform – were not the only ones to suffer during this relatively fallow period in the UN's existence.

As a result there was little coherence in efforts at reform beyond acknowledgment that something had to be done. Each effort, particularly in the decades of the 1970s and 1980s, tended to introduce an additional layer of bureaucracy to an administration which was already showing signs of unwieldiness. Peace-keeping, although not yet on a scale of the late 1980s and early 1990s, was becoming an increasing drain. Yet throughout these years when it was easy to point at the organization's ineffectiveness, it was difficult to argue that the costs of the UN were outrageously expensive.

It was the ending of the Cold War, which happened to coincide with the last years of Pérez de Cuéllar's term in office and the beginning of Boutros-Ghali's, which sparked off the latest round of attempts at reform and scrutiny of the UN's finances. It involved a new feature, that of an attempt of introducing management reform techniques into the UN. But by most accounts they were, although reasonably thorough, found initially unsuitable for the UN. The US, while in no way moved by the potential usefulness of the international organization, had not yet reached the position of sole and pre-eminent superpower which modified its view of the usefulness of the UN – and therefore the need for its greater efficiency and value for money.

As so often, the change in the political environment was crucial. The attempt to make the UN the power which might fill the void left by the dissolution of the Soviet Union produced a drain on resources, not just in financing a dramatic increase in the number of peace-keeping missions but also in coping with such challenges. For the role of peace-keeping simultaneously shifted away from the traditional deployment, held to be the interposition of neutral forces – to something more complex and involving many more skills than those of the military. It became apparent that the bureaucratic administration was unable to handle this expansion and change in operation and management. The US initially welcomed the UN's new perceived role, but shifted abruptly after the humiliation of US troops in Mogadishu to a far more critical and hostile approach. It became clear that, if the UN were to function with a role within Washington's own global foreign policy it would have to be on Washington's terms. As it showed through blocking Boutros-Ghali's reappointment and obtaining Annan as his successor, it would use its political and financial power to enforce this. An important by-product of this was that many of the concepts outlined above – in particular, the notions of the universality of the UN in a democratic sense and the individual sovereignty of member states – became diminished. Value for money and efficiency became catchwords, not necessarily with the aim of achieving those goals at the expense of performance, but as a warning that in many political and humanitarian fields the UN was by no means the only provider.

Within the UN itself, the sources of funding are changing, which has both political import and is relevant to the organization being able to pay its way. Today, the examples of the US, Russia, Germany, Japan, Singapore and Saudi Arabia, in their different ways, illustrate roles and attitudes towards payments which have changed considerably over the years. The changing global positions, both politically and economically, of the US and Russia as two of the permanent members of the Security Council have left the former paramount but reluctant to continue as overwhelming major contributor unless the UN is made more efficient and to its liking. Russia, after serious defaults because of economic turmoil at home, continues to display its determination to hold onto its privileged position by catching up increasingly with its arrears. Germany and Japan, currently the main actual contributors, can both claim that they pay their assessed way in full – at least by the end of the UN's budgetary year in December and not by 30 January when payments should be in. The competition for the non-permanent seats on the UN Security Council illustrated the changing nature of the UN's financial crisis – and the politics that went with it. Japan, in the autumn of 1996, won a seat on the Security Council at the expense of India. The latter's long-term international standing may be based in history as the representative of the non-aligned world, as it used to be called, rather than financial prowess, and in the short term it paid the penalty for not signing the nuclear NPT. Its chances have been further damaged by the testing in the spring of 1998 of nuclear weapons. But, at the time, Japan's financial strength and contributions to the UN coffers, together with a close relationship with the US, were crucial factors. In addition, Japan saw it as a gradual move towards obtaining a permanent seat on the Security Council, whose expansion from 15 members has been under extensive debate. A permanent seat would mean, among other things, paying a larger contribution than it does already to the UN's budgets, in particular peace-keeping missions. Germany shares many of the same features – not least a lingering historical stigma attached to having been on the losing side in the Second World War. They are both (along with Italy), the unidentified 'enemy states' of that war in the UN Charter[7] and both search for political clout appropriate to their global financial standing.

Wealth is clearly meant to reflect influence in this context. It also draws attention to one of the weaknesses in the fundamental principle of financing the UN: the assessments of contributions on member states according to their capacity to pay. The need for the reform of this assessment method so that it reflects more accurately the current financial strength of states is illustrated by such countries as Saudi Arabia and Singapore. When oil prices are high and financial markets are strong, they can clearly afford to pay more to the UN than they do. Both derive benefits from stability in their regions to which the UN helps to contribute through peace-keeping and development programs. At the same time, the vagaries of oil prices and the international stock markets have shown how rapidly the calculations of a country's wealth and predictable income can change. It has so far defied the efforts of economists to devise a system, which can absorb and measure rapid changes in incomes. The moot point in the equation of wealth and influence in the UN is whether countries in that kind of bracket – a potentially transient one – are or should be of political weight commensurate with their calculated wealth.

The importance of wealth and contributions has gained political influence in other ways. To that extent, a key feature has been the nature of the political element in the ability to pay or not. In the earlier examples of the 1950s and 1960s, payment tended to be withheld either to show disagreement with a particular operation or as a general function of rivalry between East and West. The nature of critical contexts has changed. From a political point of view, direct political disapproval of particular missions is becoming less frequent. Whole organizations have been boycotted, as in the case of UNESCO by the US from 1985 and also Britain, which suspended its membership between 1985 and 1997, because those countries felt that UNESCO had been exploiting its position to put forward pro-Third World and anti-West propaganda and additionally because there was clear evidence of the wasteful use of funds. UNESCO eventually stepped back into line. But there have been other examples of discontent about the running of specialized agencies. The FAO has also been under close scrutiny. Financial sanctions have clearly been influential in the affiliated agencies of the UN, but not in the main body of the organization. The UNEP was another case in point. In July 1996, when it became apparent that neither the US nor Britain were keen to have the executive director of that organization, a Canadian, stand for a second term, largely because it was believed that the running was such that money was being wasted, pressure was brought to bear. In fact, some of these problems stemmed from the wasteful activities of her predecessor, Mustafa Tolba, who had been in the job for 17 years.

There has been a traceable shift in the power of political motives and the desire for tangible results. It could be in part attributed to globalization which has reduced the UN's pre-eminence. But it is also due to the weakening of the ideological concepts which helped to establish and maintain the UN through some extraordinary political crises. At the same time, there is a school of thought that maintains that, even today, the only changes in the financial problems have been ones of scale. This is true to the extent that some of the long-standing political participants used to equate the size of contributions with the weight of their say in the making of decisions. The opposite is also true, for both France and the Soviet Union, in holding back from contributions to operations in the Congo may well have hoped that the missions of which they disapproved might collapse through lack of funding. In fact, they resulted in some ingenious, though not popular, means of raising cash to keep the missions afloat. The US has been guilty of this sort of maneuvering, too, as has been shown particularly in the 1980s and 1990s using Congressional legislation as its weapon.

On the financial level, the sums involved in UN budgets have grown, but taken over the 50 years of the UN's existence, this has been at a modest and not alarming, rate. The annual regular budget for 1946 was around $20 million and by the late 1990s was averaging about $1.3 billion – in nominal terms about 65 times larger after more than half a century. Nevertheless, the overall situation has become grimmer as the sizes of the budget and the percentage of arrears have expanded. The number of major contributors not fulfilling their obligations – whether for political reasons or poverty – has increased, so that the crisis has become graver and the outdated form of the payment and assessment methods have been more exposed. But unchanged is the fact that the UN is underfunded and has to practice a form of sly self-financing and juggling between budgets – mainly between the regular budget which is at certain times of the year in deficit and the peace-keeping budgets, some of which are often in surplus – in order to keep itself afloat. These are techniques which few bank managers would tolerate in personal accounts. And in governmental dimensions it would be comforting to believe that few governments would succeed in being re-elected if their national accounts were run in such a way.

Against this background of the tension between the ideal and the practical, it is worth spending some time examining how historically the UN has survived all these years on the basis of this hand-to-mouth arrangement. It should be pointed out that in the succession of crises which occur cyclically about every six years, a feature has been not to let the organization collapse, even if it meant turning off the fountains outside the headquarters in New York at one stage as a sign and measure of economies.

But the immutable factors have remained threefold: that the UN suffers from late and delayed payments by its members; that it has been chronically short of funds in its reserves; and that, above all, politics not money dominates decisions. To this extent it could be said that the financial crisis is unchanged. And on that level alone, it is hard to raise much sympathy for the UN's predicament. The world outside feels that it has seen this happen too many times, and without probing the nature of the organization with all its myriad of global responsibilities, it has become somewhat bored. But with the publicity over the US veto of Boutros-Ghali's second term in office, there has been perhaps greater attention paid to the need for widespread reform. Annan has continued to give that idea of reform prominence, even if tangible progress has been in the short term elusive. That the US is the largest debtor has perversely drawn attention once again for the need for changes in this sector as well.

But the vital difference is the magnitude and complexity of these features which has changed over the years, and which makes this crisis more pressing than before. And with that has come a new attitude towards the running of international organizations (whether commercial or political) and a political climate which reinforces this disillusionment through its dominance by a single superpower. The US in its foreign policy makes few efforts to conceal its disdain for comparative failure. But unless a balance between a flow of funds and reform is found, the UN, even under the impetus of new leadership from within and pressure from without, could find itself on the sidelines.

3 The Ways from the Beginning

As guidance from the beginning, the words governing the financial running of the organization were remarkably concise. The onus lies, according to Article 17 of the Charter, with the General Assembly which 'shall consider and approve the budget'. Without precise definition, it continues: 'The expenses of the Organization shall be borne by the Members as apportioned by the General Assembly.' In a further clause, the General Assembly 'shall consider and approve any financial and budgetary arrangements with specialized agencies... and shall examine the administrative budgets of such specialized agencies with a view to making recommendations to the agencies concerned.'[1]

The words and their interpretation and enactment in practical terms have derived some hidden strength from an imprecision of expression which has allowed the organization to adapt to its changing functions and the growth in numbers of its members. The rules and regulations, which emerged to guide the running of the UN's finances, have never been strictly binding. Figures and plans have been debated and scrutinized at great length and at several different levels. But they have never been able to impose overall control. One adjective stands out from all others in nearly every relevant official document to describe the UN's finances: 'precarious'.

The system at every stage of its evolution over fifty years and more has fallen prey more often than not to exploitation of the weaknesses of this imprecision and periodical readjustments at the behest of the stronger member states. It has, at the same time, been vulnerable to a lack of regimented control. The result has been a steady accumulation of problems which have come to a head at intervals over the financing of early peace-keeping operations, over the functioning of funds to tide the budgets over cash-flow crises, and over the criteria for assessing the percentage contributions of member states to budgets. Some of these problems became functions of Cold War rivalries and tensions between the industrialized developed world and the underdeveloped South. Others reflected the feeling of the larger contributors, especially the US, that influence should be, to some degree, commensurate with resources provided. The consistent weakness in the whole system has always been, and continues to be, the fact that member states, largely with impunity, have not paid their dues on time. The problem of arrears is paramount.

This came to a head in the mid-1980s in the form a real and tense financial and administrative crisis over the Kassebaum-Solomon Amendment to the Foreign Relations Authorization Act adopted by the US Congress in August 1985. That was barely contained, as will be described in Chapter 6, and, more than a decade on, it has resurfaced in a new form and on a larger scale. Some of the items are familiar – the US Congress, the relative importance of the UN in US foreign policy, the UN's costs – but this time global political circumstances have changed to the extent that US calls from the UN for budgetary restraint and reform can hardly be overlooked.

The UN and all the operations coming under its aegis are financed broadly in several ways, of which three are the most important: percentage assessments on member states for the regular budget and the peace-keeping budgets (two separate but related operations) and voluntary contributions from governments, organizations and individuals to the UN special organs and programs. This last group constitutes the largest proportion of funds coming broadly under the expenditures of the UN system.[2] As the Charter makes clear, not all financial operations come under the direct control of the UN administration. The specialized agencies are a particular case in point. If the year 1996 is taken as an overall guide and *total* UN expenditure for the twelve months is estimated at $11 billion, only $3 billion (made up of $1.3 billion for the regular budget and $1.7 billion for peace-keeping accounts) fell under its control. In 1997, the overall figure for the total operating costs of the entire UN system had risen to $18.2 billion, of which the regular and peace-keeping budgets were to amount to about $2.3 billion. Critics of the system have many targets. The fact that there are clearly different recipients within the UN system of money raised in different ways from a variety of sources should have made them more selective in their attacks. Each method of raising and disbursing funds has its own particular weaknesses and quirks. The tendency has been, however, to isolate one fault and to extract from that failing the justification for a broad criticism of the whole UN financial system.

The first scale of assessments, the heart of the source of the inflow of funds for the UN, was drawn up in 1946, and reflected the dominant economic position of the US after the Second World War. The initial *assessments* for the leading contributors for 1946 and 1947 were the US with 49.89 per cent,[3] Britain 10.5 per cent, the Soviet Union 6 per cent and France 5.5 per cent.[4] At the core of the financial problems, affecting mainly the regular and peace-keeping budgets, the insufficient provision of funds to meet obligations – is that the criteria for assessing who owes what has become antiquated and out of touch with current economic realities and ability to pay, and that there is no realistic mechanism to force defaulters to pay. The regular budget and the peace-keeping budgets (when the latter came formally into existence) raise their money according to scales of assessments, which vary between the two types of budgets, and depend on the ability of individual UN members to pay.

In theory, it is the refinement of this core of the UN's financial system, which will have to be undertaken, if a start is to be made on this fundamental problem. And this reform will have to be based on a mixture of rational calculation, points of reference shifting with changing financial circumstances, and finally, on what is politically acceptable to most of the UN's members, but above all to the US. This situation is complicated by the fact that the main defaulter – the US – is also the main contributor and therefore in a special position to keep the organization under tight control or ignore it. This pattern of behavior is not always consistent and predictable as US policy towards the UN is subject to the interplay and tensions between the US government of the day and its legislative bodies.

The method of assessment has been a major subject of debate over the years. It is generally accepted that, while the mechanics can be refined, like so many other features of the UN it is non-financial factors which will determine both payment and its assessment. Refinement of this process will be discussed at a later stage. Suffice it to say that, from the very start, the catch phrase, 'the capacity to pay' has suffered from the problem of practical definition. But times and rates of payment have changed – as has the size of UN membership and the varying wealths of the new members. The US has, as already noted, been the prime contributor. As late as 1961, for example, the US payments, as opposed to assessed contributions, were as high as 47 per cent of the regular budget.[5] The US has been in the forefront of those arguing that it was unhealthy for the UN to be overly dependent on one nation for the major part of its funding. For this reason, among many others, the size of the US contribution in percentage and in kind, has, unsurprisingly, been scaled down over the years since.

These percentage assessment rates have generally, but not always, been calculated for a three-year period, during which they may differ by some measure. They range from the highest level for the regular budget with the US assessed as paying the 'ceiling rate' at 25 per cent, down to the very poorest who pay only a symbolic 'floor rate' percentage (Swaziland, for example, pays 0.001 per cent under the latest scale). This last level is something of a hollow symbol of the universality of the organization as countries of the industrialized West have dominated contributions. Indeed, the EU, in the negotiations over the most recent assessment rates, argued for the abolition of this 'floor rate'. In 1997, the last year of the 1995–7 series, after the US with 25 per cent came other high ranking/earning industrialized countries, including Japan 15.65 per cent, Germany 9.06 per cent, France 6.42 per cent, Britain 5.32 per cent, Italy 5.25 per cent, Russia 4.27 per cent and China 0.74 per cent.[6] Amid considerable controversy and debate, a new scale for 1998–2000 was adopted on 31 December 1997.

The running of the finances have been since the beginning the responsibility of the Fifth or Finance Committee of the General Assembly. It acts as a kind of parliamentary committee on which all states may be represented and through which the budget has to pass on the way to acceptance. As a result its views tend to be guided more by partisanship than a level of expertise found on other financial committees. Its activities are vetted by that Committee's standing budget review unit, the ACABQ and, importantly, the CPC, the main subsidiary organ of ECOSOC and the General Assembly for the planning and coordination of UN programs, considering the activities of UN agencies on a sectoral basis. Its membership now stands at 34 and its members are elected on the basis of regional geographical distribution. It also acts in consultation with the JIU and crucially the CPC. The CPC's role became more important as a result of

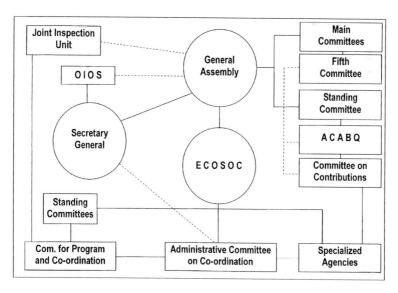

Figure 3.1   Co-ordinating Bodies of the UN System
Source: Klaus Hüfner.

the crisis over the Kassebaum Amendment (see Chapter 6). One outcome was that the budget received closer scrutiny as it passed on its way to the General Assembly. The size of its membership was increased in 1987 from 21 to 34. This coincided with a shift in the process of approving budgets from majority to consensus, thereby giving the major contributors, chiefly the US, a quasi-power of veto. Although it appeared not to have appreciated this at the time, the US had in effect brought about a change in the Charter in terms of control over the regular budget. The bodies monitoring and passing judgments at various stages reflect a mixture of the UN's membership, political interests and, particularly through the ACABQ, some efforts at impartial, expert analysis of the budgets and accounts of the UN and the specialized agencies. It advises the General Assembly on all administrative and financial questions. Its observations on the budgets of the agencies are not binding on their executive councils. Nevertheless, the role of these committees has been crucial, hampered though the 16-member ACABQ may be by its representatives not always being capable of setting aside national loyalties in favor of those of the UN, as they are in theory supposed to do.[7] Within the hierarchy of the UN, the ACABQ has represented a means for the General Assembly to assert itself against the overwhelming strength of the five permanent members of the Security Council and to have some control over the secretary-general's spending powers. Much of the work which these committees, which come genuinely close to having obtained the status of being run by international civil servants, has been worthy. But their work and workings have often been desperately slow and added to the UN's inefficiency. This has applied especially in the crucial area of the funding of peace-keeping operations.

The daily running of the organization and some of its associated bodies is through the regular, also known as program, budget. From the outset the ACABQ had as its main task to reduce as much as possible the costs of the organization and the first budgets took the form mainly of budgets of expenditure, involving personnel, materials, investments and the like, and contained limited indications of the contents of the organization's programs. Budgets started as an annual exercise. On 19 December 1967, the General Assembly[8] adopted the recommendation of the ACABQ for the introduction of a biennial budget. The aim was to facilitate co-ordination and planning particularly for medium and long-term programs and, initially, to synchronize all the budgets within the whole UN system. It was introduced first for 1974–5 but has not escaped the pressures from the General Assembly, specialist committees within the Assembly, from the Security Council, and, of course, from the continuous, but uneven, grind of the cash flow.

The budget has always passed through several stages and this has resulted in apparent, but usually slight, inconsistencies given for the regular (and, later, peace-keeping) budgets. David Singer has recorded[9] that during the period 1946–60 the budget passed through various stages: the secretary-general's estimates, the crucial CPC stage, the ACABQ's recommendations, the General Assembly's appropriation, the Assembly's supplementary appropriation, the total appropriation and, finally, total expenditure. From one end of the process to the other, the budgets of years chosen at random went from $19.63 million to $19.33 million in 1946; $33.47 million to $42.58 million (1949); $44.35 million to $43.75 million (1950); $47.77 million to $49.29 million (1953); and $54.78 million to $62.51 million (1958). Thereafter came the auditors' agreed figures.[10] Budgets undergo a similar procedure of scrutiny in modern times. Hüfner recorded biennial budgets between 1988–9 and 1996–7 through stages of appropriations and adjustments. The budget, for example, for 1988–9 started at $1 769 586 300 and ended at $1 772 313 700; that for 1990–1 started at $1 974 634 000 and ended at $2 167 974 500; for 1992–3 started at $2 404 578 000 and ended at $2 411 404 000; and for 1994–5 started at $2 580 200 200 and reached $2 632 435 000.[11]

The budget, as we have seen, derives its funds from assessed contributions from member states according to formulas that have evolved over the years and which are supposed to reflect the wealth and, above all, the ability to pay of individual countries. It has been hampered as a method by relying on a system which is overtly cumbersome and, increasingly, as the flows of wealth come and go, and globalization breaks down many of the hard and fast boundaries between countries, out of date. On the criteria for assessments, it has become generally accepted that, while the mechanics can be refined, like so many other features of the UN, it is non-financial aspects which will determine both the level of assessment and its payment.

From the very start, there have been some additional and other minor sources which provided either funds directly for the general budget, or, as in the WCF and the exceptional $200 million bond issue in the 1960s, a back-up source of finance. The former existed first at the League of Nations and was set up again in 1946. It started with initial subscriptions from member states of $20 million and this has risen over the years from $40 million (from 1963) to $100 million (from 1982) and remains in existence, but exhausted. It was to serve as a source of liquidity to enable the secretary-general to advance sums necessary to finance budget appropriations pending the receipt of contributions from member states. It constituted a form of extended overdraft facility but with the difference that it acts mainly as the current account from which running expenses are

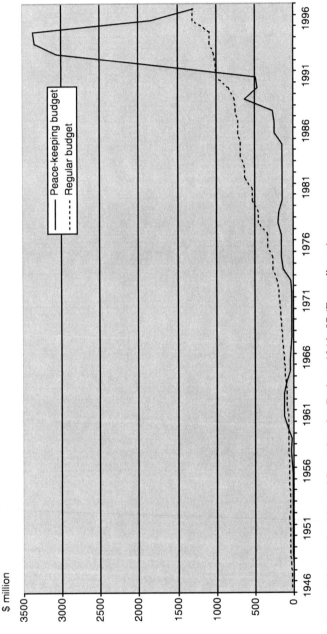

$ million

Figure 3.2   UN Regular and Peace-keeping Budgets 1946–97 (Expenditures)
Sources: for regular budget: 1946–70 Mahdi Elmandjra, *The United Nations System. An Analysis.* (London: Faber and Faber, 1973) pp. 228–9; 1971–95 Klaus Hüfner, *Finanzierung des Systems der Vereinten Nationen 1971–1995* (Bonn: UNO-Verlag, 1997), Teil 3A p. 105; 1996–7 Global Policy Forum, New York (www.globalpolicy.org). For peace-keeping budgets: compiled by Michael Renner of World Watch Institute for Global Policy Forum, New York (www. globalpolicy.org).

paid. The advances were made in accordance with the scales of contributions and the lenders were reimbursed. The secretary-general has limited ability to draw on it in emergencies. It has, over the years, fallen into virtual disuse through being exhausted by the growing size of regular budget arrears. The surpluses from peace-keeping budgets have been used to tide the organization over the lean months at the latter end of the year. In July 1997, Annan proposed the formation of a RCF of initially $1 billion, to be financed by voluntary contributions or 'any other means of financing that Member States may wish to suggest'.[12] It would be used in cases of delayed payments or the non-payment of assessed contributions, basically to ease cash-flow pressures, but only to cover outstanding amounts greater than $250 000. It passed almost without comment that this was hardly an innovative suggestion.

The bond issue was a one-off arrangement. It was not, in itself, an unworthy device and could conceivably be resurrected but the background against which it was set up – the Congo operation – was contentious. An insight into the relationship between the UN's financial state and its members was made on the occasion of the organization's 20th birthday in the context of the financial crisis which broke out in the General Assembly in 1961. It has a relevance which has applied ever since. 'It is, of course, obvious,' H.G. Nicholas observed,

> that the crisis is only in the most superficial sense a financial one. The UN finds itself short of money only because rich and powerful states have decided that it is in their interests to reduce it to such pecuniary embarrassment … Basically the dispute is over what the UN should do, not over what it should spend doing it.[13]

Elmandjra has reinforced the argument that the cost of the organization's 'collective responsibility' has been comparatively cheap – even though its expenditures for 1948 alone exceeded the total expenditures of the League of Nations during its lifetime.[14] The regular budget's expenditures (including those of specialized agencies) rose from $24.4 million in 1946 to $400.9 million in 1970 – the first 25 years. Viewed another way, in which voluntary funds and expenditures are taken into account, total assessed funds and expenditures showed between 1951 and 1970 an average annual growth rate, in current prices, of 10.3 per cent, accelerating until the middle of the 1960s and decreasing thereafter to about 7.5 per cent in 1970.[15]

It is worth interrupting the narrative to observe that, during the 1970s, the organization was marked by two related factors: an enormous rise in membership, particularly of Third World countries, and a further exacerbation of the Cold War. It provides a convenient excuse for postponing examination of a crucial development in the UN's finances – the formalization of the funding of peace-keeping operations in 1973. The missions themselves were, to some extent, frozen during the 1970s because of the ideological war but they re-emerged in the 1980s and, particularly in the 1990s, as the most visible and least flattering aspect of UN activities. The controversies surrounding these cast into relief, just as the Congo operation did in the 1960s, apart from the political complexities the anomalies and strains on the financial system and sorely exposed its limitations.

The UN system is far more than the General Assembly, the Security Council and its debates. For affiliated to both is a complicated skein of organizations and agencies with, from a financial and funding point of view, a variety of relationships. It is the money at the disposal of these organizations which bring the *total* expenditure on a current yearly basis to about $18 billion. Their importance for an examination of the UN system is in some ways peripheral. Because of their relative autonomy, which in financial terms has increased over the years, their fate should not be confused with the issue of the central funding of the UN. They certainly have their own problems but these are often derived from the running of individual agencies, their internal politics and the nature of the projects which they supervise – from transport to refugees and health, social and humanitarian affairs. In July 1998, the *Financial Times* published allegations of wasted millions of dollars donated by Western governments, incompetent management, doubtful accounting procedures and 'even possibly fraud' in the UNHCR organization.[16] Annan called for an inquiry into these allegations, which were heavily denied. This focus on the UNHCR, an organ rather than a specialized agency of the UN, was revealing in that many of the alleged malpractices involved could well have occurred also in the running of the regular and peace-keeping budgets – and on occasions have been exposed by the OIOS, established in 1994. The broad message was that the circumstances in which these large, semi-autonomous organs running humanitarian operations have to operate are difficult to monitor and control. Furthermore, a system in which appointments are often based on political patronage and regional quotas, is vulnerable to politicking at the expense of dealing with such internal problems as corruption, inefficiency and waste. It was a significant warning to but not a condemnation of the UN system as a whole.

The OIOS was introduced to mute criticism about the alleged lack of control over UN programs. The US Congress was initially skeptical about the extent to which the office had access to the records and documents of the UN and its agencies as was required under the terms of the resolution setting it up. It has identified some potential cost savings and cases of fraud and made some recoveries. Its inquiry, for example, into the Rwanda war tribunals uncovered considerable waste, improper contracting, administrative bungling and a major squandering of resources.[17] Its responsibilities extend to the offices of the UN Secretariat, the five regional economic commissions, peace-keeping and humanitarian operations, and, to a degree, the range of programs funded by voluntary contributions and administered separately, such as UNICEF and UNDP. Access to the specialized agencies with their autonomy as intergovernmental organizations has been limited.

Of interest here is the extent to which these specialized and affiliated agencies depend on the UN for money from the regular budget and voluntary funds and extrabudgetary sources, bilateral, governmental and voluntary, from outside. Voluntary contributions to the UN's specialized agencies, programs, funds and other organs has risen from $815 million in 1971 to $6.9 billion in 1995.[18] They fell to $5.6 billion in 1996 and $5.4 billion in 1997.[19] One alternative method of raising funds for the main UN budgets could be voluntary donations. This method might have serious implications for the overall running of the organization, but Article 17 does not exclude voluntary contributions and Annan has not ruled it out through the reforms he set in motion in 1997. The argued difficulty is two-fold, but it has to be seen in a broad context. Although the business surrounding agencies – whether from the UN or humanitarian NGOs – is clearly big business, the funds are finite and competition to attract these funds is considerable. There have been signs, too, for some time that the size of these funds is tailing off. In straight competition for congenial viewing on television, refugees are a more attractive target for funds than the UN peace-keepers in Blue Helmets. Furthermore, the special programs provide more precise and appear to have more immediately identifiable aims than those put forward by operations which would otherwise depend on the regular budget and peace-keeping accounts.

There have been occasions when the officials of agencies dependent on voluntary funds have in effect warned the UN proper from putting itself on the voluntary funds market. In addition, there is a conservative unwillingness to resort to voluntary funds as a source for the general budget as undermining the international character of the UN. Partly only with sarcasm, peace-keeping officials have commented that they did not want to be associated with an enforcement mission, brought to 'a certain country by courtesy of a certain well-known brand of soft drink'. But the considerable links have always been there. Between 1946 and 1970, the expenditures of ten specialized agencies for the UN's regular budget amounted to $2 billion out of a total of $3.89 billion – or 51.4 per cent. These were largely to cover administrative costs.[20] By comparison, the assessed contributions between 1988 and 1997 had risen for the UN from $1.99 billion to $2.97 billion. Within that, the amount for the 12 specialized agencies increased from $1.26 billion to $1.88 billion, with their share holding steady at about 63.4 per cent.[21] This has itself provoked problems. It has been difficult to separate out voluntary programs even though EBFs have increased, for there are bilateral co-sponsored programs and regular programs. EBFs do not, of themselves, undermine the formal authority of, for example, the WHO. But they do raise issues for the UN. Yet how sustainable would the UN, with its broader range of responsibilities, be on outside funds before 'donor fatigue' set in? The assessment system of raising funds has its drawbacks, but it does have the merit of the theoretical dependability of a regular flow.

Furthermore there can be competition between multilateral and bilateral organizations and with it the difficulty of how to maximize results attained by these funds. Hand-in-hand with this growing market can come the risk of creating a system of fragmentation through this very competition between the specialized agencies. This in turn raises an issue relevant to the reform of the UN system. The relationships between the General Assembly and the Security Council and the specialized agencies and peace-keeping operations have frequently been hampered by communications between the various UN headquarters and operators in the field. This has led to duplication and waste. Within the UN itself, the running of the agencies themselves has been fraught with unproductive competition. Management by ECOSOC, to which theoretically the UN programs, and specialized and affiliated organizations, are answerable to varying degrees, has been under constant criticism and is, also, a victim of the considerable independence these bodies enjoy. By contrast, the specialized agencies are independent, intergovernmental organizations that have their own governing councils and therefore their heads tend to act in an almost independent fashion from the secretary-general and the General Assembly.

There is a need, too, to be aware through EBFs of the possible influence exerted on what is carried out in a particular program. Particularly in the health fields, the pressing priorities still set terms which are not attractive for the donors. For example AIDS is a comparatively compelling target and focus, but, by comparison, there is less enthusiasm for combating TB. On a technical financial level, there are problems in terms of long-term planning ahead, because EBFs are given annually. In a broader context, it is necessary to gather more information from the experiences of UN specialized agencies about the impact on and role in the UN of EBFs.

Then added to these largely administrative problems is the issue of consolidated appeals. There appear to be three immediate lessons to be learned.

1. The response has been grossly and unevenly inconsistent. For example at the top of the scale was Yugoslavia where response was close to 100 per cent. It has not always been possible to sustain the momentum of generosity, particularly when there are other and newer competitors with compelling cases and claims.
2. But the majority of the responses have been at the bottom end of the generosity scale and this has posed its own range of difficulties of collection and disbursement.
3. This raises the additional issue as to whether the appeals should be consolidated, because without some co-ordination there is always the risk of considerable duplication. This, in itself, causes bureaucratic problems and probable hostility from donors, who would prefer to see their generosity go to the target of their choice.

On this similar broader front, consideration needs to be given to the issue of whether these funds should be brought into the main budget on the grounds that this would lead to greater centralization and, it is to be hoped, efficiency. There have been several protagonists of this approach, mainly in the context of wider reforms of the UN. But even if reforms were effected to bring about greater efficiency, they would be unlikely to get round the problem that most donors would give funds tied to specific ends.

The record of ECOSOC, the organization overseeing most of the specialized agencies in general, and UNDP, in particular, were notable illustrations of how there were risks of inefficiency being spread as well as duplication in bureaucracy. Their shortcomings have been one of the major targets of proposed reforms as a result of confusion in carrying out the UN's economic programs and co-ordination with agencies – both from the UN and NGOs – in the field when handling humanitarian intervention in conflicts. In this area, and it is becoming a broader sector by the day as the typical nature of wars change from inter-state to internal civil conflicts, it is much more subject to market forces than in the range of the financing of regular and peace-keeping budgets within the UN. Nevertheless, it might well be worth exploring whether this market approach could be applied to UN operations even though it has not always been easy to sell appeals for, say, the Iraqis (rather than the Kurds) or the Liberians – and those can well be projected as largely humanitarian issues. Putting peace-keeping operations or the infrastructure behind them up for privatization and competition has been put forward but these moves could raise considerable problems for the general conceptual standing of the UN.

The concept of universality raises its head again here, for its is supposed to run, in theory, through all the UN's activities. These voluntary contributions run the risk of not just being a supplement to assessed funds, but being seen by member states as a means of avoiding the obligation to provide the assessed funds which comes with membership. It is a doubtful argument because voluntary contributions have occurred, so far, largely for specific tasks or projects. They may have as a motive a desire by a particular state for a higher profile, but they seem unlikely to undermine the universal principles – among them in the Charter the contribution of each country however large or small – according to which the UN was set up. But the need for money, almost from any sources, would seem to be a short-term priority in the absence of any longer-term plan. In addition, the existence of funds followed by action would give the UN a much-needed appearance of providing action and activity. It is against this background, too, that other concepts, such as responsibility for particular missions and the blurred areas between peace-keeping and humanitarian operations have to be measured and weighed against universality. In humanitarian operations, this blurring has become increasingly replaced by definitions of shared objectives and operational methods which could result in closer co-operation in practical terms in the wider activities of newly-developed modes of peace-keeping. These will be dealt with later for, in the end, they are the linchpins for the future standing of the UN seen from the perspectives of its public relations to its organizational systems.

A special feature of this global organization is the fact that the secretary-general himself is extremely limited in his freedom to administer his official monies. His perks and income – he received a 2.2 per cent raise from the beginning of 1998 to $218 244 a year (including 'post adjustment' but not a representation allowance of $25 000) – are comparatively modest, although Waldheim and Boutros-Ghali might be held up as having yearnings for additional grandeur beyond other holders of that office. The regular and peace-keeping budgets and those for the agencies affiliated to the General Assembly and ECOSOC are, with all their shortcomings, rigid and laboriously administered. As a result, the UN has earned a largely merited reputation for slowness in responding to crises, whether they are external, such as an outbreak of fighting endangering the lives of thousands of refugees, or internal, in the form of the acute shortage in liquidity which, to varying degrees of gravity, affects the UN, threatening the payment of the salaries of staff, almost every year. But, to offset this, there are some reserve funds to which the secretary-general has access without having to pursue the full rigmarole of the General Assembly. But these funds tend to be either stopgap or start-up arrangements of a limited nature. One example is the WCF, now without funds and to be replaced by the proposed RCF. This variety of techniques of paying for the running of this organization can only reinforce the impression that it is ramshackle, guided by the concept of non-interference if it apparently defies the odds and continues to work. It also defies most of the definitions of bankruptcy, not least because there are few, if any, assets it can call its own to be taken over for someone else to administer.

Left until last at this stage are the many activities which still come under the umbrella definition of peace-keeping. Broadly this has come to mean all activities involving military and civilian personnel with a mandate from the UN. This wide definition has its obvious drawbacks. There has been a plethora of other definitions of what was once simply called peace-keeping operations, and many phials of ink have been emptied on its clarification and definition. This is because there have been great changes in the size and nature of these missions, which have become increasingly varied in nature and purpose. The divisions between civilian and military responsibilities have become as unclear as those of the UN and agencies outside its ambit. The methods of financing peace-keeping have become equally varied, and are dealt with in Chapter 5.

But in broad terms, the regular and peace-keeping budgets raise their money according to scales of assessments, which vary between the two types of budgets, and depend on the ability of individual UN members to pay. It is revision of this core of the UN's financial system which will have to be enacted, if a start is to be made on this fundamental problem. And any reform will have to be based on a mixture of rational calculation, points of reference shifting with changing financial and political circumstances, and finally, what is politically acceptable to most of the UN's members, but above all to the US.

It means, too, that the two main, formal budgets of the UN system – the regular/program budgets and the peace-keeping budgets – have to be seen in a changing context. Their size remains a tiny proportion of the total sums of money disbursed by the UN system. Yet their symbolism remains strong and, as a result, they have always been under almost disproportionate scrutiny from the outside. Their scrutiny within the various UN committees, particularly the Fifth Committee of the General Assembly in charge of financial matters and commissions is also extremely detailed, possibly far more so than any national budget. It remains to be seen whether the reforms proposed by Annan are capable of meeting the internal challenge of tighter budgeting while maintaining the universality of the intergovernmental organization and the broader demands of globalization in its widest terms.

4 The Regular Budget – an Uncertain Capacity to Pay

The regular budget, also known as the program budget, has been the consistent bedrock of the UN's finances. It is the foundation of the organization's activities not by virtue of its size, however, for it forms only a small proportion of the annual expenditure of the UN system. This has become smaller in those terms and also in relation to the sums spent on peace-keeping operations, the more visible and controversial sector. Between 1992 and 1995, peace-keeping budgets were larger than those for the regular budget.

This budget remains at the heart of the UN through its funding structure. The General Assembly elects new members to the UN after a recommendation by the Security Council. The General Assembly is the nearest body that the UN has to a parliament and a nod in the direction of universal democracy. That is the formal acknowledgment of belonging to the UN. But another feature with almost as much standing and certainly provoking as much discussion is the financial badge of membership – the obligation to the payment of dues to the regular annual (later biennial) budget as laid out in Article 17 of the Charter. The size of this contribution is based on a percentage assessment. How this percentage is reached at has been the subject of long debate and analysis, dependent on arguments and pressures ranging from the arcane to the political, emotional and ingenious. The criteria selected have never pleased all member states. The over-riding phrase, introduced by the Committee on Contributions during its earliest meetings, as a basic principle for arriving at the assessment of an individual country's membership dues was the 'capacity to pay'.

From the very start, the lasting problem with this catch phrase has been its practical definition. But times and rates of payment have changed – as has the size of UN membership and the varying wealths of the new members. The US has always been the prime contributor, reaching 47 per cent of the regular budget in 1961. Both actual expenditures and the percentage rate of apportionments have, unsurprisingly, been scaled down over the years since then, so that it is billed to pay one quarter of the regular budget and one third of the peace-keeping budgets.[1]

On one level the notion of a country's 'capacity to pay' has been unreasonable. The US had a capacity to pay, as measured as a contribution to the world's economy just after the end of the Second World War, which if taken literally would have undermined any ideas of the organization's universality. The earliest benchmarks for assessed payments reflected concerns about the ravaging effects of that war. The Committee on Contributions arrived at its conclusions and recommendations as a result of considerations including 'relative national incomes, temporary dislocations of national economies ... arising out of the war, [and] availability of foreign exchnage' for estimates of members' for capacity to pay for the years 1946–8. An account of this meeting held on 9 September 1946 recorded that:[2] 'The Committee had confined its work to making an estimate of relative capacity to pay, leaving the question of ceiling provisions and other factors *which raised political issues* to be discussed by the General Assembly.' The US accepted the renewal of the assessments at 39.89 per cent for the 1948 budget, and that was down 10 per cent on the original earlier calculations by the Committee, described as 'Relative Apportionments Based on Capacity to Pay', for 1946–8. This gave a taste of the division of labor between the statistical and political aspects of contributions. Washington repeated the conviction it had expressed a year earlier that in an organization of sovereign equals no single member should pay more than one-third of an administrative budget.

The US, as will be examined later in greater detail, played a key role in drawing up the financial mechanisms. As the country whose economy survived the Second World War in the fittest state and as the key political maneuvrer with a commitment to a world body which it did not have in the past – as its absence from the League of Nations showed – the US was firmly committed to making the finances work. David Singer observed that:

> As a prime initiator of the United Nations, the United States Government probably devoted more detailed attention to the structure and functions of the future world organization than any of the other three sponsoring powers; much of the explanation no doubt lies in the fact that, of the four, only the United States was not physically within the theaters of military operations.[3]

This factor and earlier efforts to establish a world body were central to the period before the UN's formal existence and during its earliest years. Those who drew up the pattern of assessments, the formula according to which member states paid their contributions to the UN's budgets and which was adopted when the UN was founded in 1945, had the experience of the League of Nations very much in mind. Apart from its political record, the League had suffered badly from poor administration. At the heart of this lay the question of budgetary contributions and, above all, responsibility for finances. As John G. Stoessinger wrote: 'The similarities of the financial history of the League to that of its successor organization are so numerous as to be disturbing'. He went on to enumerate:

> There was not enough money to do all the things that were considered essential; the pressure for economy was stifling; states were inclined to distrust the budgetary process, protest against their assessments, and declare that they were unjustly burdened … arrears and defaults were a perennial problem.[4]

But, with reference to the League's 'tragic financial history', he did conclude that: 'The framers of the United Nations Charter learned some important lessons.'[5]

While the Second World War was still raging, US State Department officials, among many, were attempting to plan a world order to follow the war, and the embryonic UN was to be part of it. Indeed, during the final years prior to the establishment of the system for assessing member-state percentage contributions to the UN's funding, the possibility was discussed that members should have voting power on the budget in proportion to the size of their contributions to the expenses of the organization.[6] This voting proviso disappeared amid concerns that the organization might become too heavily dependent on one single source of revenue. Gradually the authority of the General Assembly reasserted itself at the Dumbarton Oaks conversations, as they came to be known, between August and October 1944. These concerns about the size of contributions and the weight of voting power have proved to have been well-founded and the dominant influence of the US has remained a constant throughout the years. Those who drew up the pattern of assessments, the formula for which was set up originally when the UN was founded in 1945, bore very much in mind the experience of the League of Nations. The pivotal Articles 17 and 18 investing the General Assembly with the authority to consider and approve the budget (by a two-thirds majority) were in place. Harder were the arrangements for setting up a means of assessing contributions, and after a troubled period of transition it was accepted that a list drawn up by the FAO would be accepted. It was, but only as a further transitional measure until the budgets for 1946 and 1947 were established. It was at this stage that the essentials of the system in practice today were set up. An important and gradual point was that the effect of the Second

World War on the economies of member states was gradually eliminated as an aspect to be taken into account.

The principle of assessed contributions was accepted as reasonable. The system which emerged, initially applying only to the regular budget, was built on a base period, usually of three years, although this has been increased from time to time over the years. There have been suggestions that it might be increased, in the interests of presenting a stable economic picture of a country, to as many as 12 years. Into the relevant time framework have been fed calculations derived from, for a while, the economic dislocation caused by the Second World War, the GDP of a country, its total national income, its population growth and external debts and foreign exchange earnings – among many criteria. There has always been much debate and disagreement – as is still the case today – about whether floor and ceiling limits to contributions should be applied, to prevent domination from the richest countries and to protect the poorest. The guiding principle has been 'capacity to pay', and the percentages in the first years were a not unreasonable balance between perceived wealth and the political aspirations and realities of the time. The system did not begin to run into serious trouble until peace-keeping operations became politically controversial in the late 1950s and 1960s and, eventually, required the establishment of a separate but related system of budgets, as we shall see.

Inevitably, no completely fair balance and distribution of assessments could be found. The ranges of assessments for 1970 showed that the assessments of three members (the US, the Soviet Union and Britain), above 6 per cent of the regular budget, amounted to 52.7 per cent of contributions to the regular budget; and a total of 15, assessed at 1 per cent and above, accounted for 82.9 per cent. Of the total membership of 126, the 69 bottom countries (assessed at between 0.02 and 0.05 per cent) accounted for 2.85 per cent of assessments.[7] In 1980, the top five countries – at above 6 per cent – accounted for 60.25 per cent; and the 18 above 1 per cent for 86.11 per cent; and, out of membership totaling 152, the bottom 94 (at above 0.1 – 0.05 per cent) 1.36 per cent. In 1990, the top five countries (above 6 per cent rate) accounted for 61.98 per cent; the top eight countries (above 3 per cent) for 73.92 per cent; the top 16 (above 1 per cent) from 85.19 per cent; and, out of a membership of 159, the last 101 (between 0.01 and 0.05 per cent) 1.43 per cent. In 1996, the top two (assessed at above 15 per cent) accounted for 40.435 per cent; the top four (above 6 per cent) for 55.885 per cent; the top 15 (above 1 per cent) for 84.375 per cent; and, out of a membership of 185, 117 states, assessed at between 0.01 and 0.05 per cent, provided 1.67 per cent. Visually, the assessment pyramid has an extremely broad base.

The scale of assessments for the years 1998, 1999 and 2000 was based on elements and criteria which included:

- data on gross national product;
- a statistical base period of six years;
- a debt burden adjustment in 1998 based on actual principal repayments, and in 1999 and 2000 on the debt adjustment approach employed in the scale of assessments for the period 1995–7;
- a low *per caput* income adjustment, with a *per caput* income limit of the average world *per caput* income for the statistical base period;
- a minimum assessment rate of 0.001 per cent (changed from 0.01);
- a ceiling rate of 25 per cent; and
- the individual rates of assessment of the least developed countries not to exceed the existing current level of 0.01 per cent.

As a result, the top two contributors (the US and Japan – above 20 per cent) are assessed for 45.573 per cent of assessments; the top four (above 6 per cent – Germany and France) for 61.975 per cent; and the top 16 (one per cent and above) 82.029 per cent. Of the 185 members, the last 152 (assessed at between 0.001 and 0.2 per cent) accounted for 4.084 per cent.[8] From the perspective of the major donors, universality and international democracy in its UN form was often seen as coming at some kind of a price.

The record of assessments show that the highest assessments for the regular budget have, in the past, been solicited from some of the five permanent members of the UN Security Council and other leading international economic powers such as Japan and Germany. Russia since the dissolution of the Soviet Union at the end of 1991 has been hard pressed to pay and its assessment rate has slipped spectacularly. It will be 1.077 per cent in 2000. The OECD countries pay roughly for nearly three-quarters of the regular budget, with the US paying the ceiling rate at 25 per cent, down to the very poorest who pay only a symbolic floor rate of 0.001 per cent, according to the latest series of annual assessments. By the year 2000, the top five contributors are assessed to be: the US (25 per cent), Japan (20.573 per cent), Germany (9.857 per cent), France (6.545 per cent) and Italy (5.437 per cent). Britain is assessed at 5.092 per cent, Spain at 2.591 per cent and China, one of the five permanent members of the Security Council, at 0.995 per cent.

There was much disagreement in the debate over these latest assessments. The US failed to have its ceiling rate of 25 per cent reduced, having angled for it to be lowered to 22 per cent for 1998 and falling to 20 per cent by 2000. Benefiting from the effect of its large population on *per caput* income, China managed to keep its dues below 1 per cent. Japan, without a permanent seat on the Security Council and under-represented in the administration, felt especially peeved. It questioned the fairness of calculations on the basis of a six-year average of GDP data, from 1990 to 1995 (for the 1998–2000 scales) as giving a misleading picture of the relative US and Japanese shares of the world economy. A senior Japanese diplomat at the UN wrote:

> There is a growing disparity between status in the UN and the financial burden of member states. This is particularly true of the five permanent members of the Security Council. At the time the UN was created, their contributions amounted to 71% of the UN budget. The newly adopted scale will bring their share down to less than 40%. Excluding the United States, this would amount to a mere 13.7%, and yet the United States wishes to cut its contributions even more. This is a further departure from the principle of no taxation without representation.[9]

Two countries, in particular, stand out as the leading candidates for permanent membership of a new Security Council if for no other reason than their financial and economic prowess and strength – Germany and Japan. Their positions continue to be held back through hangovers from the days of the formation of the UN. They were 'losers' in the Second World War. It is a small symbol of this that neither German nor Japanese is amongst UN's official languages. The Charter refers to them in Article 53: 'The term enemy state ... applies to any state which during the Second World War has been an enemy of any signatory of the present Charter.' There is a similar reference in Article 107. 'Enemy states as a result of the Second World War' are mentioned again in Article 77 . And this is where this anachronism of the 'enemy state' has rested.

These days, this awkward aspect of that issue does not loom particularly large. These two countries raise additional problems, but for different reasons. Their wealth and political regional influence in the EU and Far East respectively undoubtedly qualify them for larger contributions. But some memories of their roles in the Second World War linger on in their two different geopolitical environments. Their war records remain of symbolic concern and, in popular minds translated into government policy, economic strength and dominance are transformed into hegemony. The circumstances of the Far East are different from those of the EU, but in both spheres it is perceived by fellow states in their regions that there should be limits on their acknowledged global power and influence.

Japan became a member of the UN in 1956 and the two Germanies in 1973.[10] For some years, these countries were limited, by their own constitutions alone, from participating in the sensitive area of peace-keeping activities, although they made contributions through financial assessments. Subsequently, the relevant parliaments have passed legislation to permit, with caveats, participation in UN peace-keeping operations; and they have done so. There has been only occasional tardiness in paying their ever-increasing assessed contributions.

The German position, given its dominant position in Europe and, in particular, the EU, evokes even more sensitive controversy both at home and abroad. Both countries, in their differing ways, feel aggrieved that their financial contributions to all budgets are not matched by their political influence both in the Security Council through a permanent seat and in important positions in UN bureaucracy.

The clue to their growing power in the UN lies in the assessments. In December 1959, the General Assembly adopted for the financial years 1959, 1960 and 1961 Japan's contribution towards UN expenses as 2.19 per cent. It had risen only slightly to 2.77 for 1966 and 1967 and doubled for 1971, 1972 and 1973 to 5.4 per cent. In 1997, its assessment for the regular budget was 15.65 per cent, second only to the US.

In 1997, Germany's assessed contribution was third at 9.06 per cent. The assessed contributions for Germany were more complicated to determine because of the existence of two separate states. Before their full membership of the UN, the separate states had participated in certain UN bodies. But for the years 1983, 1984 and 1985, West Germany was assessed at contributing 8.54 per cent and East Germany 1.39 per cent.

The assessment system which emerged was tied to a base period for calculations, often of three years but with variations over the years between one and 12, and fed into it are calculations based on the GDP of a country, its population growth rate and external debts, with the guiding principle of 'capacity to pay'. The balance between perceived wealth and political aspirations persisted so that in 1958, the main contributors (above 1 per cent) were: the US with 32.51 per cent; the Soviet Union 13.62; Britain 7.78; France 6.4; China 5.01; Canada 3.11; India 2.46; Italy 2.25; Japan 2.19; Ukraine 1.80; Australia 1.79; Sweden 1.39; Poland 1.37; Argentina 1.11; Brazil 1.02; and Netherlands 1.01. The minimum assessment at that stage was 0.04 and at that level were Albania, Bolivia, Cambodia, Costa Rica, Haiti, Honduras, Iceland, Jordan, Laos, Liberia, Libya, Nepal, Nicaragua, Panama, Paraguay, and Yemen. They make interesting reading today.

It is worth examining in greater detail the method by which contributions are assessed. The complicated system employed does not reflect accurately the current wealth of individual countries today, underestimating as a result, in particular, the contributions of some Middle and Far Eastern countries. At the heart of the problem is the elusiveness of discovering criteria which are both wieldy and relatively easy to calculate and are flexible enough not to become swiftly out of date and yet able to contain the vagaries of short-term economic and financial fluctuations.[11] Variations on calculating national wealth – essentially GNP – and pulling in such factors as population growth rate and international indebtedness have all been in use since the establishment of the UN. An element of fairness has been introduced to allow for ceilings on payments for the rich and the very poor. The approaches try to take account of social variables which often slip through the trawling net of calculations of domestic wealth. The dollar is adjudged the best currency in which to calculate all UN transactions. Given the notable record of inconsistencies and tardiness of national statistics even in the more sophisticated countries, a point of discussion has been the base period of time – ranging from 3 to 7 years or more – on which assessments of contributions should be made.

Surges of apparent wealth in the Middle East from hydrocarbons and in the Far East through attracting investment and the provision of services, have often given the lie to current assessment percentages, as even a cursory look at the current list of assessment rates show. The wealth generated in the 'tiger' economies of the Far East showed itself in 1997–8 to be of a vapid and transient nature, raising again the issue of establishing benchmarks to provide some consistency against unpredictable fluctuations.

The regular budget today accounts for roughly less than one tenth of all the expenditure that comes under or can be proved to be attached to the UN system – not just in peace-keeping, but also in humanitarian, social, economic and development affairs. Its percentage assessment system, along with a small proportion of its funds, accounts for a considerable part of the running of the UN's specialized and affiliated agencies. This does not mean that the UN budget controls them, but it does mean that the connecting link remains like lines on an administrative flow chart.

As has been shown, the budgets have more often than not suffered from shortfalls in contributions, accusations of mismanagement and threats of bankruptcy than accolades for smooth running. With rare exceptions, this may be attributed to the nature of the UN system rather than any ingrained predilection for disorder or dishonesty. It is a curiosity that the memory of the League of Nations, some of whose assets passed to the UN, has been often invoked as an example of how not to run an organization, not just from its political record, but also for its mismanagement of its financial system and information service. The League had suffered from the dispersal of authority over the determining of a budget and the approval of its accounts. Today, the General Assembly, the Fifth Committee of the General Assembly, the CPC and the ACABQ play important roles in the processing of budgets, which with some justification are subject to prolonged scrutiny more stringent than that of many national budgets. Both the League and the UN share this special feature of being often subject to small and powerful agencies such as these and, in both cases, the system of apportioning expenses – the assessment method – caused difficulties. Like the UN, the League had been faced with the problem of deciding on a fiscal year and the inevitable lag in the arrival of payments from member countries. In the end, the ultimate budgetary authority lies with the General Assembly, with Article 18 of the Charter specifically providing that 'budgetary questions' require a two-thirds majority for passage.[12] Its directions are more detailed, even if its methods of punishment for failures to pay are weak. But the planners of budgetary mechanisms for the UN-to-be in the 1940s had a science of public budgeting at their disposal through practical and academic experience, which was much more advanced than that available to the founders of the League of Nations.

From the start, the UN and its budgetary regimes have suffered from two now familiar complaints – that the organization is wastefully costly and that it suffers chronically from cash flow problems, verging on bankruptcy. The first budget was modest, with about $20 million appropriated for 1946 – and even then there were grumbles about over spending. Childers and Urquhart make the case that the reputation of historical budget matters is out of touch with reality:

> The facts about UN budget growth have often been mythologized.
>
> In 1946 the UN Regular Budget was $21.5 million. In 1992 it was $1,181.2 million. This represents an increase by 55 times during 46 years, which would not in itself be a horrendous growth for an institution that started from scratch.
>
> The UN's regular budget has always been raised from members and expressed in US Dollars, the value of which has greatly declined since 1946. Thus, in real terms the UN regular budget has grown only 10 times since 1946. The same real-terms growth pattern has applied to the regular budgets of the assessment-financed specialized agencies (ILO, FAO, UNESCO, WHO).[13]

In some senses, the pressure for no growth and indeed decline in UN budgets is little more than a cosmetic activity, particularly when account is taken of the size of expenditures by governments on defense, and the ever-growing sums needed to meet the costs of organizing and administering humanitarian aid. Juxtaposing the relative sizes of these expenditures has rarely made more than a debating point, and often a spectacular one at that. But they demonstrate that the world gets the UN on the cheap. It rose modestly to cross the $100m mark only in 1964, and $200 million in 1970. The biennial budget was introduced in 1974–5 (see Chapter 3).

The spending curve became steeper, but in 1980 the expenditure figure was only just over $600 million. Many graphics have tended to be misleading, encouraging such headlines as 'budget bloat'. Debates about both wastage and the need for more efficiency (and for member states to pay their dues on time) were often as repetitive as expensive political discussions in the General Assembly, Security Council and committees. Sometimes they had their humorous side. Jamil Baroody, the Maronite, Lebanese-born representative of Saudi Arabia for many years was a filibusterer *extraordinaire*. He delighted in paralysingly long and wandering speeches often with a needless anti-Israel tinge. On one occasion in 1976, his protracted contribution to the debate included topics ranging from King David to the Romans and the caliphs. He brought it abruptly to a halt, but promised more later, saying that he had meanwhile to attend a pressing Tunisian reception. Earlier, in 1969, Baroody had turned his rage on a journalist who had asked how much a speech to the Security Council had cost the UN in overtime payments!

The $1 billion mark was not crossed until the mid-1980s. During that period, the US, Britain and the Soviet Union attempted to halt budgetary escalation by demanding that the secretary-general put a ceiling on the 1982–3 budget and accept stringent limits on future budgets. But he was under considerable pressure from developing countries to expand various programs. This group of states has the voting power in the General Assembly to determine how much should be spent and on what, but, as has been shown, at the same time contributed proportionately the least.

By contrast, the eight richest countries by assessment – Britain, Canada, France, Germany, Italy, Japan, the Soviet Union, and the US – were paying about 70 per cent, and the developing countries a small part of the remainder. It was a situation which refueled the argument about relating voting power to the size of contribution. It was this argument in which the less prosperous pro-Eastern Bloc and the developing countries found considerable comfort and a convenient alliance of interests by promoting the important symbolism of equal voting strengths.

In the 1990s more rigid cost-restraining measures were enacted. In 1990, the regular budget expenditures were $1.03 billion.[14] They rose to

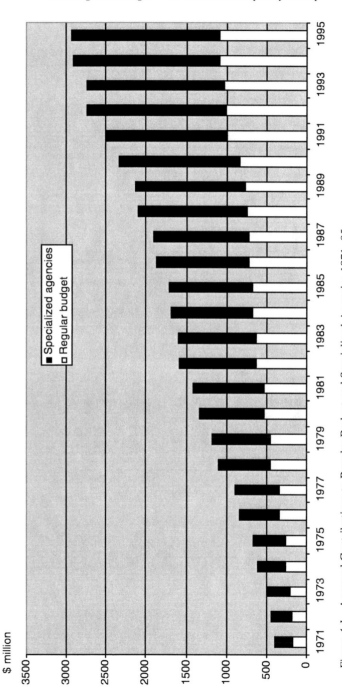

$ million

Figure 4.1   Assessed Contributions to Regular Budget and Specialized Agencies 1971–95
Source: Klaus Hüfner, Freie Universität Berlin for Global Policy Forum (www. globalpolicy.org). Specialised agencies include the IAEA; without Bretton Woods Institutions.

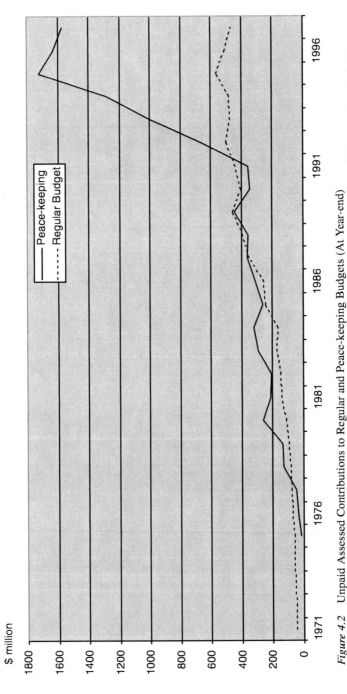

Figure 4.2   Unpaid Assessed Contributions to Regular and Peace-keeping Budgets (At Year-end)
Sources: for regular budget: Klaus Hüfner, Freie Universität Berlin, for Global policy Forum (www.globalpolicy.org). For peace-keeping budgets: Michael Renner for Global Policy Forum (www.global policy.org).

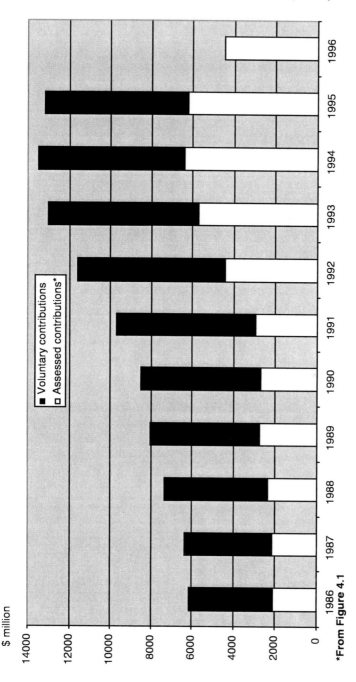

$ million

Figure 4.3 Total UN System Expenditures 1986–96
Source: Klaus Hüfner, Freie Universität Berlin.
The data includes neither the Human Rights Tribunals, which are a separate but relatively small item, nor the Bretton Woods Institutions.

*From Figure 4.1

■ Voluntary contributions
□ Assessed contributions*

$1.4 billion in 1995, but have fallen since. The biennial regular budgets for 1996–7 were estimated at $2.6 billion and for 1998–9 $2.48 billion. (Dividing these estimates by two has proved to be a plausible guide to expenditure. In 1996, for example, it amounted to $1.304 billion). The bulk of its expenditures, nearly 40 per cent, has regularly gone on salaries and the running of the organization in New York and its centers in Geneva, Vienna and Nairobi. These have become increasingly the target of criticism and the focus of cutbacks in the prolonged debate about streamlining and reform.

But earlier, during the 1980s, the regular budget had come under increasing discussion, largely under the impact of two features. The first was the emergence of a separate system for financing peace-keeping operations. An account later will show that it shares some of the characteristics of the regular budget in that its funds are raised, for the most part, by the assessment method, but with some important differences. The issue of peace-keeping operations was perforce more overtly political and subject to non-payment pressures by dissenting members. The second was the enormous rise in the accumulative arrears to the regular budget. The pattern was clear. In the 1970s, the US had no arrears to the regular budget, which rose from $44.8 million in 1970 to $95.8 million in 1979.[15]

But, thereafter the record of the US turned any concepts of budgetary stability upside down. This could be attributed directly to the intrusion of Congress which mandated spending cuts. In resorting to withholding payments, the US was, of major contributors, fairly late on the scene. But its influence was more drastic and long lasting. In 1979 and at the beginning of the 1980s, the US had made withholdings with respect to specific programs and decisions. It cited partly legal objections, and in other cases internal Congressional legislation to demonstrate its disapproval in the relevant UN organs, at political decisions seen as giving greater implied recognition and aid to the PLO and SWAPO in Namibia.

But, in 1985, the US Congress adopted the Kassebaum Amendment (of which more later). This was a quantitatively and qualitatively new type of withholding, until then not practiced by any other member state. Under this amendment, the US resorted to the threat of substantial withholdings, for Congress required the US to reduce its regular budget payments from 25 per cent to 20 per cent, starting with the 1987 UN fiscal year. The aim was not to express legal or political disapproval directly of particular programs or decisions corresponding to such amounts. This cut was to be continued until the UN adopted a system of reforms on budgetary matters by which the major financial contributors would no longer be subjected to budgetary decisions arrived at arbitrarily by the Third World majority of smaller contributors. Plainly, the General Assembly was being given a choice between bankruptcy and budgetary reform.

On 18 December 1985, the General Assembly set up an 18-member group (G-18) which reported back the following August.[16] Some changes in budgetary procedure were made which appeared to meet the Kassebaum requirements. But Congress still refused to appropriate the full amounts owed to the UN and some other UN agencies. A resolution was adopted on 19 December 1986,[17] which gave the major contributors, the industrialized countries, effectively greater control through elaborate procedures for closer scrutiny at an early stage of the budget's formulation but leaving the final decisions on UN budgets with the General Assembly. The US Congress responded reluctantly by setting the appropriations for 1988 and 1989 at $144 million – two-thirds of the assessed dues. By December 1989, despite pleas from the administration for Congress to appropriate the necessary funds, the US was $365 million behind in payments to the regular budget. This represented nearly four-fifths of the total of $461 million owed by all UN members.

The issue of the non-payment of contributions, particularly by the US, and the ensuing series of financial crises has always been a feature of life at the UN. A succession of internal review bodies had been set up in the 1960s and 1970s to confront a series of budgetary crises. The discussions were protracted, at every level of the organization and with different approaches tried and personalities behind them. None were markedly successful and, repeatedly, bankruptcy was postponed by the US paying up at the last minute. During those earlier periods, although the US, as part of its overall ideological battle with the East Bloc stemming from the Cold War and its perception that this was affecting adversely voting in the General Assembly, was critical of UN procedures, it was not the main culprit behind the UN's weaknesses.

US activity towards payments raised the more pertinent question about the UN's financial crises. The immediate cause lay obviously, and already, in the arrears of payment and the withholding of assessed contributions. But there was a larger context for the crisis of confidence in the adequacy of the multilateral structures as they had evolved since 1945. Then, as now, this raised serious doubts as to whether they were adequate for complying with the tasks facing the UN and its institutions. Whether this justified unilateral actions, such as those undertaken by the US, to bring about change is debatable in international law and at odds with the obligations of membership of the UN.

The beginning of this decade gave some signs of promise that the context of the budgetary strains might have been changing. There were hopes raised under the Bush administration, derived in part from his experience as US representative, that the UN was coming back into favor. It is an irony that peace-keeping operations have been throughout the UN years either the near-wreckers or near-saviors of its financial ups and downs. With the ending of the Cold War and some peace-keeping successes, the UN's credibility appeared to rise. Boutros-Ghali, prematurely as it turned out, promulgated it as having a role which could cover some of the conflicts which arose and which were no longer in an East-West context. This revival induced Congress in 1990 to enact new funding legislation, and President Bush promised that all back debts to the organization would be paid by 1995. It was not to be, and global recession made it difficult for member states to pay their dues. The situation of the regular budget slipped back again to one worse than that at the beginning of the 1980s, with the size of the budgets increasing and with them the mountain of accumulated arrears. The US, with the possibilities of some improvement promised under Bush, easily maintained its position as head of the defaulter's list. In the immediate term, the collapse of the Soviet Union added a new dimension. Russia's dollar cash-flow problems matched those of the UN. Ukraine and Belarus moved up the table of defaulters.

Overall figures during the 1990s were misleading, for opponents of the UN's system could derive some wry pleasure from saying that UN expenditures (encompassing, in fact, just the regular and peace-keeping budgets) were rising out of control, ostensibly from $1.410 billion in 1990 to a peak of $4.736 billion in 1994. It was only then, the critics argue, that their cries of alarm were heeded, with the result that expenditures fell to $4.6 billion in 1995 and to $2.6 billion in 1996, mainly because of the reduction in large-scale peace-keeping operations solely in UN hands. This fall has continued.[18] This rise in expenditures did in fact add an important sense of urgency to the renewed growth in the debate about overall reform and streamlining of the UN's activities. For a period, the cries of 'bankruptcy' and 'wolf' seemed almost synonymous. But while to some the peace-keeping expansion may have done a disservice in presenting an exaggerated picture of the UN's plight, individual accounts in surplus once again bailed out the UN's short-term liquidity problems. (The peace-keeping budgets have problems of their own, related to the inability to pay back states contributing men and *matériel*. These are examined in Chapter 5.)

A feature which became increasingly pronounced was the growing feeling that this situation could not be allowed to recur. The US began harking back, particularly after the distressing scenes of the humiliation of their troops involved in peace-keeping in Mogadishu, to the feeling held by successive administrations that they were the major contributor to the UN budget and had been ever since the organization was set up. In return, the US generally felt that they were not getting value for money and this attitude inevitably spilled over into a debate about competence and reform. The attempts at reassessment and reform have to be seen in these contexts. At the time of the Gulf War, there was a resurgence in the US of the feeling that, with the Cold War over and changed attitudes in Moscow, the UN did have a role. But that passed and with it came chauvinist and emotional criticism of US soldiers on peace-keeping deployment having to obey commands from non-US commanders in the field. There was even a court case involving a US soldier who refused to take orders from a non-US commander (he was acquitted). But the over-riding factor, which became strengthened as the decade went on, was the extent to which the US found the UN to be a useful part of its foreign policy armory. Clinton as the end of his presidency began to loom and domestic troubles beset him seemed to show increasingly less interest in the UN.

But already the cycle had restarted for reform of the UN and, tied into this, its finances. Boutros-Ghali has been aware of this in his *Agenda for Peace* and a number of high-level boards were set up to look at practical measures for changes in the financial system. For a time the US was right to judge that the moment to re-examine the possibilities for reform had come. They expressed it with the style characteristic of the contemporary events. From the democratic point of view, the Republican-dominated Congress had made requirements – notably legislation in 1995, but taking effect from October 1996, unilaterally reducing the ceiling on peace-keeping assessments to 25 per cent. The Clinton administration thus was able to claim that domestic legislation hampered the fulfillment of international obligations – as had happened before. They supplemented this with an approach based on the thesis that efficiency was best and would result from cutbacks. and ignoring the fact that surveys showed greater and increasing popular support in the US for the UN than its rulers and Congress cared to credit it with. Towards the end of 1997, when the rates of assessments for the period 1998–2000 were being settled, the US pressed harder, and unsuccessfully, for a measured reduction of its assessed dues from 25 per cent to 20 per cent for the regular budget. This broadened the whole range of calculations out into a wide-ranging debate about the contribution rates as a whole and those of the US in particular.

Nevertheless, it was under Boutros-Ghali that an Efficiency Board was established and that the zero-growth biennial budget in real terms was initiated. The first outlines of what the US had in mind were put forward by Madeleine Albright, at the beginning of 1996 when she was the US ambassador to the UN. They concentrated mainly on administrative reform and this reformist theme gathered in strength and determination throughout the year. In parallel, resentment at the constant state of UN's financial beleaguerement, despite Boutros-Ghali's efforts, was not confined to the US alone. The Group of Seven (G-7) industrialized nations, meeting in Lyon, France, in June 1996 had looked at both administrative reform and new methods of assessment.

The Annan approach to reform was constructed much with the wishes of the US in mind – that of tailoring payment to reforms planned and enacted. It has had a two-track approach. Both are likely to take years to be carried out. The first are being carried out in his role as chief administrative officer and involve management reforms. These can largely be effected as internal changes and adjustments. The second track involved structural reforms such as the composition and expansion of the Security Council and the system of assessments for payments to UN budgets. From the financial and reform aspects, Annan started almost like a government, newly elected but with only a modest overall majority in its notional parliament. He made his 'ministerial' dispositions, notably sticking to Joseph E. Connor as Undersecretary-General for Administration and Management and bringing in Maurice Strong to the new reform portfolio of Executive Coordinator for United Nations Reform. Both have private-sector, business backgrounds steeped in the merits of financial efficiency.

Within the first-track approach, affecting finances, his targets were realistic, but modest. As time passed it became reasonable to ask whether they were in fact little more than symbolic moves as indications of good intent. The 1998–9 budget was to be reduced by $123 million, implying real negative growth. New efficiencies – largely not filling vacant positions and using staff loaned by member states – would result in the cutting of 1000 jobs. The current level of 38 per cent of the UN's resources devoted largely to administration was to be cut to 25 per cent. Some departments dealing with economic and social activities were to be integrated. A 25 per cent reduction in the documentation produced by the Secretariat was ordered. At that stage, these moves could only be seen as a statement of purpose. Annan's first round of reforming suggestions were accepted by the General Assembly in November 1997.[19] Sadly, Congress on the very same day vetoed a bill, part of which involved the paying of some of the US arrears to the UN. It was a heavy symbol of the hazards of US-UN relations.

The regular budget of the UN also carries its responsibilities to the organizations' specialized and affiliated agencies. An important role in this lies with ECOSOC, whose writ is, as its title suggests and the Charter maintains, to establish and 'coordinate' the specialized agencies.[20] There are 16 in all (if the Bretton Woods institutions and IFAD are included) and exist as freestanding intergovernmental organizations established by inter-governmental agreement, rather than by resolution of a UN organ. As such, they are not part of the UN *per se*. They fall into three categories. The Big Five – FAO, ILO, UNESCO, UNIDO and WHO; the technical specialized agencies ICAO, IMO, ITU, UPU, WIPO and WMO; and IBRD, IDA, IFC, IFAD and IMF.[21] This is reflected in their budgetary relationship, for technically they are separate. Theoretically the General Assembly has the power to examine budgetary arrangements and adminis-trative budgets of the specialized agencies. However, it has not really exer-cised this authority and indeed the specialized agencies with their variety of systems for funding pay little more than lip service to financial 'co-ordinating' efforts by ECOSOC such is their independence. Nevertheless, their own systems are the subject of study as part of the UN system not least to see if their varied methods for obtaining funds have application for the regular and peace-keeping budgets.[22] This semi-autonomy has been a predictable cause of concern and focus of attention. The politics and inter-nal power struggles have often been given critical publicity which is not the focus of examination here. But the inevitable consensus is that in virtu-ally all agencies there is scope for cutting back on expenses by eliminating duplication and streamlining the head office staff. For these organizations depend on assessed contributions from member states for some part of their income. The approved regular budgets for the UN and 11 of the spe-cialized agencies (plus the IAEA – an affiliated agency) rose from $2.1 billion in 1988 to $3.17 billion in 1997.[23] The UN's share, at $751.5 mil-lion in 1988 and $1.1 billion in 1997 held steady at about 35 per cent. The assessed contributions were overall slightly lower, at $1.99 billion in 1988 and $2.97 billion in 1997, with the UN's share marginally higher at an almost constant 36 per cent. The methods for calculating the assessments per country for each agency vary considerably and can range from one close to that of the regular UN budget to a near-voluntary system. The WHO, for example, which was created in 1948 as the UN specialized agency responsible for international coordination in health, has changed its funding base from one predominantly dependent on the UN regular budget to increasing reliance on extrabudgetary or voluntary funding. In the WHO's case, by the late 1980s EBFs were about equal to the regular bud-get funds, as opposed to about one-quarter in 1971. EBF resources have come from donor governments, multilateral organizations, nongovermen-tal organizations and the private sector.

Back to the regular budget of the UN. There were from the start discus-sions about emergency funds to tide the system over, in the short term, without having to resort to obtaining permission from the General Assembly. Part of the inspiration for this came from the difficulties which the League of Nations had encountered. This temporary overdraft facility was intended to consist of assessed subscriptions, which remained the property of the member states making them in the form of the WCF. They should, after the contributions had been assessed, be set off against them. Indeed, in the early days when the UN first came into action, this fund was pressed into service as one of a series of transitional measures. It had become a permanent feature in 1946, set after some debate at $20 million and remained a bone of contention until the end of the 1950s. The intended mechanism was that cash would be borrowed from the fund to pay the organization's expenses, and returned as assessed dues were paid. Its working was never satisfactory with considerable gaps between disbursements and sums actually contributed. Singer, one of the earlier writers on the UN's finances summed up a sorry tale:

> At this writing, then, the [Working Capital] Fund is back at the 1946 level, and the secretary-general must still rely upon it for unforeseen and extraordinary expenses (such as those incurred in the Congo), self-liquidating purchases, loans to the specialized agencies, and of course, regular budgetary expenditures while awaiting receipt of national contributions.[24]

Plus ça change ... !

However, it did see the UN through emergencies, particularly, as indicated above, when payments were slow to come in, and in peace-keeping, when, for example, UNEF ran into severe financial running problems. Its capital was raised to $40 million in 1963. While this device has helped, *in extremis,* in reducing deficits and providing stopgap arrangements at the beginning of the year before assessed contributions start arriving, there has always been a marked reluctance to establish a settled reserve fund. The WCF has stood notionally at $100 million since 1982 and there was a recommendation by the Volcker/Ogata report[25] that it should be doubled through a one-off assessment. This was not welcomed with much warmth. But it remains much in reserve and perhaps only on paper since it can only be replenished in full when member states pay all their past dues. In addition, its size in relation to the overall budget has become increasingly small. Originally, it should be recalled, it was larger than the regular budget itself. At $200 million, this would bring its authorized level up to about 15 per cent of the regular budget. Further increases have been recommended, but probably set aside after the proposal in 1997 of the formation of a revolving credit fund.

One other experiment was tried, as a result of the crisis over ONUC (see Chapter 5). In many senses this episode, which eventually stretched over several decades, perhaps belongs better to the section dealing with peace-keeping operations. But it occurred in an era before special accounts had been established to cover such missions. The bonds issue was resorted to because the Soviet Union and France had declared their intentions not to pay their shares towards the UNEF and ONUC operations – for political reasons. The accumulated arrears on both peace-keeping operations had reached more than $80 million by the end of 1961, which was a sum larger than the annual regular budget. Mercifully in December of that year the General Assembly authorized the secretary-general to issue bonds to the value of $200 million. The bond issue kept the organization and these two major peace-keeping missions going for a year.

The regular budget remains central to the UN's functions because, on levels outside peace-keeping operations, it funds its functions, mostly in the administrative areas. However, as states continue to fail and intra-state wars proliferate, the demand on the humanitarian agencies will increase and become more costly. They will require more not less administration as peace-keeping operations take on, as they have been doing for many years, a wider range of tasks mainly associated with civilian, not military, activities. This will also put the onus of efforts to co-ordinate missions and operations with NGOs. On both the practical and symbolic levels, the UN will continue to have problems fulfilling its roles if the cash flow is irregular. Its reserves, if they exist at all, become run down and this creates uncertainty about the extent to which the UN can respond effectively to legitimate and important demands.

In the face of this evident backsliding and evasion of duties, one can only wonder at the financial durability of the UN. Elmandjra, another early explorer of UN finances, mused that: 'The legal obligatory character of budgetary decisions and the absence of a "formal veto" clashes with the attributes of sovereignty of all member States and with the political weight of the major powers.'[26] In particular, it sets this concept of state sovereignty against the principle of collective responsibility and the implications of Article 17 could be fairly far-reaching. As has been seen, it upsets Congress more than a little to realize that the General Assembly has, in theory, complete authority over the UN budget, although, in practical terms, this is no longer the case. Historically, it is hardly a surprise that richer countries should have resorted to financial weapons to counter unpalatable ideological or political disputes. Fundamental reform here, as well as elsewhere, would strike at the bureaucratic form as well as spiritual shape of the organization.

5 Finding and Funding the Paths to Peace

The peace-keeping budgets have had, over the years, an ambiguous existence and have been the most prominent of targets for discussion and controversy. These were, and continue to be, the most conspicuous activities of the UN, even if their numbers and costs have declined since the heights of the early 1990s and their natures changed considerably. They symbolize one of the central purposes of the establishment of the UN during the Second World War. The opening words of the Charter assert that:

> We the Peoples of the United Nations determined to save succeeding generations from the scourge of war, which twice in our lifetime has brought untold sorrow to mankind ... and for these ends ... to ensure, by the acceptance of principles and the institution of methods, that armed forces shall not be used, save in the common interest, and to employ international machinery for the promotion of the economic and social advancement of all peoples.

Viewed half a century later, such words might seem pretentious and cynical, but peace-keeping[1] in a variety of different forms, often vilified and criticized, has persisted. Given the fire the peace-keeping missions themselves have come under and given the inevitably political nature of their tasks, it is remarkable that the UN funding system – and at times lack of system – has survived. Two contradictory oddities persist. On the one hand, the regular budget has on a regular basis had to turn to the surpluses in individual special accounts of operations to bail itself out. This is a long-standing arrangement which is based on a silent compromise by member states on the issue of funds being raised for one purpose (specific peace-keeping missions) being used for another (the regular budget).[2] On the other, the UN system for funding peace-keeping has survived largely on the peace-keeping idealism of its active participating member states. It has its own run of arrears in assessed contributions, but the growing critical shortfall has been not through money failing to come in to the UN, but from a cash flow outwards. The UN has been increasingly unable to reimburse member states contributing soldiers and equipment for operations. The world has had its peace-keeping from the UN on tick.

Over the years, their character has passed through identifiable phases. Initially, they could have been classed as 'peace-keeping', associated with Chapter VI of the Charter. Historically this was, by and large, the case with the few initiated in the 1960s and 1970s. But even exercises such as UNEF I in Sinai and ONUC in the Congo showed that there was more to peace-keeping than interposing forces after a situation had allegedly become stable following a conflict. The focus of this chapter is less on the nature of the myriad and stream of missions which the UN has undertaken and continues to take on. Those have been ably analyzed elsewhere. The concentration will be on the strengths and shortcomings of their funding. Inevitably, the two aspects cannot be totally separated. But one word of caution and qualification is required and this applies to both the financial and practical sides of what is loosely known as peace-keeping. There should be no illusions that there has ever been a 'golden age' of such operations. That would be as great a fallacy as regarding the Cold War era as having produced a range of political and strategic certainties against which reactions and plans could be measured. Peace-keeping operations, in their broadest interpretative and practical sense, have been evolving and changing since the very first observer group was sent out, with the ending of the Second World War hardly a year earlier.

That said, some classification of the various ages of peace-keeping is required for the sake of the historical context. The first phase started with the establishment of UNSCOB (1947–54) to observe infiltration across Greece's borders in the north. This phase lasted from 1946 until 1956 and was one characterized by missions with observer together with peace-keeping functions. UNTSO in the Middle East and UNMOGIP in Kashmir, the old durables, were creations of that period. Peace-keeping became, during this formative period of acceptance, which lasted until 1967, part of the scenery of conflict involvement, if management is too strong a term. These were the years of UNEF I and ONUC, in particular. and latterly UNFICYP in Cyprus. The first largely achieved what was required, though its departure pointed up the fragile terms on which any force is present in hostile territory. ONUC, in a perverse way, proved that peace-keeping had come to stay in an interventionist way. The Cyprus mission is an amalgam of the two, vying with UNTSO, UNMOGIP and, later, UNIFIL, for the record of longevity.

During the years between the 1967 and 1973 Arab-Israeli wars, no new missions were created, in part a reflection of the rivalry between the US and the Soviet Union, directly and through their client states. In the following years to 1978, three were established, all in the Middle East, UNEF II, UNDOF and UNIFIL, the latter to join the ranks of the longer-serving operations. This could be called a period of reassertion and re-establishment, although the missions themselves were never without criticism and dispute. For the next decade, again no new UN mission was started. This was probably a by-product of a new bout of rivalry in the Cold War. But it is interesting to note that two non-UN peace-keeping missions were undertaken. The successful mission, the MFO, was the successor to UNEF in Sinai, after the conclusion of the Egypt-Israel peace treaty of 1979. It has been carrying out the physical monitoring of this treaty with success (and some questions asked about UN operations) largely under the direction of the US. The second, the MNF, again outside the auspices of the UN in two stages between 1982–4, was a humiliating failure for the US and its European allies.[3] If anything, this period served to show the limits of what, in peace-keeping terms, was possible.

The periods since have been perhaps more formative than any other in the history of UN peace-keeping, both in numbers and the nature of missions undertaken. It is sufficient to say here that with the ending of the Cold War, there were many expectations that UN peace-keepers would find new roles to re-establish peace-keeping in all its multifaceted roles as an important contributor to global politics. Broadly, the period from 1988 until today could be seen, in numerical terms as one of expansion and then contraction. In terms of new dimensions, it was a period in which there was an expansion of greater variety, reaching a peak in terms of numbers of missions in operation, troops on the ground and expenditures between 1993 and 1995. As had not become truly apparent at the time, it was the period in which peace-keepers finally grew up to the facts and realities of life. Amongst these was the realization that today's complex conflicts required more than military involvement and the intervention of organizations and resources both inside and outside the UN system. Although not fully acknowledged at the time, UN peace-keepers and NGOs, in the forefront the ICRC, had had to work together for several decades. This relationship has moved on radically as Edwin Smith and Thomas Weiss have noted:

> Making better use of NGOs in tandem with the United Nations could only help build greater public support for the world organization as an independent actor and for multilateralism more generally. ... [I]t matters little whether the focus is humanitarian relief, election monitoring, development assistance or environmental action. 'Subcontracting' may be an apt description, but the United Nations and its member states should treat NGOs not as 'contractors' but rather as 'partners'.[4]

In the early part of the 1990s, peace-keeping expenditure had consumed around one third of all peace-keeping costs since 1948. Boutros-Ghali summarized the situation as follows:

> As of June 1996, the United Nations has mounted 41 peace-keeping operations. Fifteen were established in the 40 years between 1948 and 1988; the other 26 have all been set up since 1989. More than 750,000 military and civilian personnel have taken part... Most early peace-keeping operations responded to inter-State conflict. In recent years, however, peace-keeping has more often addressed conflicts within States, sometimes where Governments no longer function. Soldiers serving under United Nations command as peace-keeping observers or troops, wearing familiar blue berets or blue helmets, are being joined by increasing numbers of civilians. Together, they have been given ever more challenging mandates. They have helped promote national reconciliation and respect for human rights, and organized and monitored elections. Humanitarian tasks have been brought within the purview of peace-keeping. Peace-keepers have even participated in the reconstruction of State institutions.[5]

As a summary it is in the main accurate, but also bald. For it reflects neither the bureaucratic strain this expansion imposed on the UN system, nor the physical and financial costs. Boutros-Ghali rarely gave the impression of standing back and wondering where it was all leading. It led, in fact, to a reassessment of the UN's roles and its system.

But from the early 1990s, with the Cold War at an end, the US the sole superpower and intra-state tensions and war in the ascendant in such countries as the rump Yugoslavia, Somalia, Cambodia and Rwanda, they expanded not only in number but also in ambition, taking on the notion – according to Chapter VII of the UN Charter – of 'peace enforcement'. The effectiveness of these roles has always been under critical appraisal, and with it have come questions about whether the money directed towards specific missions has been well spent – when it has been possible to raise it in time to meet emergent situations.

The divisions between these two early phases are not clear cut, for it is a cliché which has the merit of being accurate, that no two situations were similar. Military forces inevitably gave medical treatment to the local civilian sick. Longstanding forces in Cyprus and south Lebanon became not just one more tribe in the political jungle but also a significant economic factor. To some extent these were reactive developments. But emerging out of these two identifiable forms of peace operations has risen a third category – that of 'peace maintenance'.[6] This category, in effect, looking after the full range of aspects which go with civilian, legal, social and economic development to ensure that peace is sustained and can become self-sustainable, had been in practice, dubbed then 'multi-dimensional', already in Cyprus, south Lebanon and Namibia (UNTAG 1989–90). This would involve a considerable widening of UN operations to encompass many of the political, humanitarian and civilian roles of a full state. They could provide a framework for administering that troubled state or even just a region in a more orderly fashion until conditions for a sustainable and independent peace could be created. It raised again the issue of the blurring of boundaries between peace and non-peace operations, which have their own reflections in the sources from which their funds are drawn. The establishment of a quasi-formal governmental authority could be regarded as falling out of the peace-keeping category and, it might be argued, under the aegis of the regular budget or those of UN specialized and affiliated agencies. One factor has been, for example, that humanitarian operations have had to come to terms with the political aspect of their works and with the need on occasions for military support. Similarly, military operations have found that they too have developed or need non-military adjuncts to their activities. In financial terms, this has opened the way to what should be a major theme in the coming years. This breaking down of the theoretical boundaries between UN and non-UN territories and between the public and private domains should be seen as opening the opportunities for more and different types and sources of financing. It should mean that UN agencies are not bound by taking on larger tasks with the same or fewer resources. More funds would be available but also the responsibilities shared. It was one criticism of Annan's reform proposals of 1997 that this development had not been fully recognized and that the parts of UN system concerned with humanitarian operations, despite some changes and restructuring, was not gearing itself up towards accommodating it.

The very earliest missions – and these became the exceptions – were expected to be financed out of the regular budget. UNTSO was and still is. But UNEF in Sinai and ONUC in the Congo turned out to be complicated political and administrative exceptions. Just as UNEF established a pattern in military and diplomatic terms for a UN intervention, so it did for the evolution of financing. It was established in Sinai after the Suez operation of 1956, involving an alliance between Britain, France and Israel against Egypt. Attempts to have it, at first, funded out of the general budget plus payments from the main protagonists failed and, in the midst of the global uproar, it was eventually agreed that such operations should be funded separately. UNEF, partly as an accounting convenience, was placed in a separate *ad hoc* account covered by assessments according to similar scales as those for the general budget.

By the early 1970s, a new form of assessment, which involved putting a greater percentage burden on the five permanent members of the Security Council, was evolved; and this has remained broadly the principle according to which money has been raised. It reflects their responsibility for establishing the mandate of an operation. The General Assembly then authorizes the funds member states are to pay according to a special scale. Inevitably, this method has suffered from the same difficulties of the assessment system for the general budget. It has also been prone to exploitation for political reasons, as the focus of attention of each mission associated with peace is far more specific and liable to be controversial than the aims of the general budget. Inevitably, member states of the UN have been slow to pay their contributions with the result that some peace-keeping operations have been painfully short of money in the beginning. And wastefully so, as the process of catching up on lost time has often been more costly than prompt action and decision-making. It is an irony, however, that peace-keeping budgets have been in surplus, with UNTAG in South-West Africa as the clearest example, and the source of emergency funding for the general budget, and other budgets short of liquid assets.

The UN's figures for expenditures on peace-keeping operations on an annual basis are notional for the reason that mandates, which include financial appropriations, are renewed usually for six months and with different starting dates. This rarely coincides with a calendar or fiscal year. In addition, the inflow of funds may not be regular. Nevertheless, these UN-based figures give a guidance to the pattern of and increase in these operations. The figures for expenditure before budgets for peace-keeping became formally authorized in 1973 have been compiled and amount to $2.229 billion for the period 1947 (zero) to 1981 ($141 million).[7] In the biennium 1982–3, they amounted to $439 million. In 1988–9, they first showed signs of rapid expansion, reaching $847 million. In annual figures extrapolated from the Special Accounts for each mission, expenditure rose from $464 million in 1990, to $490 million in 1991. In 1992, expenditure quadrupled to $1.77 billion rising further to a plateau of $3.06 billion (1993), $3.34 billion (1994) and $3.36 billion (1995). A marked drop followed to $1.84 billion in 1996 and $1.3 billion in 1997. In June 1997, the General Assembly approved Special Account appropriations of $853 million for the period 1 July 1997 to 30 June 1998 for 12 active peace-keeping operations. For the same 1998–9 period, it appropriated a further, smaller sum – $636.7 million.

Expenditures will thus have fallen back to below the levels of the biennial regular budget of a decade earlier. The closing down of large operations such as those in former Yugoslavia, where non-UN forces took over peace-keeping missions at prodigious costs, largely accounted for this turn around, showing how the UN was forced to curtail its expenditures dramatically, after a surge of over-extension. More broadly and historically, they show how the peace-keepers and their managers have been consistently under strain and the target of criticism as their operations moved, as Boutros-Ghali recounted, through the various stages of responsibility, from the role of observer, to conducting full-scale war, to genuine peace-keeping and preserving and to peace-enforcement and beyond.

Consistently, one way the UN secretariat has escaped from a financial bind in the general budget has been by turning to the peace-keeping budgets to bail itself out. Peter the peacemaker has to be robbed to pay Paul the UN paymaster and custodian. To recap this role: regular budget cash balances at the end of the year have been in the red: $26 million in 1994, reaching a peak of $197 million in 1996 and expected to reach $184 million in 1998. Peace-keeping budgets registered a cash surplus of $479 million in 1994, rose to $923 million in 1995 and have declined since, estimated at $761 million at the end of 1998. For both sets of budgets the peace-keeping operations permitted a surplus of $453 million in 1994, which rose to $728 million in 1995 and which was expected to fall to $577 million in 1998.[8]

The system for financing peace-keeping had evolved from the method of paying for the regular budget through percentage contributions assessed on individual member states according to their capacity to pay. There were two basic differences. First, the five permanent members of the Security Council were subject to a surcharge amounting to about 25 per cent for the privilege of their special position. Second, related to that, the member states were classified in four groups – A (the Permanent Five), B, C, and D – of percentage assessed payments. These related approximately to their regular budget assessments. The technique of a special peace-keeping assessment was introduced with some formality in 1973[9] and was based on the methods used for the general budget. But the resolution recognized that 'a different procedure is required from that applied to meet expenditures of the regular budget'. Under the division into A, B, C and D categories, the main onus falls on the A category. These five bear the 80–90 per cent relief given to the C and D groups as a surcharge on their regular budget shares. As a result, this premium means that the Permanent Five are, in effect, assessed at rates about one quarter higher than their regular budget shares. Group D (broadly the poorest countries) is assessed at 10 per cent of their regular budget rates; Group C at 20 per cent, and Group B at their regular budget shares. The four categories have tended to be rigidly adhered to but there were exceptions: Spain and Portugal, which shifted themselves from C to B categories in assessments, partly to gain status and partly in acknowledgment of their improving economic condition, as recognized by membership of the then EC.

Since this special peace-keeping scale was adopted, the US has paid in excess of 30 per cent for peace-keeping missions. Under US legislation which came into effect in October 1996, the US payment was limited to 25 per cent. The UN, however, continued to assess the US at the higher special peace-keeping rate – about 30.5 per cent. There have been discussions with China and Russia to see if they would be prepared to pay a greater proportion of the reduction for developing countries. Agreement has been sought for the Permanent Five to a minimum or floor amount.

An important and crucial dimension which deepened the crises over Suez and the Congo was the effects of the interpretation of events by the two superpowers: the US, which was at serious odds with Britain over the Suez invasion, and the Soviet Union, which was anxious to deflect the world's attention from Hungary. In the Congo, these two were keen to seek international support in the East-West ideological conflict they saw being enacted on the ground. The mandate of UNEF I was in effect and practice far simpler to enforce than that of ONUC, which found itself sucked into a civil war. There were political interests and intrusions at every level, which were as complicated as any today, although perhaps on a comparatively smaller scale.

These intrusions showed themselves in ways which have direct bearing on the conduct of modern peace-keeping operations. The first intrusion was the funding of these operations and how these began an evolution towards what is normally practiced today. The second, closely linked to the first, was that, in inducing one of the UN's earliest financial crises, questions arose about reform of the organization. Funding procedures were the most relevant because both they and the financial crises became embroiled in a mixture of arguments. At the time of the UNEF issue, Dag Hammarskjöld, the Secretary-General, attempted to have a special account established to cover UNEF's expenses – aside from the regular budget. For a while the Soviet bloc argued that the burden should fall on those countries, which had precipitated the Suez crisis – Britain, France and Israel. A compromise formula was found, with the US bearing most of the burden. This formula produced a partial form of assessed separate special account and established the principle of collective responsibility through a fund of up to $10 million initially.[10] For, with high anticipated mission costs and emerging problems in the collection of regular budget assessments, the secretary-general had proposed that financing be based on the principle that a state providing a unit to the force would be responsible for all the costs of equipment and salaries, and that all other costs would be met by the UN, outside its normal budget.[11] This meant, in effect, that UNEF I would be financed through a special account. Separate financing arrangements for peace-keeping had been born. It was duly endorsed by the General Assembly in November 1956,[12] and the resolution the following month held that all expenses of UNEF, other than for forces provided for by states, would be borne by the UN, and that such expenses up to $10 million would be apportioned among all member states on the basis of the regular scale of assessments for 1957.

The point about this resolution was that it underlined the principle of collective financial responsibility and the idea that peace-keeping was a collective obligation, although it was not formalized until some years later. As a result, its costs had to be borne collectively and on the basis of compulsory, universal payments by all member states. In this case, a two-thirds majority in the General Assembly of those present and voting delivered the binding obligation. In theory it bound governments to pay the share of operational activities whether they supported them or not. The principle was not observed in practice. It was the start of a long tradition of payment delays to troop-contributing countries as a result of the UN's lack of resources.

The financial structure of the UN organization itself was not threatened, but it almost tumbled under the impact of ONUC. In the protracted wrangles to find a formula for financing, both the Soviet Union and France declared their intentions not to pay their shares.[13] By the end of 1961, the accumulated arrears on both UNEF and ONUC had reached more than $80 million, which was a sum larger than the annual regular budget. This deficit was the result of these missions having gone far beyond any previous peace-keeping missions in size and function. In December of that year, the situation was eased by the General Assembly exceptionally authorizing the secretary-general to issue bonds to the amount of $200 million – with the interest (2 per cent per annum) and principal to be repaid in 25 annual instalments. It did the trick and actual sales, beginning in 1963, amounted to $169.9 million when the issue was closed. Under terms set by Congress, the US was permitted conditionally to purchase up to half the issue. It was an exceptional example of the UN resorting to extrabudgetary methods for raising money for its running expenses. Significantly for the principles of obligations to pay, additional difficulties arose, for those states refusing to pay for UNEF I and ONUC eventually began to withhold portions of their assessed contributions to the regular budget in proportion to their shares of the bonds. But in the short term, the bond issue did ease the cash crisis.

These two crises contained not only overtly political problems, involving the Soviet Union and France but also internal UN implications for the legally binding nature of the organization and articles of the Charter. The refusal by France and the Soviet Union raised the possibility, at one stage, of those two permanent members of the Security Council losing their voting rights in the General Assembly under Article 19. Fortunately, the ICJ had reached an important decision upholding the principle of collective financial responsibility for peace-keeping. On 20 July 1962, the Court ruled, by a vote of 9 to 5, that the expenditures authorized in the General Assembly resolution dealing with peace-keeping financing 'constituted "expenses of the organization" within the meaning of article 17, paragraph 2 of the Charter'.[14] In other words, all member states were responsible for all expenditures appropriated by the General Assembly, pertained to UNEF I and ONUC.

The two exercises made the stark point that the UN was not yet properly organized to cope with financing peace-keeping operations. But from these crises also came the first stages towards formalizing an assessment scale adapted from that for the regular budget for individual peace-keeping missions. The process of regularizing to some extent payments for peace-keeping operations moved on in 1973.

There have also been some anomalies such as those involving Yemen and the Iraqi border with Kuwait, paid for, in the former case, by Egypt and Saudi Arabia and, in the latter, two-thirds by Kuwait, rather than by contributors or assessments. In addition, voluntary contributions continued at a low level (mainly for specific items), but these do not alter the present system which has held for about 40 years that individual missions are covered by special accounts raised by assessed contributions from the member states.

Under the category of peace operations there is another group, including, notably, the mission in Cyprus (UNFICYP from 1964), which was financed at first on a voluntary basis by the contributors to the peace-keeping force and not from general assessments for a specifically created budget. But the majority are now paid for out of contributions assessed on UN members. The formation of UNSF and UNFICYP were departures from financing precedent, if indeed an active one had been established, as a sort of recognition that mandatory assessments based on the regular budgetary procedure had run into an impasse. The expenses of UNSF in West New Guinea (West Irian), created in 1962, were shared equally by the two parties directly involved in the West Irian dispute – Indonesia and the Netherlands. On a technical point, UNSF was the last peace-keeping force acting under General Assembly authorization. Thereafter, the establishment of peace-keeping missions became the prerogative of the Security Council. The same method of sharing expenses by the parties involved was employed, as we have seen, for UNYOM in Yemen (1963–4), with the costs shared by Saudi Arabia and the United Arab Republic (Egypt).

UNFICYP continues today. Originally, it was the only peace-keeping operation to be funded by a combination of money from voluntary contributions and payments by troop-contributing governments. Latterly, as contributions slipped behind and the arrears passed the $100 million mark, the system has been changed to contributions from assessments plus money from troop-contributors, and from Cyprus and Greece. It is a form of payment half way to the special individual budgets, which have become the norm as what is generally classified as peace-keeping operations have increased in number.

A Special Account, into which voluntary contributions were made, was set up in 1965 and reinforced in 1972, and has remained as a means to help cover cash shortfalls since.

These solutions virtually saw peace-keeping financing through the first 30 years, even if it was sometimes closer to *ad hoc* solutions than a coherent system. Ironically, the Cold War climate at its height meant that the opportunities for missions were limited. Thereafter emerged a pattern of peace-keeping operations, which were by and large matched by the financing arrangements. Much depended on how the parties to operations saw these missions. For some countries, like the Scandinavian countries and Canada, they were part of the ideological aspect of their foreign policy. They did not, in any overt way, help their national security. Their contributions were almost certainly a net drain on resources. The recipient countries were, in effect, not consulted about the costs of peace-keeping (although there is a school of thought which says they should be contributors in kind). The crucial aspect of financing lay in the hands of the largest contributors, such as the US, and their concerns for value for money. In this context, it was not so much the actual costs, as the role within US foreign policy which was dominant in US support. The costs to the US were used as an excuse for not seeing worthwhile political returns. These views were reflected more in the official attitudes, especially those of the US and its domestic legislation, towards paying for the UN as a whole. Problems with the financing of the general budget found their echoes in the peace-keeping budgets. Again, within this context, came broader pressures for reform during the latter part of the 1980s under the Reagan administration. Some relief and reversal in this tone came under President Bush when commitments rose with the ending of the Cold War – and a new cycle of financial crisis re-emerged. The combination of over-commitment, the expansion of new operations involving a broader spectrum and range of activities and skills outside those normally deployed by peace-keepers and the US becoming firmly ensconced as the one and only superpower in political, military and economic terms altered the context of UN financing radically. Coincidental was an outbreak of areas of conflict and tension worldwide, in parts of Africa, Russia's border areas, former Yugoslavia, and the Far East.

Meanwhile, other parties had been working to accommodate the problem. The EU proposed in January 1996 a plan under which the US assessment would fall to 28.75 per cent. Initially the US reacted strongly against this, for it was caught between two conflicting pressures. On the one hand, it was trying to cut back on its expenditures to the UN – and to the peace-keeping operations in particular, in the wake of the traumatic experience of Somalia. On the other, it recognized that, with a cutback in contributions and even if they more than dwarfed those of other countries, they might be interpreted as reflecting a lessening of Washington's influence on and interest in the UN.

In practical terms, the process for dispatching a new mission is painfully slow. One study has traced the 'final decision making process of a peace-keeping mission start-up phase'.[15] On average, it takes 6–8 weeks for preliminary estimates prior to any decisions of the Security Council. Politics determines the length of the next stage, in which the Council approves the mission through a resolution and then has to seek General Assembly financial authority. The secretary-general has the authority to spend up to $10 million annually per mission as part of his general 'unforeseen and extraordinary' spending authority. These have to be taken from existing funds such as the $140 million Special Account Fund, or the $100 million WCF, or the $150 million Peace-keeping Reserve Fund. Up to four weeks can be spent as the Secretariat prepares the mission budget for submission to the ACABQ. The latter's approval and recommendation to the Fifth Committee takes two weeks or less. One week for approval is followed by two days for General Assembly approval and authorization for sending out the assessments letters to all member states requesting their contributions. The author concludes: 'On average only 30% of peace-keeping assessments are paid in the first 3 months and 60% in the first 6 months.' Overall, nearly four months could have passed before the financing show is on the military road. In addition, equipment has often been swifter in the ordering than in the supply. Troops have been, on the whole, slow to arrive. Delay has meant that the situation has deteriorated and become more expensive to cope with, especially in transport.

Boutros-Ghali has explicitly made the point which could have been absorbed by those analyzing the costs of these activities that many of these expensive roles, or incidents resulting in UN involvement or intrusion, might have been avoided through preventive diplomacy – ranging from better intelligence and co-ordinated political analysis to an active stand-by force for quick reaction. Indeed, the subtitle of his *An Agenda for Peace* reads 'Preventive Diplomacy, Peacemaking and Peace-keeping'. He wrote:

> The most desirable and efficient employment of diplomacy is to ease tensions before they result in conflict – or, if conflict breaks out, to act swiftly to contain it and resolve its underlying causes. Preventive diplomacy may be performed by the Secretary-General personally or through senior staff or specialized agencies and programs, by the Security Council or the General Assembly, and by regional organizations in cooperation with the United Nations.[16]

But the irony is that, even without this sort of preparation, at every stage the UN has been hampered by having insufficient resources to carry out the role it has been thrust into, or has chosen to adopt. Slow bureaucracy and inefficiency has held back the start of operations requiring a quick response.

The implication that many of these outgoings could have been precluded or reduced by preventive diplomacy measures has its limitations. It is an attractive thesis and it presupposes that steps taken ahead of the development of a crisis will be effective. Furthermore, preventive diplomacy, involving information and intelligence gathering, analysis and staff in New York and on the ground require expenditure. These costs have to be justified and accepted by the UN's secretariat. They suffer from an acute disadvantage which makes them less attractive, that they are precautionary expenses as an insurance against events which might not happen. The members of the UN have been chronically averse to voting money for activities which do not appear to have a clearly defined goal. It should be added that this applies also to the proposal that the UN should have depots of pre-stocked *matériel* (already in existence in Brindisi, Italy) and a standing army ready for immediate rapid deployment in response to an emergency.

Since the foundation of the UN there has been a sustained debate, and not just on the military side, about the merits and disadvantages of establishing a standing, rapid deployment force, which would be ready to be dispatched at short notice to any conflict. In 1948, Secretary-General Trygve Lie proposed the creation of a small guard force at the disposal of the Security Council. Brian Urquhart, a distinguished long-time international civil servant unobtrusively at the heart of political matters, indicated years later that he was thinking of a light infantry force of about 5000 which might cost in the region of $350 million a year to equip and maintain. Other estimates have been lower. Boutros-Ghali recalls: '[T]he special agreements foreseen in Article 43 of the Charter, whereby Member States undertake to make armed forces, assistance and facilities available to the Security Council for the purposes stated in Article 42, not only on an ad hoc basis but on a permanent basis.'[17] The report of the Independent Working Group on the Future of the United Nations, approved in May 1995, recommended the establishment of such a force, with an initial target figure of 10000 to be deployed on the decision of the Security Council.[18]

UN diplomacy is by its nature rarely if ever independent, unless the parties to a conflict wish it to be so. Above all, its assets for starting up and maintaining a mission of whatever practical or political hue are limited. Once on the ground, on the whole these days, its troops are in a purely UN guise, in other words not as in the Korean and Gulf wars – unable to prevent physically a military conflict. In those two missions, the global politics of the time permitted the UN to undertake what was essentially a mission for the US, even though it was carried out through an alliance of forces, as in Haiti and the Gulf. The UN depends muchly on prayer, not a wing, for logistical administration has rarely been a strong point, and diplomatic skill.

Elsewhere, the anomalies are testing to those who defend the role of UN peace-keeping operations. Stories from the field tell of the irresponsible waste of equipment. This seems to stem partly from the inevitable difficulty of raising a sense of commitment which might arise in a national army, fighting for a national rather than an international cause. It comes, too, and this may be typical only of the smaller missions untypically financed by the countries with main interests in their presence, from a sense that others will be paying the bills. In operations such as Somalia and Cambodia, some of the recognized bad behavior of peace-keeping troops has spread to theft, in one notable case worth several millions of dollars of computer equipment. There have been national disgraces, which have had effects on the performance and morale of troops provided, especially, by some of the poorer developing countries. Their troops may have greater social affinity than those from more developed countries with the local population. They also rarely see the hard currency bonuses for their service, which go directly to their governments. The reimbursement rate for countries providing troops and equipment has also become intolerably bad, to the extent that those debts are almost as much as the sums coming in for the financing of operations.

Within the UN system, the costs of operations are misleading on two levels, in particular. Special allowances are made available to serving troops, depending in part on their ranks. These are the fees which some soldiers from the developing countries do not see. The status of equipment is often moot (and hard to calculate). Some elements are taken for granted as coming with units dispatched. But others are seen as legitimate charges for compensation which should be paid back to the contributing countries. Countries like those in the Scandinavian region with not only a highly developed sense of international military service but also one which has become a regional responsibility, often write off the equivalent of as much as 40 per cent of claimable costs as lost reimbursement. It is almost regarded as an alternative form of foreign aid. The point is frequently made that this failure of the UN to put this part of its accounting procedures to rights may well have the additional effect of deterring countries from volunteering to supply troops for a peace-keeping mission. This is, too, a point which the US raises from time to time in the context of being already the largest supplier of funds to peace-keeping.

Yet it is apparent that the irregularity in cash flow leads to many difficulties. The start-up phase of operations – operationally a crucial period and one in which delay means that costs can escalate enormously – hamper them as much as the stages for approval an operational budgetary decision has to go through. It should not be necessary for member states to be called on to make extraordinary payments as they did in order to permit the dispatch of UN observers to the Iraq-Iran front following the conclusion of an armistice in 1988, ending eight years of war. Overall financial squeezes can cause cut backs in the back-up legal, financial, personnel and logistical functions in New York. Mercifully, with the expansion of those offices and a reduction in the number of operations, the pressure here has been eased. Arrears, as has been noted, mean delays in the reimbursement of states contributing troops contingents and equipment. In 1993, the UN owed $334.8 million to such countries as Britain, Canada, Finland, Sweden, Denmark, Argentina and Nigeria. This rose to $927 million in 1994 (involving reimbursement for troops, equipment, letters of assistance requesting specific services, and death and disability payments), to $1.39 billion in 1995 and has since declined to $1.18 billion in 1997. The main countries owed reimbursement at the end of 1997 were: France ($151.2 million), the US ($109.2 million), Britain ($65.9 million), Italy ($62.5 million), Belgium ($58.1 million), Canada ($50.4 million), India ($47.4 million), Pakistan ($45.4 million with the largest amount owed for troops alone – $20 million), and Russia ($36.1 million).[19] Overall planners of missions are hampered by the problems of arriving at realistic estimates.

The estimates for the operation in Namibia, starting off at $650–70 million, ended up costing overall after cuts in plans, overall, $383.5 million – casting doubts in the process on both the methods and tactics of calculating costs.

But not all changing political circumstances need be harmful. Just as the nature of the tasks of peace-keeping has changed, so has their monolithic New York-based format evolved. This could be absorbed, to some extent, by the spreading and sharing of costs through more collaboration with regional organizations and humanitarian organizations which benefit from the presence of peace-keepers. There must be a look at cost-sharing and the changing balance between just military operations and those involving NGOs. Closer co-ordination with those organizations involved in humanitarian actions will need to be further developed. The potential partners of the UN are many – NATO, OSCE, OAU, CIS, OAS, ASEAN and ECOWAS are the obvious examples.

There is another aspect of change, which has worked to some extent but clearly now needs a measure of readjustment. The main reason lies in the need for reducing through technical means the ever-present threat of financial crises. Any reform would have also to reflect the way that the UN has become a force among others in dealing with humanitarian, political and social problems. It should be added, to be fair, that suggestions for reform have been considered many times but those ideas have been pursued and enacted only to a limited degree. This could well involve greater co-ordination with NGOs and the private sector. The extent to which privatization could be extended to the military side of peace-keeping has its limitations, but has been explored.

In the end, the peace-keeping budgets share with the regular budget the vital weakness that assessed member states should and must pay their contributions. The two are not inseparable for, as we have seen, shortfalls in the latter have been, hitherto, made up by surpluses in the former. But both are subject to uneven surges in cash flow and vulnerable. This vulnerability has increased and will continue to do so unless some of these proposals are enacted. This in turn would argue in favor of quarterly payments for peace-keeping into a single unified annual budget. Ideally such a budget should include a margin for unexpected new missions. It would also be a guard against the uneven surge of payments in from countries whose financial years do not coincide with the UN's calendar years. If the past has provided anything for the UN to learn from, it is the regular pattern that in trying to cope with peace-keeping from both a military and a financial point of view, it has tended to react to changing circumstances and adapt to them. On both levels, this has protracted any ability to change, so that the UN appears to be trailing behind.

The future offers operations of greater variety than ever before. This should open the way to a greater variety in the sources of funds. Voluntary and mandatory funds are no longer as forbidden topics as in the past. Some operations, notably in Russia's 'near abroad', challenge the concept of international peace-keeping and therefore, by implication, the notion that they should be financed by the UN. (Whether expenditure on those operations should be offset against the host state's formal contributions to UN peace-keeping operations is open to doubt.) The result is that the costs of peace-keeping operations as formally and traditionally set out in the budgets of specific missions are becoming increasingly remote from peace-keeping as redefined by governments, scholars and institutions looking at these operations. As one study put it succinctly: 'Without efforts to identify costs and reconsider principles for meeting them, the legitimacy and the credibility of the principle of collective financial responsibility may come into question'.[20] That may have been a few years ago, but it applies with greater urgency today as peace-keeping operations develop with greater speed and variety than before, and because the UN needs to tackle the issue of fundamental restructuring and reform more effectively than has been apparent in the previous cycles of financial crisis. There are additional points: the size of the problem of most of the peace-keeping missions is not as large as say those of IFOR, or the Gulf operation. By comparison, UN missions are a cheaper option though their political effectiveness largely brought UN peace-keeping into acute disrepute. It needs to be repeated that the UN's problem lies largely in the peace-keeping budgets; there are fewer difficulties in the regular budget.

A detailed look at proposals for streamlining the procedures and operations of peace-keeping missions will be presented later. These have become more complicated as each period moves into a new stage. But it is clear from a preliminary assessment that the ideal would be greater co-ordination between the individual peace-keeping budgets and the establishment of a standing fund to cover both starting procedures and short-term emergencies. In the circumstances of today's missions this will also require increased co-operation with the other agencies, particularly those dealing with humanitarian and development activities. This would go hand-in-hand with the need for some examination of other sources for funds, such as sharing facilities with humanitarian agencies and regional security groups and from voluntary contributions. As successive crises in former Yugoslavia have shown so painfully, the UN is not the sole repository of financed peace-keeping operations.

In the broader perspective, it would seem that Boutros-Ghali grievously overlooked the implications of taking on an unprecedented expansion of peace-keeping commitments. It has had a harmful effect on the finances and credibility of the UN as a whole. But it became equally apparent that the increasing demand for the UN's peace-keeping services was not matched by support from the member states, especially the US. There are proposals which are examined later which could reform and streamline the planning and running of such operations. The clue, in the end as elsewhere, will lie in clearer political leadership from within the organization and more unstinting support both financially and, above all politically. In Kofi Annan's favor in this particular aspect of his stewardship is that he came in with goodwill and the experience of having been in charge of peace-keeping operations. He raised high hopes for reform, at a moment when peace-keeping operations have been cut back drastically and changed their nature in a way which will put a lighter burden on the UN's finances.

The responsibilities of peace-keeping are undergoing changes – the size and number are being reduced. There have, also, been some considered successes, even if their solutions may not always have lasted long, such as the Gulf War, Cambodia, Mozambique, El Salvador and Haiti. Somalia, Rwanda and Bosnia were failures. The UN cannot be an eternal presence. As a result the sums are coming down. If it were possible to raise the amount coming in from assessments, some countries might in fact find themselves receiving smaller bills. The year of 1997 had been hailed as one of decision. That overstates the situation. If it turns out to have marked some transition, it will hardly have come from the direct effects of any reforms that Annan put forward in detail. Peace-keeping was hardly mentioned at all as such but rather in the context of wider operations connected with humanitarian and civilian intervention. This was because peace-keeping has taken on many other dimensions. These involve sharing operations with other agencies – and implicitly costs. New mechanisms for meeting these costs will have to be recast in the context of broader administrative reforms. It will not be easy to set in position new procedures specifically for peace-keeping.

6 Washington: the UN's Dear Donor and Delinquent

We are told that it was Franklin D. Roosevelt himself[1] who thought up the name 'United Nations' after the Japanese attack on Pearl Harbor in December 1941. Early the following year, he secured Winston Churchill's approval for the term after bursting into his room at the White House while he was taking a bath. Apocryphal or not, the tale sturdily illustrates the vividness of the US relationship with the concept of the UN even before it came into formal being.

As in almost every sphere of the UN, Washington's financial relationship with the organization has swung between remarkable generosity and selfish manipulation. It has contrived itself the unique position of being simultaneously the largest contributor of funds and the largest debtor. This critical and influential role has never been more important than in the wake of the dissolution of the Soviet Union and its power bloc after the ending of the Cold War. These developments left the way open for the emergence and consolidation of the US as the world's predominant superpower.

At the start of 1997, there were all the components of a seminal year in the making for the development of the UN system as a whole and perhaps for its financial disposition and stability. On the level of leaderships, there was an unprecedented coincidence of personalities and events. Annan was appointed secretary-general in succession to Boutros-Ghali on a reform ticket. On the US side, President Clinton had won re-election to a second term and appeared domestically to be in a stronger position to counter the demands of a Republican-dominated Congress and its antipathy towards the UN. But after promising so much, the year ended, in terms of US-UN relations, in sterile disaster.

Against this background, Annan had announced, in July 1997, plans for a comprehensive restructuring of the UN. With perhaps unnerving prescience, he said: 'Starting today, we begin a quiet revolution in the United Nations'. Among the 'revolutionary' items might have been proposals, which could have a long-term impact on the management of the finances of the UN. But, at the heart of its solvency lay, as always, the mixed blessing of the relationship between Washington and the UN. From the start of this round of reform, a clear difference in approach of the two parties was

94

apparent. Annan pronounced the reforms to be 'a process, not an event' and tried to make this process subject to UN member states' paying their assessed contributions. The US, by contrast, made payment implicitly dependent on the progress shown by the reform measures. It has long been true that it would have massively reduced the strain on UN finances if the US paid both its arrears and provided its current contributions on time. But the problem is infinitely more complex.

Since the beginning of the UN's existence, the financial responsibilities and contributions of the US have been enormous and this factor cannot be overlooked in any consideration of its role. For example, it was initially assessed at providing 49 per cent of the regular budget in 1946 and 1947. This level was in fact readjusted by 10 per cent. Since then its theoretical contribution has been around the one-third mark. This has been a chronic problem which has become acute in the 1980s and is at its most severe as the UN begins its second half century of existence.[2]

As we have seen, the US position has been driven historically in different directions. Politically, it has always been aware of being the host country. This paramount geographical position has been an unending source of envy both symbolically and in fact. There have been over the years considerable concerns about the security risks of having this extraterritorial being in its midst. Espionage and doubts about loyalty have been a constant feature invading both the UN itself and spilling over into domestic US politics. McCarthyism reached even into the UN. Another constant has been the complications this has introduced into the role of the UN secretary-general. An independent-minded incumbent such as Dag Hammarskjöld, with a determined drive to give the UN and its civil servants an independent standing and authority, was regarded with suspicion and hostility. Lesser men were either ignored or put under pressure. No secretary-general has been successful in avoiding the trap of becoming a feature of US domestic politics. This became blatantly the case during the presidential re-election campaign in the autumn of 1996.

There were difficulties already well before and this has made it difficult to explain why and how the US altered its views of the organization, which it was so instrumental in helping to set up. These changed views translated themselves into actions which almost without exception resulted in the pattern of curtailing funds followed by efforts at reform and then a renewal of the flow of funds.

One reason was that the US constantly had to take into account different constituencies. With fair consistency, Congress applied the brakes on US expenditure for a variety of reasons. The State Department tended to be the agency most favorable to the UN, not least because the funds passed through its budget. The Pentagon had its own views, predictably about peace-keeping and the costs of providing *matériel* – too often, they felt – for free and for unjustifiable causes. A succession of presidents had a whole succession of views, which were often conditioned by the circumstances of their presidency, dominated by the Cold War and the explosive increase in the numbers of new UN member states from the developing and newly decolonized world, and by their judgment of popular opinion about the UN. This was often out of tune with the polls. Surveys consistently showed that the majority of Americans when polled routinely expressed support for the UN. In a 1997 survey 64 per cent of Americans – opinion leaders and the general public combined – gave the UN a favorable rating. This figure had fluctuated between 62 per cent and 76 per cent for the previous few years.[3]

The US view, as reflected by its willingness to pay its assessed way, was guided by two intertwined guidelines. The first was whether the administration felt that it was getting value for money inside and outside the UN. The second was the extent to which the UN was deemed to be a useful arm of US foreign policy. The actual sums involved have never been a burden – although the way it has sometimes been painted, it would seem the opposite.

There is, too, a third element, which John L. Washburn, a US diplomat with long experience of international organizations and multilateral affairs in both the State Department and the higher echelons of the UN, has described:

> In UN experience… [M]any countries naturally are profoundly self-convinced of the rightness of their causes and see perversity in those who will not agree with them or support them. However, in the United States this is joined by a strong sense of possessiveness in attitudes toward the UN. Americans recall vividly that the United States was the chief creator of the UN and that the similarity in names is no accident. This leads to the assumption that the United States is uniquely qualified to pronounce on what the UN is and what it should do.[4]

But, predictably, it is politics which ultimately govern the state of the financial relationship between the US and the UN.

The 1960s and 1970s saw the membership of the UN double from the 76 backbone countries of 1955. For the US this was accompanied by the worry that, against the background of the Cold War, it was losing ideological influence to the Soviet Union as expressed in the General Assembly. In active politics and crises on the ground, the experiences with two peace-keeping operations – UNEF I on the Egypt-Israel front and ONUC in the Congo – aroused broader ideological worries and involved the US in helping the UN overcome acute financial and administrative problems. In 1962 and 1963, the costs of the UN including assessments for the regular budget, peace-keeping operations and specialized agencies plus voluntary contributions amounted to about $500 million. The US provided 46.91 per cent of contributions, while its assessment scale was lower at 32.02 per cent.[5] At the same time, Stoessinger reckoned that, in 1962, 'an annual amount of roughly $82 million accrues to the American economy primarily as a direct result of the United Nations Headquarters location in New York'.[6]

Despite these two key examples, this was a period of comparative calm in financial relations between the US and the UN. During the 1970s, as William Durch has observed, the UN

> had increasingly come to be seen as a tool by which the new voting majority of poor, 'Third World' or 'non-aligned' states, with the voting support of the socialist bloc, could press an agenda designed to redistribute wealth from North to South. UN bureaucracy grew as the General Assembly's majority established programs and agencies that the West was obliged to pay for, but over which the West maintained little political control and from which it saw little apparent return on investment.[7]

This was the period when the General Assembly voted, in 1975, to equate Zionism with racism (rescinded in December 1991), and a little later, in 1984, when the US withdrew from UNESCO on the grounds of the latter's pro-Third World bias and to set an example of protest against the 'politicization' of UN agencies. Figures show (see Figure 6.1) that the US had virtually no debts in relation to total debts outstanding to the regular budget until the beginning of the 1980s decade.

But politically, under Reagan, who became president in 1981, Washington had taken a more overtly critical view of the UN's activities and of multilateral diplomacy as a whole. The Heritage Foundation, a conservative think-tank, exercised mounting pressure through criticism of US membership of organizations where its values and policies were perceived to be under attack. Rosemary Righter observed: 'The radicalism of the Reagan approach lay not in its complaints, but in its open questioning of the value of these global institutions to the United States'.[8] In June 1982, one of the five guiding principles for US policy towards the UN was defined by the State Department as zero growth in UN budgets – a view not out of step with those of the 12 western governments who were financing three-quarters of the UN's regular spending.[9]

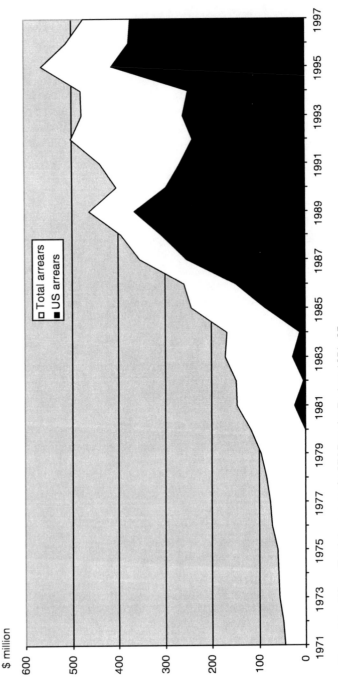

Figure 6.1 US vs. Total Arrears to the UN Regular Budget 1971–97
Source: Klaus Hüfner, Freie Universität Berlin (compiled from UN documents).

During the 1980s, both the regular budget and the peace-keeping budgets came under increasing pressure as a result of political argument and the accumulative arrears of non-payments by member states. This applied to the regular budget in particular. The pattern was clear. In resorting to withholding payments, the US was, of major contributors, fairly late on the scene. But its influence was more drastic and long lasting. From 1980 onwards, the US had made withholdings with respect to specific programs and decisions, citing partly legal objections and, in other cases, political disapproval, disenchantment with UN activities and a perception of the UN as a marginal player in international politics.

Since the mid-1980s, the US has been the greatest offender in withholding assessed contributions, stemming from cuts authorized by Congress. The unprecedented Kassebaum-Solomon Amendment to the Foreign Relations Authorization Act, adopted by Congress in August 1985, has already been mentioned.[10] Its aim was to reduce US regular budget payments from 25 per cent to 20 per cent. Later developments in Congress, in particular the Gramm-Rudman-Hollings Balanced Budget and Emergency Deficit Reduction Act of December 1985, further reduced Congressional appropriations for international organizations.

It was not a happy period for Javier Pérez de Cuéllar, the UN Secretary-General during 1982–91. He wrote of the Reagan administration's 'ideological distrust' of the UN as a body that would limit 'American freedom of action and compromise its capacity to defend democracy'.[11] The secretary-general felt that there were forces aiming at the US withdrawing from the UN and that this view was shared by some in government. His tenure was plagued by financial problems and when he raised the topic with Reagan, the response was vague or took the form of anecdotes. Pérez de Cuéllar sensed that relations seemed to improve towards the end of the administration 'as if in preparation for the new flowering of the relationship' with President Bush. But this did not lead to arrears being eliminated. He concluded: 'It remains for me a matter of great regret that I had to devote precious time in almost every conversation I had with Presidents Reagan and Bush to dunning the United States to pay its bills'.[12]

The deadlock over US payments was broken by the General Assembly passing a reform package late in 1986 that, among other items, called upon member states to reach 'consensus' at each step of the budget process. This gave all members an effective veto over objectionable budgets and the handful of large contributors like the US effective leverage. This had been one of the recommendations of the Committee of 18 (C-18) – the High-Level Intergovernmental Group of Experts to Review the Efficiency of the Administrative and Financial Functioning of the UN. This, along with other measures proposed by this group set up on the initiative of Japan, was perhaps the most comprehensive set of reform proposals offered to that point. It pleased Reagan, although consensus fell short of the authority of 'weighted voting', based on the size of contributions.

For the US, some of the traditional images of the UN lingered on – as inefficient and with an overbloated staffing system. But the ending of the Cold War and some relatively small and reasonably successful UN operations in Afghanistan, Central America and Angola, and between Iran and Iraq, Boutros-Ghali's succession to Pérez de Cuéllar in 1992, and perhaps Bush becoming president with his previous experience as US permanent representative (1971–3) – all these factors seemed to offer some hopes of an improved public role for the UN. The Bush administration, against the background of the dissolution of the Soviet Union and the emergence of the US as the leading world power, viewed the UN more favorably, with the high spot being the Security Council's stamp of approval for the prosecution of the Gulf War. Congress was in 1990 to enact new funding legislation and Bush promised to have all back debts paid by 1995. By the end of 1992, the US regular budget obligations for the past years had been reduced to zero, although $240 million was still owed for 1992, and there was $80 million in arrears for peace-keeping operations.

US measures towards payments raised more nagging questions about the UN's financial crises. The immediate cause lay obviously, and already, in the arrears in the payments and the withholding of assessed contributions. But there was a larger context, for the crisis of confidence in the adequacy of multilateral structures as these had evolved since 1945. Then, as now, this raised serious doubts as to whether they were adequate for complying with the tasks facing the UN and its institutions. Whether this justified unilateral action to bring about change is debatable in international law and at odds with the obligations of UN membership. Indeed, the US has at times contemplated, as it did during the Reagan administration, a reduction in its assessment rate. This would have been negotiated with, but not imposed by, the UN – a questionable approach to treaty arrangements and one offensive to other member states of the UN.

The intrusion of politics together with pressure for reform became more acute during the 1990s than at any other time in the UN's history. It was personified in the blocking of Boutros-Ghali from a second term as secretary-general and in his succession by Annan, the US choice.

At first when Clinton assumed the presidency, UN hopes ran high.[13] He had promised a positive relationship during the 1992 presidential campaign, but peace-keeping operations proved to be its downfall. It came abruptly, in October 1993, with the death of 18 Rangers in the Somalia debacle. In policy terms this was translated into a measured approach towards such operations in the cautious directive on multilateral peace-keeping operations, PDD-25 issued in May 1994.[14] While it highlighted the problems the US has with these operations, it also drew critical attention to the more general role of the UN in US foreign policy. Republican successes in the Congressional elections of 1994 made life difficult for both Clinton and Boutros-Ghali. The UN's position came under scrutiny in relation to its costs. Publicly, this tension became played out in a curiously personalized way. Rivlin wrote: '[Boutros-Ghali's] many detractors have found him to be disdainful, confrontational, too stubbornly independent and bent on self-aggrandizement'.[15] It came to a head in Clinton's campaign for re-election in the autumn of 1996. The near-abusive exchanges with Madeleine Albright, then the US representative at the UN, and the tasteless bandying of jokes about Boutros-Ghali's name marked a new vulgar low in US-UN relations. It made it impossible for him to confront the US with the inconsistencies and meanness of its policies. It would seem, too, with hindsight, that he never grasped the delicacy of the relationship between an American administration, US politics and the secretary-general of the UN.

Earlier, in an article published in the *New York Times* on 8 April 1996, Boutros-Ghali laid his version on the line of how he saw financial developments. This probably sealed the fate of any aspirations he might have had of a second term as secretary-general. Under the headline 'The U.S. Must Pay Its Dues', he wrote:

> The United Nations is on the brink of financial disaster. Americans need to know what's going on, because their country took the lead in creating the organization, and its delinquency in paying arrears is threatening it.
>
> When I took office [in 1992], major challenges lay ahead. With the cold war over, vast new responsibilities were heaped on the United Nations. But resources needed to carry them out were inadequate because many member states were not paying their dues. In addition, the Secretariat, which was underproductive, needed reform.
>
> For four years, the Secretariat has carried out its mandates under near-impossible conditions. A perpetual but not very successful effort has been made to convince members to pay up.
>
> In this period, the organization has been streamlined – as far as the Secretary-General's powers permit. The staff is leaner, procedures have been simplified and waste and duplication have been sharply reduced.
>
> For 18 months, I have focused on reducing the operating budget. My proposed $2.5 billion budget for 1996–97 is $98 million less than

the previous year's budget. In December, the members asked for $154 million more in cuts. Since then, we have identified $140 million in cuts, and the rest can be found'.

Boutros-Ghali outlined the approach towards the cuts in the number of staff; adding: 'The General Assembly, which approves the budget, will not help matters if it nit-picks'; and returned to his main theme:

The financial crisis has not been made any easier by the refusal of many to pay dues. The United States and Russian Federation dominate the past-due list. I am grateful that the Federation decided last month to pay $400 million, including its full regular assessment of $46 million for 1996. But America owes $1.5 billion in dues and assessments. Thus, even with the Russians' payment, the United Nations will run out of money by the end of 1996. Incredibly, our cash on hand is under $100 million.

Borrowing from the peacekeeping budget to meet regular operating needs cannot continue much longer. Huge sums are owed to states that have provided troops and equipment for peace operations. Besides, while we carry out old mandates new ones keep coming.

Boutros-Ghali moved onto the offensive in his final paragraphs:

It would be counterproductive to cut off important operations such as democratization in Haiti and the promotion of human rights in Guatemala. These operations are precious for the peoples involved. They are also United Nations success stories.

Still, the stark truth must be faced. Something has to give. If the Haiti and Guatemala operations are to go forward, other obligations must be scaled back or dropped. The members must make that hard call. If they don't, we will run out of money before long.

When the League of Nations collapsed, many members were surprised. They had not understood the depth of its problems. Today, the United Nations, created 51 years ago, is in deep trouble. This time around, there should be no surprises.

It is little wonder that, by comparison, Annan was greeted as a distinguished hero on his first visit as secretary-general to Washington at the beginning of 1997 even though the essential problems remain unchanged and unsolved. Annan hinted that he would not be seen as Washington's man, even though Congress made some more conciliatory steps in June 1997. In an initial reaction to these moves to pay, Annan implied that the US reaction was less than what the UN deserved. At the same time, one lesson has become apparent and this is that no UN chief can afford to become embroiled in the domestic politics of Washington. He has so far always tended to come out the loser. During the Clinton years, he has had to contend with a popular Democratic president outweighed by a Republican-dominated Congress. The problem for Boutros-Ghali was how to confront the US. He could not afford to become involved in what was essentially a domestic political quarrel with the Republican-dominated Congress. At the same time, his own personality and style of administration made him unpopular, not just with Washington, but also within the UN itself.

On the US domestic front, the UN has been hard to sell. Logically, it need not be so. Opinion polls have regularly shown that there is far more popular support for the institution than Congress is prepared to take notice of. One side that is presented is its costs. In 1946, during the discussions on how expensive the brand new organization might be, the point was made that its costs amounted to only one hour's worth of US defense expenditure during the Second World War. There have been constant similar parallels over the years, comparing the UN's costs with global defense spending and the costs of running the Corporation of London, among examples often cited. But today the point is also made that, in peace-keeping terms, for the US, it costs only $1 for every $250 it spends on its national defense budget. But it still remains a difficult topic when it comes to discussing and approving its share of the budget of the State Department, from which the UN's allocation comes. Indeed, in 1997, movement towards producing the statement that seemed to open the door to paying off arrears had been held up and, on occasions, lost in the argument between the State Department and Congress over repayment. To Albright's credit in this, she fought hard for her department's argument that, for US relations with the UN to have credibility debts should be paid.

The Clinton administration campaigned for a cut in UN expenses and a cut in the budgets so that for the 1996–7 biennium the regular budget was only $2.603 billion – in other words, no increase in nominal terms. The General Assembly appropriated $2.532 billion for 1998–9. But for the chief contributor to be still owing then one-third of its contributions for 1994 and all of 1995 while, at the same time, asking for cuts in the UN, not surprisingly, evoked strong criticism, not just from Third World countries but also from its closest allies in Europe.

Article 19 of the Charter has remained, in effect, a threat rather than a punishment against countries falling into arrears that equal or exceed assessments due for two years. In theory, they would then be deprived of their vote in the General Assembly. This has rarely occurred.[16] But it loomed as a possibility for the US from the beginning of 1999. Notably, this provision was not put into practice when the Soviet Union qualified in the 1960s over the issue of ONUC's expenditures. The US has never directly challenged Article 19 in the action but rather in the spirit, and, as we have seen over the ONUC issue, reserved the right to show its political objection in financial terms. Washington has grown to believe that it has a form of immunity and special position entitling it to use domestic legislation to curb its financial commitments to the UN. However, payment of assessments has been almost universally accepted as an unequivocal treaty obligation in international law, particularly after the ICJ judgment of 1962 over the funding of the UNEF and ONUC peace-keeping operations.

Legislation enacted by Congress (Public-Law 103-236) limited US contributions to UN peace-keeping operations to 25 per cent with effect from 1 October 1996,[17] eliminating for the US the 'permanent member premium' and for the UN's accounting process adding some percentage points of assessed contributions to be redistributed to other member states. These measures met widespread criticism from the G-77 group of developing countries and the EU for attaching conditions to payments. The charts make pellucid the extent to which arrears in both regular and peace-keeping UN budgets are caused by the US, and how this has persisted until today. In October 1997, the total amount owed to the UN was $2.3 billion, of which $648 million was for the regular budget, $1.6 billion for peace-keeping, and $19.6 million for International Tribunals on ex-Yugoslavia and Rwanda. Of the overall unpaid assessments, the US owed about 60 per cent, and of the regular budget around three quarters. The main debtors by country (at end-June 1997, when total debts were over $2.3 billion) were the US with $1.47 billion, Ukraine $247.7 million and Russia $237.4 million. On 6 February 1997, the Clinton administration submitted to Congress for fiscal 1998 a request for $1.02 billion to pay off accumulated arrears to the UN.

After much debate a deal was struck in early June 1997 ('the Helms-Biden agreement'), whereby the aggregate sum of $926 million in arrears was acknowledged but only the payment of $819 million of the US figure of the amount owed – not the $1.2 billion the UN claimed – was authorized by the Foreign Relations Committee on 12 June 1997. (This was to be spread as follows: $100 million in 1998; $475 million in 1999; and $244 million in 2000). The administration agreed to 38 conditions in the 44-page bill. This marked a new level of special treatment demanded, as the US legislators issued a tick-off list of conditions for the $819 million to which they had agreed.[18]

In year one the UN had to accept the US figure of the amount owed – not the $1.2 billion the UN claims – with no encroachment on US sovereignty through international taxes or a UN standing army. In year two, there would be a reduction of the US share of the regular budget to 22 per cent with a further reduction to 20 per cent in the third year; and a reduction of the US share of peace-keeping budgets from 31 per cent to 25 per cent.[19] In the third year, there would have to be:

- a ceiling of 20 per cent imposed on the US share of the regular budgets of the UN and all its specialized agencies;
- an inspector-general in the big agencies – ILO, FAO and WHO;
- the imposition of 'general accounting and financial regulations' on the UN and its agencies;
- a procedure to identify programs in the UN and its agencies that needed to be ended;
- a US seat on the influential 16-member ACABQ;[20]
- access for the GAO of the US and Congressional Office of Management and Budget to audit UN programs;
- personnel reforms, including a code of conduct and merit-based hiring and performance assessments; and
- an overall reduction in the budgets of all specialized agencies.

Viewed objectively, few of these suggestions are in disagreement with the thinking of reformers within the UN. But both the reformers and the member states have reacted strongly against their being imposed as a condition for full financial participation by one – admittedly, the dominant participant – state alone. It was hardly surprising that Annan's initial reaction was reserved.[21]

Figure 6.1 and 6.2 shed some light on the donor and delinquent aspects of the US role in UN finances – mainly those of the regular and peace-keeping budgets. However, the chart for 1995 actual contributions to the UN system including specialized agencies illustrates that, in current payments, while the US made none to the regular budget, it was the largest voluntary contributor of the top 15 countries.

Initially in the 1970s, the US debts to the regular budget were negligible. In 1981, they accounted for 16.1 per cent, reaching 35.3 per cent of total outstanding debts to the regular budget in 1985. Thereafter they averaged between 50 and 70 per cent, reaching 60.6 per cent in 1991, dipping to 51.6 per cent in 1994 and rising again to 73.8 per cent at the end of 1996. The correlation between total and US debts are clear on an annual basis between 1992–7, where the UN's total arrears fall sharply towards the end of each calendar year (the US fiscal year starts on October 1) – averaging about 35 per cent in January, rising to about 60 per cent around August and then falling again – although in 1996 and

The New Politics of Financing the UN

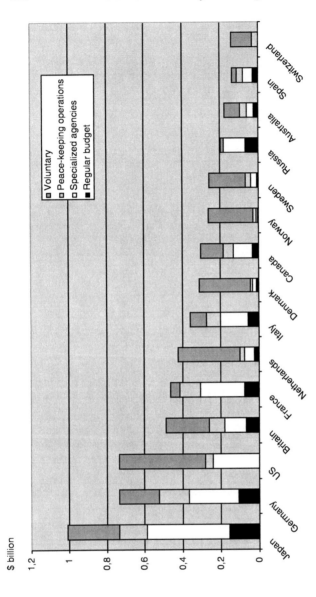

Figure 6.2 Contributors to the UN System 1995: the Top 15

Source: 'Administrative and Budgetary Coordination of the United Nations with the Specialized Agencies and the International Atomic Energy Agency', UN doc. A/51/505, 18 October 1996 with A/51/505 Corr. 1, 6 December 1996 in 'St.meld. nr. 43 (1996–97) FN – på terskelen til et nytt århundre' [Parliamentary Report No. 43 (1996–97): The UN on the Threshold of a New Century], Norwegian Foreign Ministry, Oslo, p. 54.

The figures are based on the UN's statistics for actual payments to ensure comparable figures. The US is not listed in the UN survey of contributions to the UN 1995 regular budget because its payments are recorded as arrears for previous years. Switzerland is not a member of the UN, but participates in a number of the UN's specialized agencies. Voluntary contributions in cash and kind include the UN's funds and programs (UNDP, UNICEF, UNFPA, and WFP), UJNHCR and UNEP, and voluntary contributions to the most important UN specialized agencies (WHO, ILO, UNESCO and FAO).

1997, the trend was upwards towards 70 per cent. Similarly, the US share of debts in regular and peace-keeping budgets has remained consistently high. Connor on 23 January 1996 produced some telling figures, saying that the US paid its contributions as if its assessed rate were 12 per cent, not 25 per cent, to the regular budget and 14 per cent not 31 per cent for peace-keeping operations! Today, it is worth noting that, as the expenditures of both these budgets is projected to decline in the coming years, so will the size of the US cash contribution.

The US may have been reluctant to hand over money to finance the UN, but there has been also debate and advocacy of a reasonable approach from the US towards the UN; and not all Washington's concerns are parochial and self-serving. The range of views presented here represent the tenor and serious flavor of the debates about the place of the UN in US hearts. All too often, the influence on Congress and the White House of those advocating a generous attitude was, at best, minimal, but at least the debate remained alive. US Ambassador Princeton Lyman, Assistant Secretary of State for International Organization Affairs has summed up many of his country's attitudes towards the UN at a time when Annan's reforms were just evolving.[22] In terms of reforms, the budgetary aspect came third, after eliminating the duplication of activities and focusing the UN's activities on what it does best. But Lyman reckoned that Annan had a better chance of getting his reforms enacted because, contentiously, of the financial problems. On these, he said somewhat fallaciously that there had been a tendency to allow the budget to grow 'without a great deal of discipline. With some 14 countries now paying 80–90 percent of the budget, one has to look at whether the budget system has enough discipline.' The impetus for reform was the financial crisis and the crisis in peace-keeping in the 1990s brought on by 'the perceived failures or shortcomings of … operations in Somalia, Bosnia and Rwanda'. But, he emphasized, reform should not just be concentrated on the UN headquarters in New York, but on the large specialized agencies with worldwide operations and budgets.

Lyman described the dilemma facing the US:

> We have reached a point where our ability to get needed reforms is clearly jeopardized by our failure to pay our arrears. It creates resistance on the part of others who feel that we are making demands on an organization without paying our way. It creates animosity, which colors people's objective views of the reforms being put forward and causes them to question our motives.
>
> People may ask if the United States is really trying to make the United Nations more effective or if it is just trying to weaken the United Nations

so it doesn't have to pay more money. Clearly, it is the first reason, but if we don't pay our dues and arrears, people may think it is the second.

This was a far more measured view of the US role than that reflected in the sometimes wild and chauvinistic debates in Congress. The moves proposed in June 1997 for the payment of arrears, although extremely limited, reflected some headway at the time by the State Department in their own difficult negotiations with Congress over the UN.

As a former ambassador to South Africa and Nigeria, Lyman was aware of the developing world's perception of US attitudes: that support for development might be threatened by reform proposals. The US aim was to reduce the money spent on administration in such areas as overheads, the headquarters and conferences, and increasing the amount spent on delivering assistance to people in developing countries. He cited an increase in US payments to UNDP as an example.

On the troubled question of changes in the assessments to the UN budgets, Lyman wrote:

> There are two objectives. First to make the United Nations less dependent on one country – the United States. We pay 25 percent of all the regular costs of the United Nations. We are assessed more than that for peacekeeping. And there is a feeling in the United States, certainly in Congress, that our share should be reduced; we think that is good for the United Nations.
>
> Second, we have to look at the way the United Nations is financed. The 95 poorest countries don't contribute much, and that is understandable. But as a whole, they contribute less than one percent of the cost of the United Nations. When you take the next 60 countries – which include all the members of ASEAN (Association of Southeast Asian nations) and OPEC (Organization of Petroleum Exporting Countries) – they contribute altogether 12 percent of U.N. costs.
>
> While we recognize the problems of the least developed, we think that this financial structure of dues paying ought to be reexamined. The world economy has changed. Individual countries have made progress. We need to come up with a better sale of dues. Our proposals will still leave the United States as the number one donor to the United Nations. The United States now pays 25 percent, and we would like to reduce that to near 20 percent.

John R. Bolton held Lynam's position in the Bush administration. He expressed views often reflecting the skeptical opinion voiced by many Americans, in considering a different side to US dilemmas.[23]

For many around the world including close friends and allies of the United States, the skepticism of many Americans, especially members of Congress, about the United Nations is puzzling. In virtually every other nation, support for the United Nations at both the popular and policy-making levels is almost unquestioned, at least rhetorically. According to the conventional wisdom, assessed contributions are paid regularly and fully, many people aspire to work in U.N. agencies, and the United Nations is perceived as a higher and better institution than the nation-state.

The contrasting attitudes of American skeptics are unique to the United States, deep-rooted, and will not change any time in the near future. Skepticism about the United Nations is another aspect of what scholars have termed American exceptionalism, the idea that the United States is, simply stated, different from other countries.

Bolton argued that the US position was misunderstood if the problems facing the UN were primarily those of money and withheld contributions, for 'the U.N.'s real problem today is a crisis of legitimacy, not of money, and it was caused, in part, by grave doubts about the world organization within the United States'. It is that point, expanded philosophically into the argument that a people which harbors doubts about its own government is bound to question an organisation of 185 governed states, that lies at the heart of the question of the UN's authority. 'This deep philosophical disjunction between the prevailing ethos of the United Nations and the fundamental American approach to governance is not something that will change in the foreseeable future.' He mentioned, too, such examples as the adoption by the General Assembly of resolution 3379 in 1975 which equated Zionism with racism, repealed only in 1991.

Perhaps most relevant to Washington's thinking was Bolton's comment that 'the United Nations has been associated with major policy failures that have made it an unattractive vehicle through which to conduct American foreign policy'. The peace-keeping operation in Somalia, where 18 US soldiers were killed, was given as an example. His conclusion was stark but important because it represented an ever-present trend which colored influential policy-makers – and ultimately the US willingness to pay its assessed way. 'I believe,' Bolton wrote,

> that the United Nations can be a useful instrument in the conduct of American foreign policy... No one, however, should be under any illusions that American support for the United Nations as one of several options for implementing American foreign policy translates into

unlimited support for the world organization. That is not true now, and it will not be true for a long time to come, if ever.

Later, in an article in the *Wall Street Journal,* Bolton, citing a number of court cases, argued strongly against the assertion that the US failure to pay its 'arrearages' to the UN 'is "illegal" under the "treaty commitment" the U.S. entered into by ratifying the U.N. Charter in 1945'. In particular, he invoked a US Supreme Court judgment to counter any argument that Article 17 of the Charter (concerning the allocation of UN expenses among its members) 'strips Congress of its normal constitutional power and discretion over financial matters under the Constitution's Appropriations Clause (Article I, Section 9).' He went on: 'Congress can legitimately override any treaty provision it chooses ... The correct conclusion is that the U.S. should meet its commitments when it is in its interests to do so and when others are meeting their obligations as well.'[24]

In the electronic journal, David E. Birenbaum, a former US representative to the UN and an active supporter of its financing, made a different plea:

> The United States should pay its outstanding arrears ... That is our legal responsibility under the U.N.Charter. As the world's leading proponent of the rule of law, we can do no less. It is also our moral obligation.

He argued that keeping commitments to the UN did in fact serve important US foreign policy interests and that these could only be furthered through reforming the UN of its weaknesses. He acknowledged that the American people were not prepared to provide an open check for the US contributions to the UN neither through assessed contributions nor support on a voluntary basis and other services.

He wrote:

> Here we come to the heart of the matter. The Congress has for some time – whether controlled by Republicans or Democrats – treated funding for the United Nations as discretionary spending. But it isn't. Along with all other member states, the United States undertook a legal obligation to bear its share of the expenses of the United Nations 'as apportioned by the General Assembly in accordance with Article 17 of the Charter'. That obligation ranks equally with the duty of countries 'to accept and carry out the decisions of the Security Council' imposed by Article 25 and to conform their behavior to the norms established in the Declaration of Human Rights. And it is indistinguishable legally from the host of other international commitments made by this country.

He went back in history to the status of Article 17 as considered by the International Court of Justice in 1962 in connection with an advisory opinion on the responsibility of the Soviet Union and France to pay for peace-keeping operations in the Congo. The Court, he recalled, confirmed that assessments under Article 17 were legal obligations of UN member states.

The arguments range between the politically practical to the philosophically moral in their mustering of support and fighting off opposition. In the present mood of the US as displayed in its forthright assertion of its foreign policy rights and perceived obligations, the former trend dominates the latter.

But there should be no belittling of the size of its contributions. The US positions on contributions to the regular and peace-keeping budgets have been noted. Its involvement in humanitarian activities and other agencies has been formidable, but, as in the case of UNESCO, not without political sanctions held in reserve. FAO receives 25 per cent of its money from the US in accordance with the regular budget scale; the US through government and private funds is UNICEF's largest donor; it contributes enormously to the world's refugees, primarily through UNHCR; it gives almost one third of voluntary contributions of commodities and cash to WFP; and there were concerns about the US large annual contribution to WHO.

The US, if it has to select one characteristic above all others by which it has to measure its participation, would almost certainly nominate efficiency. It is this goal which drives its pressure for reform and makes it its main precondition for financial participation. From the practical and politically emotive aspect of US involvement, peace-keeping operations capture the imagination of the taxpayers and leave evocative telegenic images which outstrip almost any other UN activity. Such operations also involve a considerable outlay of money. Figures compiled by the Congressional Research Service show that the US contributed $1.3 billion or 26.8 per cent of the total costs of UN peace-keeping operations funded from special accounts or voluntary contributions from 1956–89.[25] In a later report, it showed that the US had contributed $2.74 billion, or 25.7 per cent, of the costs of $10.61 billion of all operations between 1948 and the end of 1993, and $2.08 billion, or 23.8 per cent, of the $8.72 billion current operations.[26] Although below the rates of assessments, these were sizeable contributions.

The US has had problems with UN peace-keeping operations before those of recent years, such as the mission to Somalia. The cost and effectiveness of peace-keeping operations and their relationship to US interests have become major issues. The US General Accounting Office,[27] which is a respected and thoughtful critic and auditor of US government

expenditure, has turned its attention to missions of over five years standing
and these involve UNTSO, UNMOGIP, UNFICYP, UNDOF, UNIFIL,
UNIKOM, UNAVEM II and III (in Angola) and MINURSO (in Western
Sahara). Up to the end of 1996, these eight missions accounted for about
$6 billion, or 35 per cent of the $17 billion total of costs incurred by
peace-keeping operations since 1948. Partly because of their longevity,
five of these operations are among the 10 most costly UN operations ever
undertaken. In 1996, their costs amounted to $588 million or 42 per cent
of the estimated $1.4 billion for all operations. (Only 30 US military per-
sonnel were deployed out of the total of 14 897.) The estimated US share
of about $148 million[28] raised all the issues which have surfaced over the
years in relations between the US and the UN – the apparent intrusion
of international authority into national legislation, the dominance of US
foreign policy objectives and, above all during the last decade, efficiency
and value for money.

The GAO conceded that there were limits to passing analyzed judgment
on whether missions had been 'successful' (UNDOF and UNIKOM), 'partially successful' (UNTSO, UNFICYP, UNAVEM II and III), or 'not successful' (UNMOGIP, UNIFIL and MINURSO) because they might
not adequately capture the multidimensional and complex interest in each
mission. The GAO noted that:

> At this time, however, U.S. officials see no reasonable alternative to
> continuing these operations indefinitely, given their assessment of the
> potential harm to U.S. foreign policy objectives if the underlying con-
> flicts resumed, balanced against what they considered to be these opera-
> tions' relatively moderate cost. In continuing to support what have
> become essentially open-ended commitments to peacekeeping, how-
> ever, the executive branch does not appear to give adequate considera-
> tion to other factors articulated by U.S. policy that seek to ensure that
> peacekeeping operations are limited in duration, linked to concrete
> political solutions, and have exit criteria and identified end points for
> U.N. involvement.[29]

It was a reasoned and plausible presentation of the choices facing the
makers of US foreign policy. It concluded that the US secretary of state
should work towards this objective with the Security Council. 'This
should be done,' the report said, 'in a manner consistent with PDD-25,
balancing the need to bring closure to these operations with other U.S.
interests, such as stabilizing conflicts that pose a threat to U.S. foreign
policy objectives.'[30] The GAO concluded by not proposing 'immediate
ends to these operations', but rather an assessment of their foreign policy

worth. Criticism of the costs of these operations, which were looked at in detail and extensively, are notably absent from an organization whose primary task is to monitor expenditure. It is the Defense Department which comments that the report could be strengthened by elaborating on the steps the executive branch had taken to reduce the costs of these operations or help spur the disputing parties to resolve their differences. The GAO report reinforced the impression that, in certain, visible areas of the UN's activities the issue of costs was important, but not central, to the debate over the repayment of arrears.

The political leadership from Washington tended to be reactive. The consistent theme was the desire to have the secretary-general of the day responding to US foreign policy objectives. There have been strong and weak UN chiefs, but none that fell comfortably into the category of following Washington's wishes. There emerged instead a parallel contest to that between Washington and the UN, that between the White House and Congress. At crucial moments, Congress has been able to intervene, largely on the financial level, as seen in the Kassebaum legislation in the 1980s and that effective from 1 October 1996, capping contributions to peace-keeping budgets to 25 per cent compared with the UN assessment of around 31 per cent. The involvement of Congress has often been tinged with a patriotic theme, emphasizing the inviolability of US law and the role of the UN's activities in US foreign policy. They have often coincided with the cyclical financial crises and the linked calls for reform. What made this latest round of US self-assertion special is the confluence of its paramountcy as a world political leader and the expansion of its economy. It is little wonder that the emphasis on reforming the running of the UN centers around the ideals of business practices. Efficiency reports from the UN write of mission goals, percentage targets met and efficiency illustrated through neat graphical boxes.[31] It is deliberate that the prime movers of reform were Joseph E. Connor, inherited by Annan from Boutros-Ghali as Under Secretary-General for Administration and Management, and Maurice Strong, appointed by Annan to be Executive Coordinator for United Nations Reform. Both come from private-sector, business backgrounds steeped in the merits of financial efficiency.

The GAO has again had its interesting say through a report based on five years of studies of UN peace-keeping operations.[32] Given the background of operations ranging from the Gulf War to former Yugoslavia, Haiti and Somalia, its conclusions were apposite and contained flavours of the US demands of the day. The report made much of the operational and organisational limits on the UN's ability to lead missions to enforce peace under Chapter VII of the Charter. 'These limitations have been overcome when a nation with sufficient military prestige, credibility, and the commitment of military forces necessary to conduct operations has taken the lead role in the U.N. operation.'[33] These contained illusions to modern operations in Haiti and Eastern Slavonia and historical contrasts with the Congo, Rwanda and south Lebanon. While the GAO repeated such operational constraints as insufficient troops and armaments, uncertainty about orders given by a UN commander in the field being obeyed by national contingents and the UN's lack of an approach to guide the use of force, it made little reference to financial difficulties as a whole. When mention was made, it was more about budget procedures and its effects on the availability of advance funds. Crucially, the GAO acknowledged that: 'The United Nations is at its core a political body of individual members and not an organization that has independent resources and power of its own'.[34] This lies at the heart of a gap between a nation which has the resources, apparent efficiency and decisiveness to attempt to do what it wants in its own interests and an international organization of member states which has these elements, at best, only as an aspiration. It helps to explain why the US has always wavered between being a generous donor and a delinquent to the UN.

Robert W. Gregg has written eloquently about the need for congruence between UN and US policies. Seen from a perspective which takes into account the financial aspect, he wrote:

> US assumptions as to what constitutes efficient and frugal management of the United Nations have, of course, always been closely tied to UN performance on substantive issues. When other US expectations are met, UN efficiency and frugality are less salient for US policymakers; when the UN fails the United States in other areas, however, they are quite likely to be invoked.[35]

In this context, the early reactions to Annan's proposed reforms as a whole and where they affect financing in particular have been muted and tinged with disappointment – although passed on 13 November by the 1997 special session of the General Assembly. To some extent they became lost in the protracted debates in the General Assembly. They were further confused by the search for new assessment rates for 1998–2000, with all the implications these rates carried for influence through weight of payment.

To judge by the content of the General Assembly debate and subsequent reactions, the US dual donor/delinquent role is clearly resented. If there is to be a more stable and predictable base for the UN's finances and therefore worldwide activities, some plan has to be arrived at that accommodates some of the special demands of the US. Washington has to be persuaded that, in organizational terms, the UN is entering a new era, well aware of new demands and realities.

But in mid-November, the prospects of 1997 reaching a happy conclusion looked remote and it turned out that way. On the plus side, the General Assembly gave approval on 13 November without a vote to a package of administrative reforms Annan can enact within his powers as secretary-general. Agreement on the newly assessed rates for contributions to the regular and peace-keeping budgets for 1998–2000 did not placate the US which had argued for a reduction in its 25 per cent level.[36] But on the same day, both houses of Congress voted against a plan negotiated with the Clinton administration that would have authorized overdue payments to the UN and additional money to the IMF for dealing with international crises. The domestic reason was the linking of aid to international family planning programs which might have involved abortion. As a result of the adjournment of Congress, start on the process of permitting the US to pay off more than $1 billion in arrears was stalled until 1998. This reflected the fact that, for the administration, it no longer carried any of the political urgency displayed at times earlier in the year. The White House spokesman said: 'It is utterly boneheaded for Congress to fail to meet the commitments that the United States has at the UN in terms of our arrears.'

On 14 November, Annan said:

The failure comes during a week when the United Nations Security Council has been seized by the crisis regarding arms inspection in Iraq, in which the UN plays a role that is indispensable to international peace and security as well as to the vital national security interests of the United States.

He went on: 'And it comes only a day after the United Nations General Assembly endorsed a major component of my program of institutional reform'. With understandable bitterness he added: 'It is both unreasonable and regrettable that the legislation was held hostage to the entirely unrelated domestic politics of abortion'.

This Congressional decision was a source of embarrassment and some confusion. The first half of 1998 was spent attempting to renegotiate positions with Congress which might have eased its implacable hostility towards settling the problem of arrears. The aid bill was drawn up and maneuvering started with a view for appropriations. The US debt position became unchanged at about 60 per cent of all dues owed to both the regular budget and peace-keeping budgets. There remained the remote possibility that the US might lose its voting rights in the General Assembly from the beginning of 1999. The final word about the confused relationship of the US with the UN was probably best left to Michael Douglas, the actor, who was named in July 1998 by Annan as a UN 'Messenger of Peace': Douglas said he was 'deeply embarrassed' by his country's debt to the UN 'As a member of the wealthiest country in the history of civilization, I think that most Americans are deeply embarrassed and humiliated that this debt is tied up in a controversy that should not exist.'

7 A Gallimaufry of Money-Raising Devices

It was Ted Turner, the chief of CNN, who most dramatically illustrated many of the oddities and contradictions of the ways in which the UN system funds itself. On 18 September 1997, he made an offer of $1 billion over ten years as a contribution towards UN humanitarian programs.[1] It is reported to have made Jane Fonda his wife and former film star, cry at the time. It certainly caught UN officials on the hop. A spokesman pointed out that the funds would not offset the $1.5 billion the US owed the UN at the time, because the world body could not accept contributions from the private sector. In fact, Article 17.2 of the Charter does not say that private non-governmental contributions may not be received. More formally, Joseph E. Connor said on 3 October that a trust fund would be set up, as it was the only way the UN could receive voluntary funds from individuals. One was, headed by a former State Department official, to dispense the $100 million a year (just income from yearly interest from Turner's fortune). One official remarked that Turner's contributions would make him, were he assessed as a state, the fourth largest contributor after the US, Japan and Germany. James Gustav Speth, UNDP's Administrator, described Turner's action more ethereally, as a 'godsend'. He added:

> It is a wake-up call to those governments that, citing domestic priorities, are slashing their development and humanitarian assistance. It may even nudge governments that now owe the United Nations some $2.5 billion (including more than $1 billion owed by the United States) to pay their debts.[2]

Back on earth, this episode underlined a theme, which has been present since the earliest days of the UN that the door should not be shut to outside contributions. One report in the 1950s by the Commission to Study the Organization of Peace suggested that:

> *the United Nations develop a program budget, combining all programs – such as relief, welfare, and technical assistance activities – falling outside the realm of standard or normal operations, and clearly distinguished from the administrative budget. For the present, the program budget should be supported by the voluntary contributions of*

Members States and by such other revenues as the Organization may receive, while the administrative budget should continue to be covered by assessments upon Member States.[3]

Ironically, and that was written in the era before peace-keeping budgets were set up separately, this division between 'program' and 'administrative' budgets would have saved future generations considerable trouble. To a certain extent, the system has evolved through the link between the regular/program budget and those of the specialized and affiliated agencies. This budgetary link is now confined mainly to administration, since they raise much of their money themselves – through the voluntary contributions alluded to. It does not quite go as far as to suggest that the regular budget should be open to non-assessed contributions, and it labels individual donations as 'undependable', nevertheless the tone suggests that they might not be excluded.

The US has always been, and latterly more strongly than ever, a proponent of greater encouragement of voluntary contributions and their integration into the financial system. It is a view that sits well with a variation of this, that the UN should not turn aside too easily suggestions for alternative means of providing finance – outside the established systems.

Kofi Annan proposed for his reform program of 1997 a 'two-track' approach. The first-track reforms were to be carried out in his role as chief administrative officer and involved management reforms. The second meant working with the member states, which had to make up their own minds and give the Secretariat their backing for structural reforms. The former was the easier proposition and its enactment was met by comparatively slight opposition. Financial reforms would have to fall under these two categories for as long as the Charter provides the basic constitutional guidelines. In terms of streamlining the inflow of revenues and scrutinizing expenditures, his suggestions were slow to get off the mark and were deferred for further discussion. If there was some innovation it was in the direction of closer contacts with business. This has become increasingly apparent to both the UN and other intergovernmental organizations as they realize that they have to confront the new challenges of the global economy with business to help them.

The years have thrown up a large number of suggestions for putting the UN's finances onto a sounder footing. They range from attractive but sometimes implausible devices of levies and fees, which might raise a large quantity of ready cash in a short period as a single indulgence to more fundamental reforms. These might make sound financial and practical sense but they might also involve changes in the UN's management and structure. Sustained imaginativeness seems to have eluded the would-be reformers from the latter sector.

For the present, scrutiny of how the costs of running the UN could be more fairly shared out are to be laid aside in favor of an examination of how the UN could swell the contents of its coffers. At the same time, the whole system of committees needs badly to be redefined in such a way as to ease the path to streamlining bureaucracy with the attendant cutting in costs and to make the system more responsive to the global needs of the day. To some extent, Annan's proposals aim to fulfill that through putting as much emphasis on development for the developing countries and the fight against crime and drugs. This trend was also being emphasized by strengthening the position of the secretary-general by creating a single deputy, whose main roles would be to administer (aided by a second 'cabinet' tier of managers) when he was off on his frequent travels and to take over in the short term, when the organization's chief was unable to carry out his tasks. There was particularly strong criticism that Annan had not devoted sufficient attention to making real changes in the operational structures and offices dealing with humanitarian operations.

At first sight the Annan proposals did not appear to have changed much of the structure of the financial system. Assessments remain at the heart of raising money. Controversy remains over how these assessments should be made and their fairness. The politics of paying, which applies mainly to the US, has not been seriously tackled. The sectors which may be most affected lay outside the immediate scope of this book in the areas of the main large agencies and the politics behind attempts to make their operations more efficient and coordinated. But attention must be paid to assessing the realistic outlook for the proposals and to make an estimate as to whether they could give greater shape and order to the running of finances and, above all, free the secretary-general for the overall and particularly political administration of the UN.

The proposals of devices for getting the UN out of difficult short-term cash-flow crises have the appeal of immediacy and action. They are often linked to easily identifiable events and sectors such as defense spending, tourism, air and sea travel, the environment, fossil fuels, currency exchanges and stock markets. There will always be adverse factors. They will inevitably require a complex measure of administration, and this will inevitably be complicated because of the need for the co-operation of many, and in some cases all, member states. Each new measure might well need a new office to administer its affairs. There are some measures, for example those involving tourism, which would not affect states equally. There are others, involving financial tools, which would be almost exclusively in the sphere of influence of the many financial centers. Above all, many propositions would offend tightly held views on sovereignty and universality. If it is possible to talk of the UN's sovereignty – or perhaps on a less inflated level, the authority of the General Assembly – then there are those who would argue that some measures would be beyond the direct control of the UN, even if the object was the benefit of that organization. On the level of individual states, the US would be in the vanguard of those maintaining steadfastly that a ruling passed by or for the UN cannot supersede national legislative authority. Both these concepts have been tested in law in relation to the UN over the years. And what Annan himself has said about sovereignty could call into question whether it still has its former strength. Universality still, however, holds some sway.

In an eloquent passage in presenting 'Reform at the UN – Track 2' in July, Annan said:

> The greatest source of strength enjoyed by the United Nations stems from its universality of membership and the comprehensive scope of its mandate. And the most encompassing manifestation of this strength is in the normative realm. Norms that approach universality for a principled basis on which to assess and guide practice within the community of nations. Such norms have not only a moral import. They also provide the institutional underpinnings of daily life within the international community: expectations as to rights and obligations, the mutual predictability of behavior afforded by the rule of law, the specification of best practices, a nearly endless array of standards without which the conduct of routine international transactions would be inconceivable.
>
> Its universal character and comprehensive mandate make the United Nations a unique and indispensable forum for governments to identify emerging global issues, to negotiate and validate common approaches to then, and to mobilize energies and resources for implementing agreed actions. The convening power of the United Nations has produced impressive results in a great variety of fields, including trade and development, environment, human rights, the progressive development and codification of international law, gender equality, population, as well as in peace and security, and disarmament.[4]

It is interesting to note that he has backed away from this position somewhat, particularly when it comes to the need for closer contacts with the operations of business.

But more critically, the strength of globalization in both financial transactions and companies' activities and the development of regional organization such as the EU have worn away the edges of notions of national sovereignty. This should make these money-raising devices for the UN the more plausible and worth serious practical consideration.

It should be pointed out that reviews of how the UN could better run itself, and in particular its finances, have been around some time. In its report, the Commission to Study the Organisation of Peace, after a passage suggesting as sources of funding

> fees for special services performed by international agencies in the interests of governments or private concerns... levies on the operation of governmental services having an international character, and... revenues from the exploitation of the natural resources of areas such as the bed of the sea (beyond the continental shelf) and Antarctica,

wrote: '*We urge the United Nations to promote continuous and intensive exploration of possible new sources of revenue to supplement governmental contributions and to take timely action to exploit such sources as circumstances permit*'.[5] It did, at the same time, recognize 'the primary role of national governments as the financial supporters of international agencies'. Nevertheless, in the details of its suggestions (for example, on direct taxes, defense expenditures, and fees for international radio licensing among others) it indicated an early willingness to propose alternative methods of financing the UN.

Later some of these suggestions have been taken up by the UN itself, notably in Boutros-Ghali's *An Agenda for Peace*.[6] There he wrote of other proposals for raising money:

> These ideas include: a levy on arms sales that could be related to maintaining an Arms Register by the United Nations; a levy on international air travel, which is dependent on the maintenance of peace; authorization for the United Nations to borrow from the World Bank and the International Monetary fund – for peace and development are interdependent; general tax exemption for contributions made to the United Nations by foundations, businesses and individuals; and changes in the formula for calculating the scale of assessments for peace-keeping operations.

Some of these suggestions perhaps sit more easily in the category of structural innovations, as is understandable coming from the secretary-general. For he goes on to the vital central theme:

> As such ideas are debated, a stark fact remains: the financial foundations of the Organization daily grow weaker, debilitating its political will and practical capacity to undertake new and essential activities. This state of affairs must not continue. Whatever decisions are taken on

financing the Organization, there is one inescapable necessity: Member States must pay their assessed contributions in full and on time. Failure to do so puts them in breach of their obligations under the Charter.

Few would contest that any of these are original. Debates from the earliest days contained comments about expenditure on defense as a point of reference, not just for the small scale of the UN's costs but as a source, through a percentage global tax, of additional funds. Each one of these funds and their authorization raise the issues mentioned above, those of sovereignty and universality.

Yves Beigbeder related[7] how Boutros-Ghali turned to the Ford Foundation which convened an independent international advisory group of experts – the Volcker/Ogata group – in September 1992 to examine the financing of the UN with a view to creating a secure long-term financing base for the organization.[8] The 11-man group, under the experienced guidance of Brian Urquhart, included such luminaries as Paul Volcker, the co-chairman and former Chairman of the US Federal Reserve, Shijuro Ogata, the other co-chairman with 30 years' service in the Bank of Japan, Raymond Barre, a former French prime minister, Abdul Aziz Al-Quraishi, former governor of the Saudi Arabia Monetary Agency, and Olusegun Obasanjo, a former president of Nigeria. It is an interesting insight into the perceived size of the UN's problems that there was some difficulty in persuading these eminent persons that the size of the crisis was certainly in billions of dollars, but in twos and threes, not tens or hundreds – their more usual fare![9] It is worth quoting at length this group's conclusions on 'additional financing for the future' for their measured judgment indicates how they were both far-sighted and yet, at that time, hampered by still conservative attitudes of the time. The report wrote:

> The most pressing financial questions before the U.N. involve paying the bills for ongoing operations and raising the funds to pay for its foreseeable obligations in peacekeeping, humanitarian relief, and sustainable development. For now, these obligations can and must be financed by governments.
>
> But the U.N.'s current operations are still in many ways quite limited. It has been suggested that there may come a time when the U.N. will face exceptional needs that can only be met by exceptional means, when the level of expenditure for essential activities will force the U.N. to seek financial support from the private sector, and from individual citizens. Proponents of additional means of financing the U.N. have recommended levies on airline traffic and shipping, which have a stake in the maintenance of international peace, as well as taxes on arms sales and

on the production of hydrocarbon fuels. Some have proposed the establishment of an international U.N. lottery, others an active campaign to encourage private donations to the organization.

The advisory group nevertheless believes:

- Current proposals for additional, nongovernmental sources of financing are neither practical nor desirable. For now, the system of assessed and voluntary contributions provides the most logical and appropriate means of financing the U.N., as it permits and encourages member governments to maintain proper control over the U.N.'s budget and its agenda.

With the passage of time, as confidence in the effectiveness and efficiency of the U.N. grows, governments might look more favorably on more direct means of financing some activities of the world organization. In the longer run, the U.N. may be asked to assume much larger financial obligations in an area such as sustainable development. Those obligations could be of such magnitude that they could not easily be supported by its current financial arrangements. It would then be useful and timely to explore what alternatives might eventually prove feasible. The group believes, however, that the future needs of the organization can be met with assurance and foresight at this time without resort to new and inevitably controversial initiative.[10]

These views have been overtaken to the extent that the pressure has grown for recourse to new methods outside the traditional source. At issue, of course, also is the extent to which the financial independence of the UN is regarded as a virtue in itself and there are advantages to be gained in the UN having some leeway between itself and its own members. As Riggs and Plano have observed:

Suggestions for new sources run the gamut from those that would provide minor amounts of supplemental income to those that might in themselves finance most or all UN activities. As might be expected, sources that offer the greatest potential for substantial income are also the lest feasible politically.[11]

To this should be added the factor of how to make their suggestions enforceable.

The authors went on to list other potential sources for the UN including:

- private contributions in the form of individual gifts (as in the Turner case), inheritances, and foundation grants encouraged through a joint policy of making such contributions deductible from national taxes;

- charges levied by UN agencies for services as weather forecasts from the World Meteorological Organization or for fees for international licenses from the International Telecommunication Union;
- tolls for transportation and communication, facilitated by UN programs;
- fees for international travel imposed through levies on passports and visas or through surcharges on national customs duties;
- profits earned through implementation of the 1982 Law of the Sea Treaty by which a UN international investment corporation could exploit the mineral and other forms of wealth in international waters and seabeds;
- charters sold to private companies or governmental agencies authorizing them to exploit the resources of seabeds and Antarctica, with royalty rights reserved by the UN;
- fishing, whaling, and sealing rights in international waters, assigned to countries or private companies upon the payment of 'conservation' fees to the UN;
- rights to outer space, or the operation of outer space programs by the UN, aimed at producing revenues through communications satellites, meteorological systems, and the future development of resources on the moon and the planets;
- taxes levied directly on member states, collectible by their governments, and based on ability to pay judged by national income;
- taxes levied directly on individuals through the cooperation of member states, based on income and with a mild gradation of rates;
- the issuance of an international trading currency, backed by national reserves, that could serve the dual function of financing UN programs and providing a supplementary international monetary unit to encourage greater trade.

Others have contributed their suggestions of unorthodox methods of finding funds. Childers and Urquhart repeating some of the items mentioned in the Volcker/Ogata report observed that: 'Schemes for additional financing of the UN are, however, easy to suggest but would not be at all easy to implement. In addition to other schemes, they mention: a fractional levy on all transnational movement of currencies and consideration given to designating one day in each year as 'United Nations Communication Day', when all postage charges and telephone calls – and possibly a fraction of broadcasting advertising revenues – would carry levies accruing to the UN. They made the point that each member government would have to agree to levy any such taxes, and collect and transfer them to approved parts of the UN system. Thus, international taxation revenue would essentially rise through and stay under the control of member states. It remains moot whether this would apply to a UN lottery, which others argue would emphasize the UN's principle of universality by going straight to the peoples. But soberly, they concluded:

> Some guiding principles for serious exploration of any alternative financing would seem essential. First, any such financing of the UN and its System should be *supplementary to a more healthily apportioned, and a fully honoured assessment system.* Secondly, there must be representative governance of any such additional contributions. Thirdly and closely connected, any such additional financing must be transparently accountable to citizens.[12]

This provides about as comprehensive a check-off list of sources of funds as wit could contrive,[13] and should not be dismissed out of hand, for the reason that through its last round of financial stumblings and attack on reform, the exclusive side to the UN's nature has been, to some extent, breached in the same way that notions of national sovereignty are not what they were. Secretary-General Annan said as much, both shortly after coming into office and again in June 1998. What he said has broader implications. If sovereignty can be breached in areas connected with humanitarian rights and international security, it can be extended to ideas of collectivity that the UN values governing the centerpieces of the principles for financing that organization, then it should follow naturally that alternative and less orthodox means of raising money should be seriously entertained.

The traditionalists still have their supporters. In an interesting if vociferous attack on deviation from the system of assessed contributions, Muchkund Dubey wrote: 'One of the most unfortunate developments in UN financing has been the steady growth of voluntary contributions.' His targets were in particular agencies carrying out development, but the arguments have been wielded against the principle of unorthodox payments as well. Briefly, they were that voluntary contributions:

- distorted the priorities of recipient governments; introduced uncertainty in programs;
- gave a 'tremendous fillip' to conditionalities;
- undermined the democratic process of decision making in the UN;
- introduced a donor–recipient relationship absent from the regular budget process;
- held back the growth in regular budgets of UN organizations;
- had failed to mobilize additional funds for financing UN activities.[14]

But back to the more practical realities of devices to raise cash for the United Nations. Beigbeder's conclusions are important, not because they are prescient in indicating how attitudes towards the financing of the UN were changing, but in underlining the point that the Ford group's views were weighty and well-considered, but that they already look to have been overtaken by global developments in both the political and financial fields. For Beigbeder wrote:

> Contrary to the Ford Foundation Group's position, the prospects of additional, non-governmental sources of financing the UN should be seriously considered. There is no reason why Member States could not 'maintain proper control over the UN's budget and its agenda', if the UN was to finance part of its expenditures through sources other than governmental contributions: the practices of the European Union, of the EPO [European Patent Office], and, in the UN system, of the WIPO, show the direction to take, if the UN is to establish a broader and more solid financial base. The UN (and its specialized agencies) cannot continue to depend exclusively on the good or bad will of Member States for its financing: a 'third source' should be created besides the mandatory assessments and the voluntary contributions.
>
> Here, the Secretary-General's 'other ideas' should be pursued: a possible levy on arms sales, on international air travel and shipping, on the production of hydrocarbon fuels – tax exemption for contributions made to the UN by foundations, businesses and individuals. The establishment of an international UN lottery does not appear too serious.
>
> Any of these technical remedies will fail if Member States do not show more commitment to the Organization's role and activities in global politics, economics, the environment, human rights and other areas of concern to the international community: overall commitment includes dependable financial support.[15]

These will depend, in the end, not just on commitment to these ideas but also commitment to the extent of being able to organize the collection and enforced payment of such funds. Ingvar Carlsson, when Prime Minister of Sweden and co-chairman of the Commission on Global Governance, added a note of caution about the global approach to taxes: 'It would be much more realistic to recognize that in few, if any, countries does the UN have the kind of strong political constituency that can support its claim on the national budget against the competing claim of domestic constituencies.'[16] This places the onus of being a worthy recipient of such funds on the UN to prove that its own record has changed to the extent of being able to begin to compete with local national rather than international concerns in an individual country.

The UN itself has not held back from exploring new sources of funding. A report by the secretary-general was delivered to a session of ECOSOC in Geneva in the summer of 1997 on this topic.[17] It was developed in co-operation with the UNDP and was aimed mainly at the agencies and programs outside the UN regular and peace-keeping budgets. Indeed, it said: 'At the outset it should be stressed that funds generated by new and innovative ideas should neither be viewed as a substitute for official development assistance nor as a source for financing of the regular and peace-keeping budgets.'[18] Nevertheless, the report discussed a variety of options under such headings as collateralized bond obligations, micro-credit, investment incentives and aid, and the developmental responsibility of private enterprises, charges and fees on pollution, and IMF gold holdings and SDRs that suggested at least a willingness, despite the initial caveat, to explore alternatives.

These medleys of suggestions over the years throw the arguments back onto the existing mechanisms of the UN itself. For the bulk of those already mentioned are largely supplements to an existing system. They lie beyond the belt-tightening resorts such as savings through reducing expenditure on bureaucracy, ranging from eliminating the number of languages into which documents are translated and printed to slimming down the number of civil servants and the contracts which they enjoy. The use of computerized technology should, in theory at least, cut down on paper and shift some costs to the recipients of information about the UN. Instances such as these have become the bread and butter of the reform debate, which has broken out again in the last few years, protracted by the promulgation of reforms. Any resolution of these issues must have a direct bearing on the ways and means of reducing the UN's chronic financing problems.

On a broader level, however, the first approach might be to integrate both the general and peace-keeping budgets into one single budget financed by assessments. This would have to be an ultimate ideal and one which would be likely to be sternly resisted on the grounds that, first, it would be too unwieldy and difficult to manage and, second, it would involve making demands on contributors towards undefined aims, particularly in the peace-keeping area. The most that could be practically handled would be a tidying of the existing regular and peace-keeping budgets, with predictable recurring payments, for example, in the setting-up stage of an operation, being gathered into an annual reserve. At the same time, there have been several suggestions that it would be an advantage to drop the denomination of contributions in dollars through calculating the UN's finances in SDRs. The IMF already uses these as a means of evading the fluctuations in the dollar's value through this basket of the world's major currencies. The UN's budget has been under particular exposure since the floating of the dollar in 1973. But it is questionable whether this would be a sufficient hedge against fluctuations and it would require a fundamental change in the institution rules to permit it to deal with the UN – a non-government.

A second, much discussed approach is the one involving incentives and disincentives. The incentives should combine those that cover positive financial incentives and constitute fair measures towards prompt payers, and those intended to be more directly binding and bringing pressure to bear on states unwilling to fulfill their commitment through contributions towards the UN. These would include crediting budget surpluses for a given period to member states which had paid their contributions and not to members as a whole; or the refund of interest on the investment of assessed contributions which were not immediately required; and discounts to states paying in full and on time. In peace-keeping, countries contributing troops and equipment should be reimbursed first. Disincentives would include stricter implementation of Article 19 and the charging of interest on arrears (taking into account national budgetary cycles different from the calendar year, genuine difficulties causing late payments and the application of interest charges to avoid early payments subsidising member states with poor payment records). Disincentive schemes should be applied on a sliding scale, with higher penalties on larger contributors and lower on smaller ones, with no penalties on least developed countries. Other suggestions could include the representatives of states in arrears becoming ineligible for election to or recruitment to employment in UN bodies; and not awarding contracts to companies from states in arrears. Some of these would be challenged in law.[19] The theory is easier than the practice, with problems of added administration and enforcement the most obvious disadvantages. For how do you get delinquents to pay their arrears? It has been patently obvious that threats on any level do not work. Penalty payments, too, are unenforceable. Parallel with the concept of punishment runs the concept of disincentives, but these too run into the problems of enforcement – although incentive payments for the delivery on time of outstanding debts would not be rejected.

It has reached the stage where one of the more ludicrous suggestions was that the flag of a defaulter should be lowered outside the UN. It would be neither noticed nor have any impact if it were. Neither shame nor embarrassment has played a notable role in any UN operations – particularly when it has come to money – at any time.

The third approach would be to express greater and more open interest in voluntary contributions. There have been notable changes on this front. This had become the more pressing as, first, many organizations have been successful in financing their budgets largely from sources outside the formal UN system – largely voluntary private and governmental contributions. Second, as, particularly in 'peace-keeping' operations, the UN has had to work closely with non-military and non-governmental organizations which naturally derive their funds from elsewhere and as a result costs may have to be shared. In this case, it would help the UN to examine whether in some circumstances it would not be to its benefit if it raised its finances from similar sources. The problem here is that this could be seen as undermining the direct authority of the UN itself.

As has just been remarked, most individual organizations under the aegis of the UN already derive their funds that way, and have been relatively successful, but the reservations about this approach have been outlined elsewhere. There are difficulties here as well. The UNHCR is cited often as an example of success but drawbacks occur because finance ministries will in effect only authorize mandatory payments. There is an element of chance in voluntary funds, for they tend not to work on a whip-round basis and need to be formalized. There thus lies a problem in both the UN itself and donor governments recognizing more formally this new arrangement.

A fourth approach would be to raise finance through a taxing assessment technique on sectors in individual countries and regions, which depend directly on UN operations in these areas. These might be raised regionally – as in health or refugee questions or directly on countries such as Saudi Arabia or other oil and gas producing countries, which need national protection from an international force to guarantee income from a specific resource. In the Gulf War, this was successful but almost exclusively outside the remit of the UN. Some financing was worked out on a bilateral basis between the oil-producing countries and their allies in the field. Japan and Germany paid up in lieu of military participation because of domestic constitutional constraints. In Japan's case this amounted to $13 billion and in Germany's DM 18 billion[20] – considerable sums for non-participation in a war which had disputable UN authorization!

In the context of UN-backed intervention to preserve stability, there have been discussions about raising taxes on financial transactions (the Tobin Tax) and defense and tourism activities. These supra-sovereignty approaches have their attraction and would undoubtedly raise more than sufficient funds. But they have already raised objections that the UN is not a global government but rather an association of nations. The idea runs swiftly into the complaint that such actions would be infringements of sovereign authority. With that come again the difficulties of enforcement.

As a variant on the issue of increasing regional involvement and co-operation, there have been suggestions, notably in the autumn of 1996 by the US in the context of Africa, of devolving military preparedness and peace-keeping operations on to regions. In Africa, ECOWAS' efforts in Liberia have been notably unsuccessful in admittedly difficult circumstances. The African response has been muted in voice and, in practice, extremely hesitant – even if the manpower and facilities were fully available. The trail of disastrous events in Rwanda and Congo/Zaire holds little hope of an African regional peace-keeping force developing for several years. The Gulf Consultative Council, in connection with an ill-defined Arab deterrent force, has a wide range of arms at its disposal; has made sterling assertions that the Arabs should be left to look after and settle their own disputes; and has pronounced readiness to join forces to deter any invader. But their active achievements have been unco-ordinated and markedly unconvincing. They were impotent during the Gulf wars. On the civilian side, their regional counterparts are under heavy suspicion of being too partial to be dependable for the distribution of aid, not to mention to feed into any preventive intelligence network. Nevertheless, it is an alternative form of load sharing which needs to be explored further especially where finances are involved.

A fifth approach, not unconnected to the fourth, would be the levying of taxes on such specific sectors as tourism and defense expenditure, or, as has been proposed in some Scandinavian countries, the raising of taxes on air fares (since airlines are obviously dependent on the preservation of peace and security). This could be expanded to international taxes on foreign currency and stock market transactions. There could, indeed, be an international lottery, which would have some marginal attraction for the populists in appealing over the heads of government direct to 'we the peoples' of the UN Charter. With imagination the range of alternatives is vast – though their enactment and practicability are limited.

Sixth, the UN could turn to the sale of such items as stamps and coins on a far larger scale than is carried out at present. This would have the merit of boosting public relations, which tends to be looked down on and regarded somehow as being debasing. But the earnings here would probably be on a marginal scale.

Finally, it has been proposed many times that the UN could act like other major international concerns and turn to the money markets and some of the international institutions such as the IMF and the World Bank for loans. Again there are reservations about this and also practical obstacles. Where the World Bank is concerned, this course is at present forbidden because that organization does not lend to non-sovereign entities. One idea has been that debts overdue should be sold at a discount to intermediaries, like some Third World countries' debts.

As for financial functions and the practicalities of monitoring them both as a positive exercise and as good public relations, the JIU and the OIOS need to be strengthened to eliminate waste and corruption, and to monitor the administration of both regular and peace-keeping budgets and of organizations of the UN system. The JIU, in action since 1968, needs an overhaul. It has only 11 inspectors, many of ex-ambassador rank and seniority, appointed by the General Assembly. It lacks the mandate to pursue extensively and aggressively the details and implementation of budgets. It could become more effective if there was a JIU unit for each agency or regional inspectors. The OIOS, started in 1994, has a larger staff and broader range of activities in collaboration with the auditors. It has also the means of checking expenditures.

But where peace-keeping is concerned an important factor under consideration has been preventive action. It need not be very expensive, for example, to improve the use of computer technology and raise the level of communications. This could improve efficiency and, above all, help to cut down on wasteful duplication of activities. Voluntary funds and contributions in kind could find their niche here. If the problems in the peace-keeping sector are seen as more of a 'wasting sickness' than a congenital problem, then this puts things in proportion. There may have been many ways suggested but it is apparent from the inertia and lack of inventiveness in practice that there has not been the necessary will. There seems to be an immutable gap between areas for innovation and structural changes in the existing UN system. The comparatively small section in Annan's reforms devoted to financial reforms confirmed this.

8 Reassessing the Budgets

The devices outlined in the previous chapter have their marked merits and disadvantages. Almost all share the starting-point of being bounded by the conflicting interests of the international idealism, which the UN is supposed to embody, and day-to-day practicality. They cannot be introduced as a single package for, as the debate and narrative have shown, they all potentially cut across different attitudes, principles and national interests. But some features stand out. Both analysts and practitioners have over the years urged the use of, or at least serious interest in, such alternative means to financing the UN. Devices will not provide a solution but they are far more acceptable today than in the past. There should have been some learning from the experience of the specialized agencies and programs which have had near autonomy in financial terms and in the running of their budgets from the beginning. This has lead to acute problems in the running of programs, but, in terms of the financial structure of the UN, it is taken for granted that they are virtually their own masters. The theoretical paramountcy of the General Assembly has, in this way, been long eroded and emphasized by the globalization of the world economy and by the swiftness and broad extension of financial and economic flows. But, in theory, the Assembly shares the task with ECOSOC of co-ordinating the policies and activities of these affiliated agencies and offering suggestions about their administrative budgets. Examination of agency budgets by the General Assembly is, by and large, confined to a broad review. These budgets were initially to have been included in the consolidated general budget of the UN, but this practice was never seriously pursued. No practical steps have been taken for the UN to collect contributions on a regular basis for specialized agencies, although related percentage assessment rates are in operation. The operators and comptrollers of the regular and peace-keeping budgets could have learned from their relationship with the budgets of the UN agencies something which might have had useful application to their own budgetary exercises.

This evolution in financing as carried out by the agencies has had some influence on the key factors of the UN's regular and peace-keeping budgets, for it has thrown the burden back onto the organization to look again at these fundamentals. The UN's financial situation in the run-up to the annual session of the General Assembly in the autumn of 1998 reflected a sense that the overall situation had changed little in terms of arrears and cash flow prospects. A year earlier, Annan in presenting his reform package to the General Assembly had warned that: 'The United Nations is not working as it should. Our Organization has been slow to reflect changes in geopolitical realities.'[1] A year later in the financial sector, beyond a new cabinet-style management in the Secretariat, the trimming of jobs and biennial budgets, there was little to show of substance reflecting the new approaches or practices promulgated.

But for the moment, it is almost certain that, whatever the will and climate for reform, some aspects of the running of the UN's finances will not change. The basic structure of two separate budgets, one, the regular budget, somewhat misleading entitled also the program budget, and the other, the group of special accounts for peace-keeping budgets, is unlikely to be modified beyond the establishment, or rather re-establishment, of reserve funds to provide some leeway for late payments and shortfalls in the cash flow. The other budgets – the third category – affecting mainly the specialized and other affiliated agencies, are likely to keep their percentage links with the General Assembly, based on assessed contributions, but will probably continue the trend of depending increasingly on extra-budgetary funds derived from voluntary contributions and bilateral and multilateral private and governmental funds.

The common thread which runs through these three types of budget[2] (the fourth – voluntary programs – by its nature excludes itself) is the system of contributions. These are assessed, as is well known, on a complicated capacity-to-pay basis. The debate about their calculation affects the regular and peace-keeping budgets more than those of the specialized agencies. The problem with this method of raising funds falls fundamentally into two parts, which are only notionally linked. The first is structural and concerns a range of assessed rates which have ranged now from 0.001 per cent to 39.89 per cent for the regular budget over all the years of the UN's existence. The relative fairness of this apportionment[3] has long been under scrutiny and a strong focus of debate. As will be shown later, there is considerable room for flattening out the unevenness of this assessment system and of the calculations on which it is based.

The basic and longstanding problem is the wilful decision by member states to hold back their assessed payments. In the early days of peace-keeping operations before separate budgets were established, as in the cases of ONUC and UNEF I, there were clear-cut political motives behind the withholding of these payments. This has tended to be the main excuse, although hedged about, in the vital case of the US, by protracted, domestic legislative niceties. National incompetence, bad temper and insolvency have been other frequently invoked explicit or implicit reasons. Resorts to *ad hoc* methods, such as the WCF and the UN Special Account, among

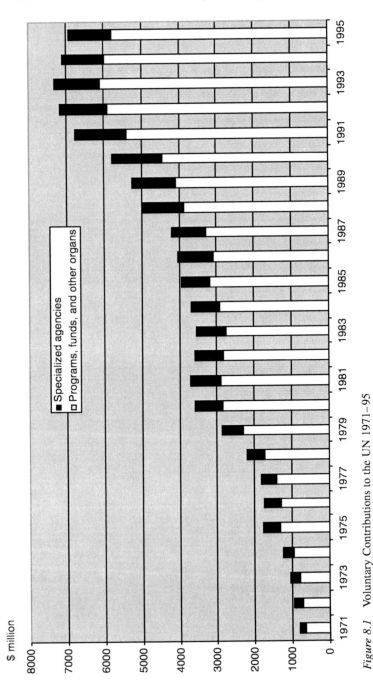

Figure 8.1 Voluntary Contributions to the UN 1971–95
Source: Klaus Hüfner, Freie Universität Berlin for Global Policy Forum (www.globalpolicy.org).
The major Specialized Agencies include the ILO, UNESCO, WHO, UPU, ITU, IMO, and UNIDO. The major programs, funds and other organs include UNCTAD, UNDP, UNFPA, UNHCR, UNICEF, UNIFEM, and UNU.

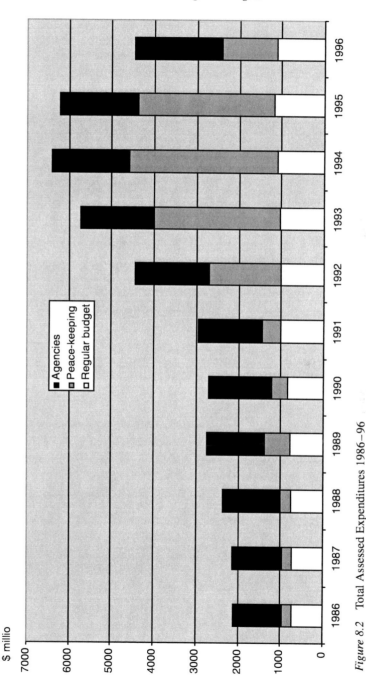

$ millio

Figure 8.2 Total Assessed Expenditures 1986–96
Source: Klaus Hüfner, Freie Universität Berlin.
The data includes neither the Human Rights Tribunals, which are a separate but relatively small item, nor the Bretton Woods Institutions.

others, have been no more than that – *ad hoc*. Annan's \$1 billion RCF, based on voluntary contributions, looks suspiciously like a larger variant on this approach. Their main merit is that they might help to get round a problem of the fortuitous lack of synchronization between the UN's fiscal year and those of individual states by providing a safety cushion against an uneven (although largely predictable) cash-flow problem towards the end of each calendar year.

The non-payment of assessed arrears is likely to remain the insoluble heart of the problem. Since the late 1980s the UN's regular and peace-keeping budgets have borne a higher proportion of the shortfall in appropriated funds than have the UN specialized agencies. Incentive and penalty payments have been mooted. The idea never caught on. But both the incentive and punitive approaches have superficial attraction.[4] Penalty systems have applied at some of the more technical and specialized UN agencies with some, measured success. But their introduction on a broader basis to the UN as a whole would pose distinct problems. They could be voted down, especially by the possible offenders. Those who were unable to pay for understandable or legitimate reasons might find themselves put on a par with those who withheld payments for political reasons. Above all, the US, or its Congress, would not brook what it might well see as further anti-American moves and continue not to reduce the payment of its arrears. As for the encouragement of early payments, incentive schemes have been implemented by ICAO, introduced in January 1987, and followed a year later by UNESCO, IMO and WMO. But early payments might well take the pressure off those countries, which are late in fulfilling their dues. In all, incentives for paying on time and penalizing schemes for late-paying members through fines, including interest on non-payment of contributions have been used by the ILO, FAO, UNESCO, ICAO, WHO, UPU, WMO, IMO and ITU but, in the end, with only mixed and limited results for punishment of late-paying offenders. It is noticeable that in the agencies where the assessment schemes are self-regulated and where technical services are provided the payment rate is, unsurprisingly, much higher.[5]

It has been difficult to work out whether the results of prompter payments have in fact had a measurable effect on the competent running of these organizations. The incentives themselves are on such a scale, that if translated into mainstream budgetary terms would probably have only a negligible effect. These are weapons probably best kept in reserve.

Closer to the heart of the full range of the problems are the assessment procedures and the budget periods. But, it is worth repeating, ever since its inception, the UN has had no practical means of enforcing its authority on those who defy its authority. In theory, late payments or defaulting can be punished. Under certain conditions of Article 19 of the UN Charter, members can be deprived of voting rights in the General Assembly.

For the regular budget, the system of assessing contributions, which has been under discussion for as long as it has been in existence and that was before the UN came into being, will have to be reorganized extensively and on a more realistic basis of what constitutes the wealth of individual countries. The major payers should in theory welcome this, not least because it would reduce the burden on them and also criticism at home. It has been broadly shown that some countries are paying way below what they could and should. The acknowledged fact is that as long as the guiding principle seems to be to keep a balance between a flow of money to keep the administration and most of its programs going, the financial democratic universality of equal membership and a statistical base to keep account of all these features (not all of them measurable), there cannot be a perfect scheme. A broader base for estimates might be used through the incorporation of the HDI used by the UNDP in its annual *Human Development Report*. This relies on national estimates reported by the UN and its agencies among other sources. But this index, although more 'human' in its points of reference than GDP or GNP *per caput* statistics, can be exploited and misread like other indices.

The UN budget approval process is long and complex.[6] The effect of the process is that the industrialized countries, which are the major contributors, have had, since the end of 1986, a major say over programs in the regular budget as it is reviewed by the CPC (see Chapter 6), whose role in scrutinizing the budget on its way to the General Assembly was strengthened by being able to operate through consensus rather than a majority vote. The contents of budgets could be subject to closer scrutiny and control by the reforms suggested by Annan in July 1997. Under these, the budget will be more results-related rather than setting an overall ceiling. Against this background, it was hoped, the size of the budget would not just be held steady through 1996–7, but was actually to fall in 1998–9. The 'zero real growth' cap on the regular budget has had the inevitable effect of reducing financial resources for everything funded through it.

The 18-member Committee on Contributions has the thankless task of submitting the scales of assessments to the General Assembly. This it does according to existing criteria, while formulating new proposals for change. The UN scale is adopted by the General Assembly for three years (although there have been variations within these periods, notably in the new series). A new list of rates for 1998, 1999 and 2000 was reached and accepted by the General Assembly after prolonged discussion and the current assessment rate. It is a process and outcome which is fraught with both political and financial implications. The mantra is the 'capacity to pay' and it is also the determining factor for the ultimate scale. National income data provided by all states for a ten-year period is one starting point. Allowances have to be made for high degrees of external debt. The rates of assessment, it is decided, may not be lower than a floor rate of 0.01 per cent (now changed to 0.001) or exceed a ceiling of 25 per cent. The scheme of limits is aimed at avoiding excessive variations of individual rates of assessments between successive scales. The calculations are made more complex in that, as a first step, each country's national income is worked out in the national currency and converted into US dollars. Artificially inflated exchange rates and fluctuations add further uncertainties.

The thankless role of the US at the earliest stages of the development of the UN's budget system provides a useful insight into the political problems of the capacity-to-pay regime. Originally the floor-rate was 0.04 per cent and the initial US assessment should have been at nearly 50 per cent, but this was reduced by negotiation to 39.89 per cent in order to lessen the financial dependence of the UN on a single member. It is now 25 per cent. Over the years, the US has been pulled between wanting to reduce the size of the burden it carries and yet fearing to have its influence eroded. Inadvertently, its position finds support from the less developed countries, which are unwilling to take up the slack in finance caused by the US contribution being reduced. Occasionally, the US has contemplated, as it did in 1988 during the Reagan administration, a reduction in the assessment, which would have been negotiated with, but not imposed by, the UN.

The world's sole superpower flexed its old reactions when the EU proposed on 25 January 1996 some changes in US rates and other means to get payments made on time. It proposed overhauling the dues system, in part to ease the problems of member states with genuine payment difficulties (including a schedule of repayment over a fixed period not exceeding five years), so that the US would pay substantially less, while others like Japan and Germany would pay more. By redistributing the peace-keeping percentages, the Permanent Five share would fall from 51.54 per cent in 1997 (with the US contributing 30.86 per cent) to 45.69 per cent (US 28.75 per cent). In more detail, the proposals directly involved the assessment procedures and levels. Reforms in the percentages assessed proposed the EU as a single unit with the resulting calculation that the EU combined accounted for 34.4 per cent of the regular budget and 36.7 per cent of peace-keeping operations – the largest group contribution by far. On the basis of the EU proposals , the US would pay no more than 25 per cent of the regular budget. Asia would have to pay more – South Korea's share, for example, rising from 0.82 per cent to 1.5 per cent by 1997, and that Japan's share should rise from 15.65 per cent to 17.78 per cent. The EU also suggested that there should be penalties on those who did not pay arrears. The US at that stage owed $1.2 billion out of a total of $2.3 billion. The US and other delinquent members would be required to pay their bills on time. If they did not, they would be liable to such possible penalties as suspension of their voting rights, late payments charges and a ban on the UN's hiring of their citizens or the buying of goods or services from their nationals' companies. Such changes would have required the laborious procedure of changing the Charter. One penalty suggested was that there should be a restriction on earnings made by countries from UN contracts. Here the US was reckoned to be earning more than $1.2 billion a year. Furthermore, and this has often been overlooked in the annual row over UN diplomats apparently failing to pay their parking tickets, the presence of the UN in New York is a vital element in that city's economy.[7] Boutros-Ghali, recognizing the nature of the broader crisis, responded by promising swathing cuts in manpower, by 10 per cent. This was done in some centers, such as Geneva, with little concern for the effectiveness of the organizations' agencies. On some occasions, his efforts to dismiss officials were resisted and the decision had to be reversed. He also suggested that no contributor should pay more than 15–20 per cent towards the regular budget. but this ran into opposition from the US which again saw in this a reduction in its political power, even if it meant having to pay less money. This left the US contribution of 31 per cent towards peace-keeping budgets untouched and as an awkward anomaly, which the US Congress had already dealt with.

The US reaction was tart. In a paper entitled *U.S. Variant to the UN Scales of Assessment*, dated 3 March 1997, the High-Level Working Group on Improving the Financial Situation of the UN recorded the US suggestion that its regular budget contribution would be 20 per cent rather than 25 per cent. Outside the Working Group it was known that the US was opposed to disincentives or penalties. It was against the EU suggestion that the US should pay 28.75 per cent of the peace-keeping budget. It maintained, since Congress the previous October had unilaterally as a punitive measure cut back its contribution from 31 to 25 per cent, that no nation should pay more than 25 per cent. That action by itself was technically against at least the spirit of the Charter and unprecedented for a contributor of such importance. This self-imposed ceiling has in addition caused confusion because it effectively reduced, from US calculations, the amount it owes. In addition, the US was opposed to any taxation scheme for funding the UN, since it was seen as another form of infringing sovereignty. In popular terms, the UN was seen as both ordering US boys into battle and also imposing direct taxation on an independent nation!

The EU's proposals were supplemented further by plans proposed by the G7 at a meeting in Lyon, France in July of that year to reduce the US contribution. It again met with resistance, and the issue was largely subsumed by the more public issue of Boutros-Ghali's determination to stand for a second term and the US' successful campaign to prevent that.

Battle had been effectively joined. But underlying the US obduracy were simple, mainly political, facts. The US was uncomfortable as the only superpower - that its dominant authority was being challenged in an international forum, which it might not like but which was part of world politics. It disliked the fact that this challenge and criticism came from Europe. In addition, Washington was making the point, through its hostile reaction, that, unless the US paid what it owed, the UN faced the serious risk of, despite many previous cries of wolf over the decades, grinding to a halt or curtailing most of its operations to the point of making them meaningless. The message was clear. The future UN would have to operate in a slimmed-down form and in a manner which suited the US and the next administration.

The background against which all this had taken place was not encouraging. At the end of 1995, the WCF and the Special Account, which had been drawn on to tide the UN over shortfalls in the regular budget and to act as accounts on which the UN administration could draw during the daily running of affairs, had been exhausted. The sum of $175 million had been borrowed from peace-keeping funds to help out the regular budget, leaving a cash balance of $744 million, which would run out by the end of 1996. But, as on many occasions before, the crisis was averted with Congress releasing in October some of the arrears, permitting a breathing space – yet again. The cycle looked to be beginning again in 1997 and has persisted into 1998. In short, the existing methods obviously did not present in an edifying way that there was in use an effective and accepted system of running a serious global organization.

This raises the question of the budget structures. The most obvious easement would be to make payments tied to the timing of the UN fiscal budget, which on an annual basis, coincides with the calendar year. But that would be difficult to administer, unless member states paid their contributions as soon as was possible into a holding account which could be drawn on for the appropriate UN fiscal year. Payments are supposed to be in by the end of January of each fiscal/calendar year This would, however, not get round the problem of payments withheld. The example of the dislocation between the US and UN budgets sums up the problem. For while the UN's fiscal year is the same as the calendar year, the US fiscal year runs from October 1 to September 30.[8] This has the effect that US payments to the organization will be on assessments made by the UN the previous year. In practical terms, this means that the US only completes its payments to one year's budget in the August of the following year. This clearly makes the flow of funds – key funds at that – a problem for the UN. Internal US mechanics make the issue no easier. The US budget allocations for the UN are made as part of the overall budget for international organizations, as agreed by the House and Senate Appropriations Committee. The Foreign Aid Appropriations Bill funds UN contributions to UN voluntary programs and the multilateral development bank, while the State Department Appropriations Bill funds assessed contributions to the UN regular and peace-keeping budgets. Not just contributions to the UN proper but also to the international organizations are a source of intense internal debate. In 1997, there was clearly a division between the State Department and Congress over whether arrears should be paid, when and how much. This was in fact bridged and suggestions were made which would have gone some but not all the way towards closing the gap between what the UN wanted and the US could provide. In November, this effort was halted by Congress; legislation and efforts to pay back arrears were stalled. The US is obviously both a special and, at the same time, most crucial case for the UN. Fortunately, the other 184 members do not repeat the problems created by the US to the same extent, but the problem does point to the need for some device to cushion the budget against an unpredictable flow of cash.

Joseph E. Connor, UN Undersecretary-General for Administration and Management, on 10 March 1998 gave a briefing in which he presented the current picture and some forecasts for the rest of the year. His message was gloomy, in short that the organization's cash position was weak and becoming weaker. He said: 'In all fairness, not a lot of change.' The unpaid assessments were slowly decreasing, but the regular budget's ability to 'cross-borrow' from UN peace-keeping budgets was drying up, he added. In detail, cash (the aggregate of regular budget and peace-keeping cash budget combined) at the end of 1997 at $669 million was slightly worse than a year earlier, but reflected little change over the 1995–7 period. Disaggregated, however, the picture was somewhat different with a steady downward trend of peace-keeping cash from $923 million in 1995, to $874 million in 1996 and to $791 million in 1997. The level was expected to be lower at the end of 1998 in accordance with the decreasing level of peace-keeping assessments and consequent reduced cash inflows.

On the regular budget, Connor said that cash had been in deficit at the end of each year for the previous three years. At $197 million in 1996, it was virtually the same as in 1995. The reduced deficit of $122 million in 1997 was the result of two factors. The first was the one-off level of underspending of $54 million in the 1996–7 biennium budget. The second was the regular budget cash position benefiting from unexpected contributions received in December 1997, principally from the US. Without those unusual factors, the regular cash deficit at the end of 1997 would have been $74 million greater and once again at a deficit level of about $195 million – the pattern of recent years.

Unpaid assessments, for both the regular budget and peace-keeping totaling $2.048 billion at the end of 1997 were slightly better – down from $2.1 billion (1996) and $2.3 billion (1995). This reflected, in part, a decline in regular budget appropriations of $2.603 billion in 1996–7, down from $2.632 billion in 1994–95. In 1998–9, those would be $2.532 billion. Unpaid assessments, Connor said, was 'very concentrated' on one member – the US, which owed 79 per cent of all outstanding regular budget assessments at 31 December 1997. The US, together with Brazil and Ukraine, accounted for 86 per cent of regular budget unpaid assessments.

Peace-keeping assessments were down markedly from $3 billion in 1994 and 1995 to an annual level of $1.2 billion in 1997. The amount unpaid at the end of 1997 aggregated at $1.574 billion, down $150 million since 1995, but the 'down' did not apply to the US whose arrears had risen by $124 million in that total. He noted that Russia's performance, by contrast, had been remarkable as its arrears had fallen by $269 million. Between 1995 and 1997, Russia's share of unpaid peace-keeping arrears had fallen from 23 per cent to 9 per cent, while the US share had risen from 47 per cent to 60 per cent.

Turning to the level of debt to member states for troops and contingent-owned equipment, Connor estimated that it had been at the peak in 1995 of $1.155 billion and was down to $884 million in 1997. Since the end of 1996, it had been the intention of the secretary-general not to allow the current debt to increase by providing running compensation to contributors, but he had been hampered by continuing arrears.

This account of 1997 bore all the hallmarks of the messages of previous years – despite efforts to curb budgetary expenditures and despite the UN system being in the process of Annan's reforms. Connor's projections for 1998 were hardly more encouraging. Combined regular budget and peace-keeping cash at the end of the year was projected to drop further to $577 million. The regular budget component would be $184 million. The projection showed no basic change in recurring patterns of significant deficit which had affected the organization during the last four months or so of every year since 1995. In fact, 1998 would show a return to the deficit levels experienced in 1995 and 1996. Peace-keeping cash was also projected to continue the pattern of decrease in recent years and would be at the level of $761 million at the end of 1998.

On the combined cash position, he said that projections for the end of 1998 suggested a further increase in the percentage of peace-keeping cash to be cross-borrowed by the regular budget to offset the cash deficit in that account. At 31 December 1998, combined cash would total $577 million, the smallest amount in four years, and the organization would have to cross-borrow 25 per cent of peace-keeping cash – the largest percentage in four years – to cover the deficit in the regular budget cash. It was borrowing more and more from a smaller and smaller source. The projection of amounts owed to troops-contributing countries, he estimated, would increase slightly to $890 million.

Against that sort of background, Annan's proposals of July 1997 looked unlikely to bring about any change or improvement. The RCF was likely to provoke problems since it was in part to be dependent on voluntary contributions. This could be further backed by using and/or unifying additional funds such as the WCF, the Special Account, the Trust Fund and the Peace-keeping Reserve Fund, which, after the third category of the operations paid for by voluntary donations (a source that has not been without its own imbalances and problems), provide means for the secretary-general to have access to immediate funds with fewer of the restraints imposed at present by the General Assembly and Security Council. Reservations have been expressed about earmarking money for an undetailed, unspecified objective, just as there have been, in a conservative, unimaginative way, about the role of non-governmental support, such as Ted Turner's offer. The mechanics of paying up so that the UN can function may be improved, but the will behind them founders on the politics of the organization.

The way payments are made could also be rationalized. At present, the budget is drawn up on a biennial basis, partly on the assumption that this two-year spread helps to even out the flow of payments in and expenses out. It also provides some notional room for planning. But this theory is undermined by the fact that the problem of payments remains the same. They are paid on an annual basis, so that even if it were possible to even out the fluctuations in outgoings – and that is a debatable proposition – the inflow of finance would remain as uneven as before. This occurs in both the regular and peace-keeping budgets.

The system for assessing contributions needs to be radically revised to take greater account of short-term economic fluctuations – and this is an issue which can only be settled through the ultimate approval of the General Assembly. In calculating who owes what there is a need for a balance which makes the percentage assessment more sensitive to changes, and here the reference is to falls in oil prices and global economic uncertainty stemming from stock market and currency collapses in the Far East, in the economic standing of individual countries. Statistics need to be more up to date with greater acknowledgment of trends. In good times, this would have meant that some countries, such as those in the Middle East with their hydrocarbon resources and the Far East with their fast-developing economies, would have to pay more. It will be instructive to see how China will react to the fact that the growing strength of its economy in the world's standings is far from being reflected in its percentage contribution rates. These are way below what it contributes, both as a formidable growing economic power, and as one of the five permanent members of the Security Council with its premium payment for peace-keeping. The member states of the EU, which already as a block contribute the largest share of more than one-third of the regular budget, could well be called upon to pay more. It might be controversial, but not unreasonable or necessarily cause hardship in money terms, to ask whether the minimum floor rate should not be raised. The object of such realignment would *not* be to make the UN by itself richer, but to make the percentage contributions more evenly shared out, so that the burden rests less heavily on the US. But, as we have seen, when a serious range of suggestions comes from a group with the standing and political and economic power of the EU, the US feels strangely threatened and resistant to opportunities, which should, on the face of it, reduce its financial burden.

On the peace-keeping front, there are essentially many of the same underlying problems but with particular differences. The contributions, as outlined in Chapter 5, are based on the regular scale of assessments, but with the difference that permanent members of the Security Council (Group A) pay more and less developed countries pay less. Group B, the developed countries, contribute the same rate as they do for the regular budget; Group C, the less developed states, are assessed at 20 per cent of their regular rate, and Group D, the least developed countries, at 10 per cent. The permanent members make up the difference. The inevitable criticism has been raised that these four groupings do not adequately reflect the economic circumstances of every country in each category as a whole. It would clearly be invidious to bring in (and impossible to enforce) what would amount to an additional penalty assessment on a strategic country for being in a volatile, sensitive geopolitical region. At the same time, it is equally clear that some countries, with for example wealth from hydrocarbons, pay seriously below their assessed level and that, as a result, others – not just the US – bear a disproportionately higher burden.

A single annual accounting period has been advocated, ideally in the form of a single, unified budget for all peace operations. Such a suggestion should be enforced with recognized pay-in times, possibly on a quarterly basis to reduce the pick-and-choose approach at present which leads to uneven surges and falls in income over a fiscal period. Ideally such a budget would include a margin for unexpected new missions. The enormous disadvantage of this single peace-keeping budget approach is inevitably political, for those who might be prepared to help finance an operation in Haiti, might be decidedly unhappy at the prospect of their money being used in a Far Eastern mission. Furthermore the overrun of costs is more likely to occur in peace-keeping operations than in the regular budget. Unless peace-keeping settles into a more regular pattern, it will be hard to argue for a regular unified peace-keeping budget, which should cover most foreseeable contingencies.

To this should be added other aspects which give the financial expenditure systems a bad name. Inefficiency has been one accusing cry and corruption has been another – both of which have been taken up vociferously by Congress. Undoubtedly both have been operating, but whether the UN knowingly wastes money through corruption rather than inefficiency is still debatable. Sizeable frauds have been turned up and rightly pursued but these arguments are often used as additional weapons with which to attack the UN without looking at more fundamental areas which, if reformed, would make inefficiency more difficult. Inevitably, cases of black-marketeering and fraud can be and have been found. But the problems are probably more attributable to mismanagement and the overlapping of functions rather than systematic criminal activity. Nevertheless, these abuses need to be corrected and in 1994 the OIOS was set up to pursue waste and mismanagement. Its findings hitherto have been small, but a start has been made. In this context, the mindless slashing of budgets and staff by a certain percentage does not increase efficiency. It has been seen increasingly since Annan's reforms as being a potentially hurtful exercise, more designed to please the US Congress than to bring about substantial and lasting improvements. One might propose that the first department to be examined (and possibly streamlined) should be that governing personnel. But given that the US has been over the years the chief agitator for change and greater efficiency, it is likely that its calls for nominal 'zero-growth' budgets (a decrease in real terms) and reform will take precedence.

The fact that peace-keeping operations have long ago left behind their interpositional role – if that ever really existed – and become more complicated should be reflected in the methods for financing them. Multidimensional operations involve considerably more than soldiers and when taken to potential extremes, the concept of peace maintenance, whereby the UN would be involved in setting up and helping the development of a whole administration, means that the use of these budgets and the mandates of these operations would need to be redefined. It is a process in which the issue of development is also involved. The UNDP is, for example, helping to implement peace accords in Guatemala after 36 years of civil conflict, and support comprehensive judicial reforms to improve criminal justice procedures and administration, enhance human rights and help integrate former combatants into civilian life.[9] These are clearly political activities not, *per se*, directed at peace-keeping or development, which raises the whole issue of what these budgets are for, whether they should remain separate or, even, in a separate category, connected with the UN General Assembly and Security Council but established for the funding of these mixed exercises. This in turn raises the question of the administrative structure – for might not these new operations perhaps sit more happily in with the specialized and affiliated agencies and programs, which have their own special form of funding?

The question of a standing army has been contentious enough already and argued about over the years. The suggestions have taken several forms and, in recent times, there has been growing enthusiasm for devolving some of the UN's peace-keeping duties onto regional forces, which presumably would be expected to pick up some of the costs. But many of these schemes still lack firm definition. It is almost certain that the US, as the largest provider, would argue that Congress would not agree to the allocation of funds under such imprecise circumstances. In peace operations, a single budget could be run less controversially in parallel with preplanned arrangements, such as trained men on a national basis (but, probably, not a standing army) and *matériel* ready for new operations, prestocking arrangements, standardized advance cost estimations and the like. In those more clearly defined areas, it would be possible to establish paid-for reserves in both cash and kind. But it would seem that otherwise UN peace-keeping operations – in their more traditional form – are condemned to individual 'ad hoc arrangements' – or mission budgets. But just as the tasks undertaken by 'peace-keepers' have changed and absorbed a wider range of dimensions, so must future funding take account of this. It need not necessarily be translated into larger and unwieldy budgets, but greater co-operation with individual agencies and NGOs to avoid unnecessary duplication.[10]

Boutros-Ghali's suggestions in *An Agenda for Peace*, followed up in his supplement[11] remain worth studying, even though events, people and the circumstantial structure of the UN have moved on. He wrote:

> The contrast between the costs of United Nations peace-keeping and the costs of the alternative, war – between the demands of the Organization and the means provided to meet them – would be farcical were the consequences not so damaging to global stability and to the credibility of the Organization. At a time when nations and peoples increasingly are looking to the United Nations for assistance in keeping the peace – and holding it responsible when this cannot be so – fundamental decisions must be taken to enhance the capacity of the Organization in this innovative and productive exercise of its function. I am conscious that the present volume and unpredictability of peace-keeping assessments poses real problems for some Member States. For this reason, I strongly support proposals in some Member States for their peace-keeping contributions to be financed from defence, rather than foreign affairs, budgets and I recommend such action to others. I urge the General Assembly to encourage this approach.[12]

Subsequently, he might have pressed for member states to involve other ministries connected with social affairs as sources for UN funding. Many would regard this as interference in domestic affairs, but they were proposals worthy of consideration. They have hardly been approached since, even in Annan's proposals for quiet reform. Boutros-Ghali had other suggestions which were connected much more closely with the UN's running of peace-keeping operations. They (and some were, he acknowledged, inherited from Pérez de Cuéllar) included:

- the establishment of a temporary Peacekeeping Reserve Fund, at a level of $50 million, to meet the initial expenses of peace-keeping operations pending the receipt of assessed contributions;
- the establishment of a UN Peace Endowment Fund, with an initial target of $1 billion, created by a combination of assessed and voluntary contributions, with the latter sought from governments, the private sector and individuals;[13]
- agreement that one third of the estimated cost of each new peace-keeping operation be appropriated by the General Assembly as soon as the Security Council decided to establish the operation, thereby giving the secretary-general the necessary commitment authority and assure an adequate cash flow – the balance of costs would be appropriated after the Assembly had approved the operation's budget;

- acknowledgment by the member states that, under exceptional circumstance, political and operational considerations might make it necessary for the secretary-general to employ his authority to place contracts without competitive bidding.[14]

Like many of the suggestions put forward, they were not without intelligence and practical application, but discussion and movement have tended to proceed with such slowness that events had often passed by the suggestions for which they might have been intended.

The Ford Foundation's Independent Advisory (Volcker/Ogata) group ran through the disadvantages of the existing system, among them: the slow arrival of assessed and approved funds; the lack of a continuous program to get round the problem of starting each operation from scratch; and the frequency of financial requests at odd times in budgetary cycles.[15] Again, its recommendations, suggestions and ideas were sound:

- the establishment of a much larger revolving fund, set at $400 million, financed by three annual assessments, to permit the UN to fund the starting costs of several large missions;
- a regular appropriation for peace-keeping training 'at a level the U.N. considers appropriate to enable its staff and military contingents provided by member states to deal with the increasingly complex duties they are assigned';
- the consideration of 'the merits of a unified peace-keeping budget, financed by a single annual assessment' (as the overall costs of missions decline this becomes increasingly feasible and it would have the advantage of being able to respond to unexpected emergencies);
- permitting the secretary-general to obligate up to 20 per cent of the initial estimated cost of a peace-keeping operation once approved by the Security Council;
- the phasing-in over several years of changes in Group B assessments to include from the Group C countries, those with above average per caput incomes. Group B members pay the same rate of assessment for peace-keeping as they pay for the regular budget.

But in the end, and this cannot be repeated too often, the whole budgetary imbalance would be eased if countries paid their arrears, as Connor's projections for 1998 and review of recent years showed. At the end of June 1998, the sum $2.474 billion was outstanding from contributions to the regular budget ($0.921 billion), peace-keeping operations ($1.528 billion) and International Tribunals ($26.1 million). Of these, the US owed $0.569 billion, or 61.8 per cent, of the regular budget arrears, and $0.966 billion, or 63.2 per cent, of the peace-keeping arrears. The other chief overall delinquents were Ukraine ($ 235.1 million), Japan ($164.4 million), Russia ($136.6 million), Germany ($61.3 million) and Belarus ($56.8 million).[16] The US' first response to Annan's arrival was not encouraging – a mere $100 million under the proposed 1998 budget for its debts to the UN and $912 million in 1999; and the payments are contingent on a level of reform that the administration and Congress have yet to define. The offer in June was, in its own way, restrained – some $819 million of arrears to be paid off, but subject again to conditions and only over three years.

In a way, the peace-keeping budgets could well turn out to be a key to progress. They have bailed out the regular budget in the past. But, expenditure on peace-keeping has fallen sharply and with it has grown the sense that peace-keeping in its various forms should be shared with others. The UN will therefore no longer be able to depend on these peace-keeping bounties to anything like the same extent to offset their debts elsewhere in the system. It will have to look elsewhere for funds and non-traditional means of raising funds towards its regular and peace-keeping budgets.

9 The Discomfort of the Run-in with Reform

If Childers and Urquhart have calculated right, then the reform package put forward by Secretary-General Kofi Annan in July 1997, was the twelfth time that the financing and management of the UN has been under evaluation and reform. Member governments have initiated eight and secretaries-general four.[1] It is never quite that clear-cut and for that reason Annan stated that what he was initiating, as reform, was a process and not an event. Indeed, the current process of change could be dated back to 1991–2 under Boutros-Ghali who recognized that in the changing global circumstances at the end of the Cold War, the UN both had and must play a different role. Whether he misjudged that role, despite his thoughtful writings in a series of Agenda reports, has been extensively debated elsewhere.

Those in charge of UN peace-keeping, in particular, had to confront the fact that their tasks had been changing for years. But at the beginning of the decade, the scales of change had become abruptly different. These changes – and the UN showed painfully after the Gulf War of 1990–1 it was not equal to their challenge – had their greatest effect in the peace-keeping sector in its broadest interpretation but with additional and substantial reverberations on the financial and budgetary fronts. Arrears of money owed by member states, already in a dire state, crept up further. The US role became more demanding and dominant. The scene was set for reform or, at least, radical adaptation, but this became eventually subsumed under the growing alienation between Washington and New York. In the end, it became an almost personalized feud with Boutros-Ghali failing in his attempt to win a second term as secretary-general. Nevertheless, the mechanisms for reform, largely encapsulated in cost cutting and efficiency seeking techniques had been set in motion. But like other attempts at reform before, this has to live in the shadow of the fact that, in spite of a whole series of reforms, none have succeeded in removing widespread doubts about the effectiveness of the UN system.

The year 1997 might well be seen later as the moment when the UN appeared to take decisive steps towards turning itself into a credible bureaucratic and political international institution. But by inference, Annan's remark acknowledged that, in the short term, Boutros-Ghali had, in his own way, started the reform process already. Indeed, this latest attempt at reform could be seen to have had its beginnings almost as soon as Boutros-Ghali became secretary-general in 1992. The tenor of his pronouncements implied realistically, too, that changes and reform had been and always would be marked by evolution rather than by sudden and spectacular change. In such processes, it has always been impossible to extract the financial system from the rest of the UN's structure. Indeed, changing the system through which the UN finances itself has proved to be the most stubborn aspect of all.

In *An Agenda for Peace*, Boutros-Ghali acknowledged openly the need for the system to adapt in order to meet the challenges that the post-Cold War era had presented for the UN. At the time when he was writing, the pattern of the cash flows was regular, providing an unhealthy but at least consistently unhealthy picture. The dips into deficit were relatively brief and below the $100 million mark, and until the beginning of 1994, although in visual graphical terms somewhat jagged peaks approaching the $200 million level, there seemed to be some predictability. But underlying trends had begun to deteriorate. From the beginning of the decade, unpaid assessed contributions to the regular budget had risen gradually until they were topping the $500 million mark, reaching $564 million at the end of 1995. Payments owed to peace-keeping operations had tripled over that same period to $1.7 billion. Within the regular budget, the number of member states owing more than the current year's regular budget assessment had risen from about 30 to over 40, so that while assessments and payments may have matched each other in 1993–4 there were still payments owing from 1995 and earlier years. By contrast, in the peace-keeping budgets there was a change in 1990 and 1991 when payments actually outstripped assessments, thereafter there was a regular shortfall. In all this the US share of arrears had remained consistently high. For the regular budget, this backsliding had begun in earnest in 1985 when it accounted for 35.3 per cent of total outstanding debts to the regular budget. Thereafter it has averaged between 50 and 70 per cent, standing at 60.6 per cent in 1991, and dipping to 51.6 per cent in 1994. Connor, as quoted in the last chapter, filled in the picture for the period since then. It is clear that the US holds the key to any long-term stability and predictability, for reform and the UN's finances.

While this may be a sketch only of a period of less than a quarter of the UN's total existence, it bears familiar traits that have been with it all that time. For successive secretaries-general and their secretariats have had to become adept at short-term improvisation rather than any longer-term planning. The change has been in the size of the shortfalls and growing pressure of changing duties which have to be undertaken. During 1994 and 1995, under orders and statements from Boutros-Ghali UN working parties, later halted and adapted by Annan, had been looking at ways of tightening the financial system, drawing on many of the ideas outlined above, and enacting methods of streamlining the overall, complicated and often overlapping structure. It was a period which was rich in debate and in a measure of serious and well-thought-out suggestions – but little concrete change. It was, however, apparent, that, as at several instances in the past, the mood for change was building up. Finances are often the most visible evidence of this, and as has been shown there seemed to be a clear deterioration that surpassed previous real or imagined crises. As in the past, these crises took on many of the political ramifications, which were not entirely related to financial mismanagement. They led to the crisis becoming gradually personified in Boutros-Ghali and ultimately led to his downfall, helped by the US. They coincided with a related increasing focus on the UN's role and, in particular, its apparent inability to cope fully with large-scale peace-keeping operations in former Yugoslavia and elsewhere. The fact that it took about five years for a serious and comprehensive set of proposals for a process, not an event, indicated how difficult it has always been to effect change at the UN.

But the move towards reform and change gathered momentum during 1995, and as one observer pointed out that, in its 50th anniversary year the UN 'kept the lights burning only by topping up its regular budget with funds from the separate peace-keeping budget.'[2] As the year progressed, it became clear that a number of issues – ranging from overhauling the system, to member states' appointments to key committees, to the secretary-general's post and financial reform – were gathering pace.

In November 1995, guided by the Efficiency Board, Boutros-Ghali launched an effort to accelerate change in the management of the secretariat. It did achieve some short-term results, although much of its early reporting gave the impression of exhortation, early successes and good intentions. There were constant references to the need for efficiency and effectiveness. The travel bill during the first six months of 1996 had been reduced by more than 25 per cent. The volume of documentation and publications printed had been cut by 13 per cent. The zero-growth (in nominal terms) budget and savings which were needed to live within the 1996–7 biennium budget of $2.08 billion were the targets.[3]

On 6 February 1996, Boutros-Ghali told a General Assembly committee – the High-Level Open-Ended Working Group on the UN Financial Situation – that the UN was 'trapped in a downward spiral' of financial crises that threatened its very survival. The UN, by any reckoning, would have run out of money by the end of the year. Boutros-Ghali promised to pursue a rescue plan that would include deep staff cuts. He put the sum of arrears to the UN at $3.3 billion, of which the US owed $1.2 billion. He added that the UN owed about $1 billion to countries that had contributed troops and equipment to peace-keeping operations. In an attempt to win back US support, Boutros-Ghali proposed setting a ceiling of 20 per cent, or even 15 per cent, on the amount any single member state should pay.

He went on to say that certain basic structural issues had to be addressed: the composition and procedures of the Security Council; the relationship between the Council and the General Assembly; the future of the Trusteeship Council and the role of ECOSOC. Almost all of these issues resurfaced in Annan's proposals. Boutros-Ghali added that his objective was a more integrated organization, which could focus on the major tasks of peace-keeping, human rights, humanitarian assistance and development, and their growing linkages. Then the trope. Action on the financial crisis was the key to progress. As long as it remained unresolved all other efforts to cut back, reform or restructure could not possibly succeed and the fate of the UN was in danger. He pledged to do everything to find a solution but said there were decisions only member states could make. This working group continued its work until June, after which a progress report was submitted to the General Assembly through the Fifth Committee.

As indicated, by the end of April, the UN was having to turn to its usual resort of borrowing money from peace-keeping accounts to meet its regular expenses, including the payroll. Connor said, on 30 April, that cash in hand was 'zero' and that 'we're back in the borrowing business'. He had expected to have at least $79 million in the budget at that point.[4] He said, also, that he hoped the assessed contributions of Japan and Germany would be paid in June, but that a $50 million loan was necessary to tide the organization over until then. This would reduce or delay reimbursements to member states already owed more than $1 billion for providing troops and equipment in the 16 current UN field operations. Checks from Japan and Germany had been held up for 'technical reasons'. Looking ahead, Connor said that he would have to borrow again in late August and once more in December when available cash would be about $200 million less than forecast. The US did make some payments towards the end of 1996, after Clinton signed a bill in October, authorizing the payment of $660 million – half for the regular budget and the other for peace-keeping. Nevertheless, the UN ended the year about $100 million in the red in its regular budget, somewhat better than the sum of $243 million Connor had earlier predicted.

Thereafter, a 10 per cent cut in the central staff was mooted, along with the first zero-growth for 1996–7. With some exceptions, most of these staff cutbacks were put into action – in some cases not without strikes – a further indication that the US accusations that Boutros-Ghali has been slow to make reforms were misconceived. But at the time, that was written off by foes of the UN in the Senate Foreign Relations Committee, chaired by Jesse Helms, as a public relations exercise to shame Congress. To many, these twists and turns seemed an all-too familiar tale. And, in truth, it turned out that way despite the dramatics of Boutros-Ghali's deselection and the urges towards the acceleration of reform under his successor. But the coincidence of this serious, though not fatal, financial crisis and this reform movement underlined the need for a look at the provision and spending of monies.

During 1996, the main thrusts of Boutros-Ghali's adjustments, according to his report in August,[5] were reductions in the regular biennial budget of 1996–7 to the level of $2.608 billion approved by the General Assembly. These were to be reached by lopping off some $154.1 million from the initial figure of $2.76 billion and staff cutting. The sections which bore the brunt of the cuts were administration and management, peace-keeping operations and UNCTAD.

Also during 1996, there was some gathering momentum towards reform and betterment of the financial situation. On 19 August, Connor said that preliminary estimates – before allowing for inflation and currency exchange fluctuations – indicated that the UN would need $178.9 million or 6.9 per cent less for its regular budget for 1998–9 than in the previous biennium.[6] For the forthcoming biennium, Connor said that it was estimated that on average 8500 posts would be occupied at the headquarters in New York – a 15 per cent reduction since 1 January 1996 and a 30 per cent reduction since 1985.

In fact, although the US had a hand in both Connor's appointment and the running of the Efficiency Board, its criticisms were, on occasion, countered. These criticisms 'United Nations officials … say are politically motivated and based on misinformation or no information at all'.[7] Washington, it was said, had asserted that Boutros-Ghali had been holding up efforts to cut costs and streamline the organization's bureaucracy. Clinton's government, which had used their veto in the UN Security Council to block a second term for Boutros-Ghali, had said that this was one reason to oppose him. On returning from the G-7 meeting in Lyon, France, Connor said: 'Concrete results on reform are already visible, and more are to come.' He called Boutros-Ghali the 'instigator' of the reforms. 'I have been the implementer', he said. Listing steps recently taken,

Connor said the core staff of the secretariat had been cut to 9000 from 10 000 in the last year. In 1985, the secretariat had 12 000 employees. Working with its first no-growth balanced budget, the UN could no longer make improvements to its ageing headquarters beyond repairs needed to bring the building up to New York fire and safety standards. Escalators, for example, Connor said, stayed out of service for days, and dead shrubs were not replaced.

Dissatisfaction with US policies and approaches towards the UN did not stop there – or, indeed, have any noticeable effect. On 8 November, at the annual secret ballot of all UN states for membership for the coming year of the 16-member ACABQ, which makes the most important decisions about UN spending, it was decided to pass over the US for membership for the first time ever. Reaction, it was related,[8] ranged from unmitigated, almost vengeful, joy to deep concern over the longer-term consequences. The US offered no sign of humility. A US official was quoted as saying: 'The lack of American participation on the ACABQ will inevitably diminish the significance of that body in UN budget deliberations.' He went on: 'The outcome of the ACABQ elections adds even more to the importance of electing this year a new, highly-qualified, reform-oriented Secretary-General for the UN.'

The narrative and argument thus far hardly presents an encouraging picture for those in search of solutions to the UN's financing problems. For a start, it is difficult to suggest a credible single approach since the UN is an intergovernmental organization with a vast array of associated agencies enjoying varying degrees of autonomy. Its theoretical remit stretches to international finance through the Bretton Woods institutions, which fall outside the scope of this book, and its aid and development programs. Many of these conduct operations and handle and disburse money in a manner which require all the skills of purely financial and business dealers. If there are symptoms of a new era, one must be the pressure that the UN's finances should be run on a more business-like basis. Yet the UN could never be described as a financial business. Nevertheless, there have been efforts to define the UN in business terms – indeed one of the hallmarks of almost every serious attempt at reform, including the one formally outlined in the summer of 1997 have been business reform approaches to improvements and streamlining. The member states have been likened to shareholders. The budgetary deficits have been seen in terms of being 'in the black' or 'in the red'. The differing assessments for contributions to the budgets within the UN system bear a passing acquaintanceship, through the variety of rights afforded to the levels of funding support to shareholders. The major shareholders have expressed complaints and threats about the company's policies but have, in the end, a limited ability to effect lasting changes. They have been effective in some of the branches of the organization, such as UNESCO and UNIDO, in bringing about changes in political policy and waste but these moves have been warnings and not influential on the main bodies of the organization. But organizations such as these fall outside our immediate range of interest, beyond making the point that the element of politics is infused into UN financial operations on a scale which business would probably rarely tolerate.

An article, based on an interview with Connor, who had once been the chairman of the accounting firm Price Waterhouse, illustrated the different approaches of business and bureaucracy.[9] It said: 'After three years in the job, Connor can show solid gains in efficiency. But as his conversation makes clear, to think of the UN in purely managerial terms is to miss the point. It is fundamentally not a business and probably never could be.' The writer points out that: 'The UN's finances would make a corporate executive blench. It runs an operating loss equal to almost 10 per cent of turnover. It has not capital or reserves left, and is not allowed to borrow. It funds itself by the simple expedient of not paying its bills.' Connor has made that same last comment elsewhere. But he emphasized that member states largely determined how money was spent. Faced with five portfolios of UN activities – peace and security, humanitarian affairs, setting economic and social norms, development and human rights – were he the chief executive of a loss-making corporation, he would immediately ask which businesses to shut down. 'The UN does not have that option', he writes.

'From a broader managerial viewpoint, Connor says, there are three main things wrong with the UN. First, the executive structure is weak. His boss, the secretary-general, has direct authority over the secretariat, but none over the various agencies such as the International Labour Organisation or the World Bank.

Second, the funds and programmes of those agencies should be brought together and rationalised ... Third, the whole process by which the secretary-general communicates with the member states needs reform. He should report to a few institutions, instead of a host of sub-committees, as at present.'
And benchmarking?

The UN does it all the time, Connor says. But it compares itself to the public sector around the world rather than corporations ... [A]n organisation like the UN – or like any government – finds it hard to assess its results. In a business, the planning cycle has three phases: set the strategic objectives, allocate resources and measure the outcome. The UN has the first two in place. It is struggling with the third. ... Member states, Connor says, are far more strict in controlling inputs than outputs.

The account of this conversation with Connor concludes that: 'It is as if the shareholders of a corporation used the annual meeting to set next year's budget and business strategy.' It might well be that Annan's results-driven budget proposals were designed to fill gaps in measuring performance.

The analogies with company behavior and discipline thus break down, because there is no overall corporate policy, which can be imposed on an organization with such diverse interests and responsibilities. The links between the head office in New York and its operations are in some cases so tenuous that it is a misnomer to put the Secretariat and its accounts office in the category of a holding company. A glance at any flow chart of the UN system (such as the one reproduced on page 16) might suggest that responsibilities and finance run from the General Assembly and ECOSOC to specialized agencies, programs and other affiliated bodies. But their overall contributions to these individual budgets are becoming smaller in percentage terms and in many cases nothing at all. In the context of administration the agencies fight fiercely for independence from New York. Some because of their specialist nature such as those which deal with communications, postal services or maritime affairs, are free to operate with relative independence. Others, like UNHCR, UNICEF and WHO, fight to preserve their own areas of authority, and against efforts to centralize and pool their resources with a strength that comes close to defying interference in the shape of reform. This became immediately apparent in the discussions preceding the proposals of structural reforms in 1997. The so-called holding company has, in the end, only a limited hold over its component parts and certainly not sufficient support to impose strict financial changes. The proposals that Annan made – the RCF, results-driven budgets and development dividend from internal savings – reinforced that point. At the same time, Annan has acknowledged the knitted ties between the UN and business, particularly through globalization. Addressing the World Economic Forum in Davos, Switzerland on 31 January 1998, he said:

> Peace and prosperity cannot be achieved without partnerships involving governments, international organizations, the business community and civil society. In today's world, we depend on each other. The business of the United Nations involves the businesses of the world.

But Annan stopped short of suggesting that the ideals of global society encompassed by the UN Charter could be brought closer and made more attainable through tighter financial management methods learned from business.

Annan has openly adopted a stance more favorable towards business. He has endorsed the growing importance of the private sector as a source of stability for investment and sustainable growth, and a force to impress on governments the need for regulatory frameworks to encourage international investors' confidence. While application of this approach falls mainly on the UN's agencies it implies a willingness to be part of, explore and benefit from economic and financial globalization that had not been apparent before. This attitude contains the implicit possibility of the private sector being able to have a larger role in helping to finance the UN's operations and system. In February 1998, Annan had a meeting with representatives of the ICC with worldwide representation. In a joint statement they recognized that the goals of the UN in promoting peace and development and those of business could be mutually supportive. They are already involved in many joint projects with the UN, but mainly through the UN's special funds, programs and specialized agencies. Publicly this approach has had some returns in the recognition that diminishing the organization's role or its capacity because of budgetary restrictions would be harmful. In a statement to the G-8 summit in May, the ICC said that the UN and other intergovernmental organizations 'require sufficient resources and more authority' to handle complex global problems. Wooing the private sector might also have the additional benefit of winning over some of the more conservative elements in US business which have argued that the UN was an obstacle to free trade, by promoting country-based development programs and state regulatory mechanisms. As examples of responses to and returns on this approach, the UN gives the examples of Turner's $1 billion pledge and Rotary Clubs worldwide, which have given more than $400 million to the WHO's efforts to eradicate polio.

Some parallel resort has been made to change through appeals for qualities which should be attractive to bureaucrats whether working in an international civil service or business. The watchword has been efficiency. This drive has carried with it much of the philosophy of American and international methods. It is not for nothing that Messers Strong and Connor have been the main appointed executive agents of this policy. Cost cutting is an exercise which organizations and management individuals have not found difficult to carry out. But it has often been confused with efficiency and raising the levels of production, and, on occasions, with reform. Since the beginning of this decade, as the repayment of assessed contributions slipped behind and the number and costs of peace-keeping operations escalated, this business-inspired approach gathered strength and momentum. Even the most devoted supporters of the UN have conceded that some changes in these directions were necessary. The last cycle of attempted change came to grief under Peréz de Cuéllar for many of the reasons which come up whenever this is attempted – the *sui generis* nature of a global organization.

However, broadly the problems with the UN fall into two parts. First, cutting numbers almost invariably brings with it the risk of reducing efficiency and quality of work in vital areas. Under Annan, the reductions have continued but have been masked by the controversial use of *gratis* labor, using officials on free loan from diplomatic missions (which raises the issue of divided loyalties), and by not filling positions which have become vacant. In some cases this has been governed by the fact that the UN has not been able to afford redundancy payments to dismissed employees. Often it has been seen as an artificial exercise in number cutting to fulfill one set of requirements at the expense of quality.

Second, the UN is committed to a balance in regional representation. For practical reasons, it has always been impossible to fulfill this to the letter. On one level, some countries may not physically have the manpower to fulfill their quotas. On another, the fair representation of blocs and geographical regions has been hard to enforce for political reasons and, in some cases, because certain countries feel that their financial contribution is under-rewarded in the UN administration. There are few, if any, who would deny that inefficiency, often through duplication, and corruption, do exist. Part of this stems from having to go on trying to achieve the difficult balance of representation based on 'an assessment of the distribution of the staff of the United Nations Secretariat by nationality, sex, grade and type of appointment, in the light of the principles contained in the Charter of the United Nations and the guidelines set forth by the General Assembly'.[10] The buck starts and stops in Article 101.1 of the Charter, which reads: 'The staff shall be appointed by the Secretary-General under regulations established by the General Assembly.' On 30 June 1996, the total number of staff was 33 157, of whom 14 166 were assigned to the UN Secretariat and 18 991 to the secretariats of UN subsidiary organs. Of the total number 9 196 occupied posts financed from the regular budget. The balancing act begins here. For 2 514, referred to as 'staff in posts subject to geographical distribution' were awarded positions on the basis of three factors – membership, contribution and population – established by the General Assembly. Efforts have been made to assess the fairness of representation by member states.[11] Between 1992 and 1996, the percentage of those reckoned to be represented within the range rose from 58 to 67 per cent. Those states unrepresented were Andorra, Kuwait and

Tajikistan. Among the underrepresented were Albania, Italy, Japan, Norway and South Africa. Other inequalities were shown up by dividing the member states up by major geographical regions, development classification – and by women. The latter's share of all postings subject to geographical distribution rose from 30.56 per cent on 30 June 1962 to 35.08 per cent on 30 June 1996. This is a microcosm of the task faced by reformers, who want also to preserve an element of equitability. As a result, these two issues, in particular, have been consistent themes for debate, year after year. One of the most radical attempts to confront a crisis occurred in the 1980s when techniques recommended by management consultants were introduced, but with limited success. In Annan's reform package there were further commitments to staff-cutting measures.

It is not for nothing that the formidable Yearbook of the United Nations devotes a sizeable section to personnel, with particular emphasis on the global division of the UN's work force, and on which jobs go where. The organization's character is universal by decree and inspiration of the Charter, but universality is no guarantor of excellence – a situation that the US, for one, seems reluctant to recognize. Nevertheless, there has been some counter to the business-management approach towards finding an approach through streamlining and reform. It plays on the potentially more positive side of universality – but one that is hard to project. Hammarskjöld as secretary-general pressed hard for the status and recognition of the international civil servant. He saw this as having not just a role for international diplomacy, but also in developing a class of people whose loyalties, in the end, would be more tied to running the UN as an efficient organ than to any residual national loyalties. The point about these discussions is that inefficiency and bloated bureaucracy have a direct impact on supposed savings and therefore UN expenditures. In this context, there was criticism of Annan's proposed reforms that he did not tackle closely enough the possibility of buying in more expertise from outside the UN's resource rather than rely on existing staff.

To some extent this issue of trying to develop for the UN an independent standing through having its own international civil service comes down to leadership. Whatever the personal standing of a UN secretary-general, part of the task of his office will be to create an independence which will enable his staff to mould the demands of a weak financial system to its own real demands, rather than attempt to follow those being indirectly imposed by the US. This has become all the more pressing in a time of globalization. In some senses, the UN, as a global organization, should have been better prepared than most to accommodate this new set of circumstances. It signally has not although belatedly it has begun to make concessions. Internal communication has been weak, leading to duplication of activities. For the dilemma comes up which makes the UN different from other international organizations. It can be termed in the form of a question about how independent the UN could or should be of its member states. Probably because of the parlous state of its finances, the power of the purse is, within the UN, the most effective instrument of control. That power is vested, through the Charter, with the support of the General Assembly. It is no surprise to learn that the Assembly will not let this power slip away easily. It is unlikely that the member states will allow the UN a degree of financial independence and still maintain control over how the funds are spent. In the negotiations and discussion which preceded the establishment of the UN, this issue turned into a debate about the merits of consensus decision-making as opposed to majority votes and linked to it – especially in the financial spheres – the General Assembly's say in the regular budget. It was this argument which came to a head in the Kassebaum amendment and the readjustments in budget-formulation which it brought about – to satisfy the US. This concept of universality is inherently and further hampered when one state, the US, has such leverage in both financial and political spheres.

The limits induced by this concept of universality have been apparent at the core of the UN's difficulties over repayment. That is the issue of how to devise a mechanism to penalize states which fail to pay in full and on time. Over the Congo, it was clear from the cunning method used that there was reluctance to confront the Soviet Union. States can get round this penalty by paying some money just before the overdue contributions fall due. The punishment approach has clearly not worked and is almost unenforceable. The US sniffs dismissively at any idea of a punishment for arrears, but might be interested in incentives. The US was a key factor in the onset of the crisis in 1986 by withholding its assessed dues. That was followed by a spurt of attempts at reform which petered out. About a decade later and in a very different political and economic climate globally, it has done the same again. The debate within the UN and outside has changed. But it remains to be seen whether it has provoked a change in attitude and approach which might reach down to such levels as paying dues on time. Technical remedies can only provide short-term solutions, which will raise cash but little, if any, continuity of approach. As Yves Beigbeder has put it:

> Any … technical remedies will fail if Member States do not show more commitment to the Organization's role and activities in global politics, economics, the environment, human rights and other areas of concern

to the international community. Overall commitment requires dependable financial support. In turn, the Organization has to deserve its Member States' and peoples' commitment in its objectives, programs and management.[12]

Like many of the proposals for changing and improving the UN system, potential action swings between the desire for money to come flowing in first on a regular basis so that the changes can be effected and the reverse. This demands that money can be assured only after the assessed contributors know what they are getting. Since the enactment of any changes have proved to be, year after year, a drawn-out process, it is hardly surprising that attitudes have changed little beyond measuring up the alternatives.

Bertrand expressed some initial surprise that theorists and specialists in the subject of world organizations were often adherents also to the view that 'governments and their representatives will support a structure which assists in the maintenance of the existing order.'[13] He measures three lines of approach: the 'realist' line, which amounted to war or a balance of power which is continuously under threat; the 'idealist' line which adheres to the concept of interdependence and concepts which could lead to a universal community and perhaps a more peaceful society; and a 'Marxist' or 'neo-Marxist' line, maintaining the theory of dependency according to which international relations should be seen in terms of domination and exploitation. As he put it succinctly: 'None of these lines of thought leads to proposals for reform.'[14] This might well lead to the conclusion that, in its own debilitated way, sovereignty and traditional methods, such as 'the maintenance of national armies, alliances, solidarity among the rich and powerful countries against possible trouble makers'[15] do remain the best means of producing security. In that kind of analysis, the chances are that the UN would have only a marginal role to play. It might lead to the conclusion that it might be pointless to modify its structure and powers. But the fact is that the UN's existence has been accepted and that it has an important role. The trend has been a form of devolution from New York, giving increasing strength to regional organizations and agencies to promote both development and security – in short, greater decentralization. But within such thinking there would have to be ideas for the restructuring of the financial system. The approach would have to be, in its own way, 'two-track' – short-term devices to ensure that money flowed in and out on a more co-ordinated basis and deeper structural reform which would reflect more closely the broad gamut of the UN's activities.

There have been so many attempts at reform during the UN's existence that there are probably no truly new approaches, only new circumstances. This would go some way to explain, in the context of finances and the UN's costs, the repetitious comparisons of UN spending with those of corporations and defence budgets. From what is proposed, often only parts survive. National and UN sectoral interests are defended powerfully by their promoters. Debate may be endless and compromises reached may end in errors that could take years to correct. Human factors are often overlooked. There has always remained a residual concern about what might happen if control, particularly over money, was centralized. Both governments and agencies have led the resistance to this.

One key to an approach to reorganization lies with the package of reforms which the UN promotes. If the UN had appeared to be trying to reach out to the US, and if President Clinton had chosen to see this as an issue of importance for US foreign policy in a league not too distant from the expansion of NATO and relations with Russia, for example, then with the improbable alliance of Congress, a more solid, not extravagant, financial base would have helped reinvigorate the sense of purpose of those promoting reform. But from the events of the second half of 1998 it was clear that it was not a foreign policy priority, except, importantly, where Annan intervened in the crisis with Iraq over the UN mission looking for weapons of mass destruction. Furthermore, Clinton's battle with Congress had a deep effect on any serious attempt to resolve the crisis over US payments of arrears. But it goes back to the UN finding an approach – even with Annan's announcements in the middle of July 1997 – which does not evoke a feeling that there is another rearrangement of the seatings and chains of responsibilities, which in turn reflect some balance between meeting the realities of the age and not undermining the organizations' innate authority and special nature. It will have to be shown to be fundamental and not a piecemeal addressing of most of the problems. The assessment, which will come later, is that, while Annan's personal standing may have risen, that of the UN – within the perspective of reform – has not.

Notionally, the largest payers should have and deserve to have some call on what happens to their money. These are, in effect, the US, but increasingly other leading assessed member states such as Japan and Germany. This may run into conflict with such democratic representation as there is in the UN system through the Secretariat and memberships of the Security Council and General Assembly. Under this measure, the assessment ratings could be seen as one, out of several, of the benchmarks of importance in the UN hierarchy. Annan's 1997 proposals would seem inevitably to have moved in the direction of proposing changes which have as their main object the pacification of the US Congress and the developing world. With these factors in mind, it might be worth a serious attempt at modifying the system of sharing out the contributions by member states. This would not lessen any political influence that the larger contributors may have. With a reduced contribution, the US is unlikely to be politically less influential. Even if Germany and Japan, with their large contributions, were to be given permanent seats on the Security Council, their political influence would not necessarily rise as individual countries, though it might as part of their regional grouping. But these issues have become less pressing as the EU moved into closer monetary union and the Far East has been the key party to a global financial crisis. Any redistribution could be worked out which shares out the load more equitably and, at the same time, protects the smallest and poorest countries which make only a token contribution. It is, in any case, questionable for the health of any organization that it should have been and continues to be so reliant on any one national source of funding. An extension of this is the possibility, which Annan's proposed reform appears to recognize, that contributions outside the assessment system should be possible.

Arguments abound about how this might undermine the universality principle of the UN, encourage others to pay less than their share and even result in a theoretical take over through a large-scale contribution – the sum of $2 billion would be easily within the capacity of countries rich in natural resources or with thriving capital and services markets – of the organization itself. But attitudes would need to shift seriously with the times. And image is important. As Childers and Urquhart have recommended: 'The image of the UN system as an intractably large and reform-defying bureaucracy is a myth of distance, ideological denigration and media distortion.'[16] But these images have persisted and, as a result, something more radical would have been needed than Annan's proposals to dispel them on both international and regional levels.

It is hard to believe that there is a collective desire to endanger the existence of the UN. Inertia probably plays a part, but that cannot provide an overwhelming reason. Politics, as has been seen, has been a constantly dominating theme. This applies at every level from the superpowers, to those who seek more clout in relation to their economic standing, to those countries further down the scale for whom the General Assembly provides perhaps the only outlet for grievances and the expression or solution of crises.

The payment process is equally painful. As has been remarked, some of the basic weaknesses, such as late or non-payment of sums due, have been a recurrent bane. The percentage of member states paying in full by the end of the year has fluctuated, but over a ten-year span there has been a discernible pattern of decrease. The high level was 56 per cent of member states paying in full in 1986. Thereafter this drifted downwards reaching 41 per cent in 1994, the lowest in 10 years. Fifteen years ago, the member states paid 82 per cent of the aggregate amount assessed by the end of the year. For 1994, that percentage had dropped to 67 per cent, which was in fact an improvement over the level of payments experienced between 1990 and 1993. Between 1980 and 1984, the norm had been at the 80 per cent level. Furthermore, an increasing number of member states are making no current payments to the regular budget year.

These non-payments have been made more severe through chronic cost overruns, but the main fault has lain with the member states not paying their assessed contributions. The members as a whole remain after all these years a deeply conservative group, reluctant to address the benefits of reform, often pleading that methods to reflect changing material circumstances run the risk of undermining the principle of universality. These attitudes are unrealistic and hypocritical, because, for years, some smaller countries which are leaders amongst the peace-keepers, such as Canada and Norway – have been bearing the burden of non-payment by less prosperous nations without recrimination.[17] There has long been an inertia which tends to confirm one view that since this system has – with all its ups and downs – continued to keep functioning, it should not be tampered with. Sadly, this characterization of its existence would not have been a recurrent theme of debate if it had not had some credence.

With surprising speed, in January 1997, Annan paid a visit to Washington where he was welcomed as the man of the moment. He went, rare at such an early stage, to Congress to talk to the UN's foes. But the US responded with slight promises and the initial conflicting approaches towards the priorities of money and reform have continued. The US wants reform first and then the money will be forthcoming; the UN says first money and then reform. A compromise has till to be found between the two approaches and already at an early stage there was disappointment expressed at the news that a reform package would not be available until July. In between, the US after detailed negotiations involving the White House, Congress and the State Department, offered some repayments, spread over three years, which Annan, to his credit, described as being less than what the UN deserved.

Annan's task, in a way, was to break with the past while benefiting from it. In his first statement, in the form of a letter dated 17 March 1997, to the President of the General Assembly, he emphasized the management and organizational reform measures which he had taken in the brief time he had been in office.[18] Some preliminary reorganization of consultative groups took place, with Maurice Strong appointed Executive Co-ordinator for United Nations Reform. Most notably, he established a Management Reform Group within the Department of Administration and Management to replace the Efficiency Board and its working group. Reform groups were to be set up in each department, fund and program 'to assist in pursuing internal reforms in each United Nations entity'. In effect, Annan was drawing on and streamlining the work of his predecessor, but with the precious advantage of being a new man, and Washington's at that. His views on the regular budget bear repetition:

> It will be recalled that the regular budget has shown a zero nominal growth since 1994. The 1994–1995 regular budget appropriation was $2,608 million. The current appropriation for the budget for the biennium 1996–1997 is $2,603 million. The overall decline of $5 million was achieved through real resource reductions of $210 million offset by output cost pressure from inflation and foreign exchange fluctuation.
>
> For the biennium 1998–1999, the General Assembly has approved a budget outline of $2,480 million based on the same price levels used in the latest reading under the 1996–1997 budget. Accordingly, **my proposed budget for the biennium 1998–1999 will contain proposals that will be around $123 million less than 1996–1997 at comparable prices and will represent a real resource reduction.** Assuming the continuation of present inflation and exchange rates, **my goal is for the United Nations to achieve a negative nominal growth budget for the biennium 1998–1999.**[19]

This report was followed by another letter, dated 21 April, accompanying the first report of the Management Reform Group in the Department of Administration and Management as 'a further indication that managerial reform is well under way'.[20] Its emphasis presented extensively in graphic form numerical estimates of increases in efficiency tied closely to the first track of reform. Its aims, affecting the financial sector in particular were accelerating and expanding managerial reform, through placing greater emphasis on effectiveness and embedding efficiency reviews, completing at least 400 efficiency projects, and achieving efficiency savings of at least $100 million in 1997 (in both regular budget and extrabudgetary expenditures); reducing the administrative costs of the organization from 38 per cent of the budget to 25 per cent by 2001 and increasing the accountability and responsibility of program managers for real results on the ground. In an accompanying Letter of Transmittal to Annan, Connor acknowledged that: 'We are building on the process that the Efficiency Board catalyzed over the last year and the efficiency projects initiated by the United Nations' managers and staff members'. In the *UN 21 report* of the Efficiency Board in the previous year, it had concluded that it

> shows that, even under the current constraints, it is possible for effective managers to do a great deal. However, even more can be accomplished. The successful first phase of the efficiency exercise leaves the Board confident that, together, the organization and its members can meet the commitment made by the heads of State and Government at the fiftieth anniversary of the United Nations to 'give to the twenty-first century a United Nations equipped, financed and structured to serve effectively the peoples in whose name it was established.'[21]

The Efficiency Board was disbanded the following year.

Yet underlying these statements of purpose and good intentions lay a state of flux. This has never helped the UN towards trying to be more active and unconventional in confronting its financial problems. Given the premise that the UN comes cheap at the price, it raises the legitimate concern about whether cost-cutting as an end in itself is a useful approach, particularly if it is dressed up in the ethos of reform. In another point of comparison, the daily costs of Operation Desert Storm were virtually equal to the UN regular budget for the whole year. The point can be made more forcibly through the hypothetical exercise of what was saved through the intervention of the UN-authorized allied force which defeated Saddam Hussein's invasion of Kuwait in costs against the losses which would have been incurred if Iraq's military adventure had succeeded in terms of political instability and prices and production of oil. The problem with this approach is that it is highly notional and it is possible too that the figures for the costs of war and the costs of the increases in the oil market do not add up.

But it does address the issue that those in a region suffering from conflict which is settled through UN intervention should pay for those benefits. This, in turn, raises the financial possibility of closer links in peace-keeping missions with regional organizations in Asia, Africa, Latin America, the Middle East and Europe. The political risks are apparent, for, while shifting and sharing responsibility with regional leaders may be an attractive aim, there is always the risk that they will use these contacts and implied endorsement to gain control over neighbors. This has occurred in Africa. But elsewhere, a devolution of expenses has already become apparent in peace-keeping operations, particularly in Europe and parts of the former Soviet Union and in the running of humanitarian emergencies and the activities of the UN's specialized and affiliated agencies. As the nature of wars in the 1990s have changed from the set-piece engagements at the end of which a peace-keeping force would be interposed to intra-state wars, so the nature of UN intervention has altered. Most wars today are not the clinical Cruise-missile led forays painted by Washington and Tel Aviv. They are often guerrilla battles in which three-quarters of the victims are civilians and refugees. Humanitarian agencies and NGOs have been deeply involved in such places as Cambodia and former Yugoslavia. They and the UN forces have not always been compatible, but they proba-bly need each other. In these circumstances, it is only reasonable to look not only at how they can join forces in administrative and bureaucratic terms, but, more important for the purposes here, how such operations could be funded. For, ideally, it would be necessary to marry the raising of UN-assessed funds with the voluntary extra-budgetary money on which the other organizations depend. For the latest assessment rates for the years up to and including 2000 preserves the perennial uneven balance of payments whereby the top seven or so countries collectively account for more than two-thirds of the regular budget.

To complement a partially inward-looking reform of its finances, through greater efficiency and the reform of assessment schedules and the regulating of members' payments, the UN will have to abandon old ways and traditions and seek new and, if necessary, unorthodox means of raising money. Few are genuinely innovative, but have become increasingly pressing because of the expansion of UN activities and because of the need to preserve the UN's prestige in the next decades against a changing background of activities not just in war zones but elsewhere.

However, pennilessness might mean that parts of the UN may be unable to operate, and this will then lead to the whole operation of the UN system being debilitated. And after the decision to appoint Kofi Annan as the next secretary-general, Madelaine Albright, who had persistently fought his predecessor's candidature for a second term, nevertheless went out of her way to praise Boutros-Ghali as a 'renowned international statesman' who had 'made his mark in history'.[22] Having got their man out and their new man in place, attention in the coming years inevitably centers on the implementation of the formal newly proposed reform package and the extent to which the US will help to make its enactment possible.

The man now at the UN's helm had this to say some years ago:

Meeting the budgetary and fiscal challenge by instituting long-needed reform is not solely the province of the Secretary-General. However, he has a major responsibility in this area of articulating the problem and exerting the utmost effort to have the Member States go along with him and take the necessary steps to extricate the United Nations from its crisis of insolvency. The Secretary-General is no magician, although at times it would seem that the Member States think him one, judging from what he is expected to do with the UN budget.

The United Nations is on the verge of becoming a more dynamic and relevant Organization. Difficult situations such as it faces in the budgetary realm often offer challenges and opportunities that, if properly exploited, could make possible gains and achievements that could not be contemplated in normal times. The spirit ought to be embraced as the United Nations is repositioned for the twenty-first century.[23]

He certainly was aware of the dimensions of the task long before he might have guessed that he would have to be implementing it.

10 And Back into the New Era

The word and concept 'reform' has been overworked in relation to the UN. Annan's package of July 1997 provoked a mass of examinations, which were probably both unjustified by their content and the advance heralding they received. Furthermore, the UN had undergone a surfeit of analysis and been fed an oversufficiency of advice on its 50th birthday. The end of the Cold War had already prompted further guidelines about political etiquette for the new political era. It has become a truism that the UN probably missed its opportunity to establish its role in this new political order. Bosnia and Rwanda are held up, in particular, as striking examples of failure by the world body. Boutros-Ghali, the secretary-general for much but not all of this era, has received much of the blame. Perhaps it only reinforced the view that his professional training, that of an academic historian, could not have been preparation to cope with the exigencies of an historical political turning-point. But he could not have been completely unprepared for he had been for some years an uneasy but important member of the Egyptian cabinet as deputy foreign minister in President Anwar Sadat's time.

The UN has missed other challenges and has survived. The calls for reform and change may have been, for a while, shriller this time round but they have been heeded. It is a moot point when adaptation becomes or qualifies for the epithet 'reform' but the fact remains that if the UN had not shown extraordinary powers of adaptation – or reform – it probably would not have survived. Thus it can be firmly argued that some concept of meeting change has been around, whether forced on the organization or not and the 11 or 12 attempts that Childers and Urquhart list bear tribute to that. In this context, Annan has fairly acknowledged that many of the proposals and actions had been put into action by his predecessor, Boutros-Ghali. To Annan fell the task, for reasons of timing and political maneuverings to promulgate them officially, as, to use his words, a process not an event.

And that is the way it has been. In broad terms, Annan has reinforced the notion that change, adaptation and reform are not dead. It is not the hyperbolical press release boast of the moment that proclaimed it 'the most extensive and far-reaching reform of the United Nations since it was founded 52 years ago'.[1] To be fair, it has not been solely greeted with critical acclaim. But in crucial areas such as the ever-mounting number of humanitarian interventions, the proposals have been strongly criticized. This is important because these operations have become the most public aspect of the UN's activities, taking over from peace-keeping as one of its derivative and closely linked activities. This sector has exposed Annan and the UN to the most detailed exposure of the complexity and confusion of its system and agencies – and the way it spends its money and that of others.

The US, inevitably, has its own, important role in this phase of the UN's development as it has had since the negotiations during the Second World War. Those hostile towards its role and its presumed exclusive influence on the organization forget – as do many Americans in places of legislative influence – that the US is also one of the UN's 185 member states. For better or for worse, part of what the UN turns out to be is the result of that special membership. Annan has been assailed for not having any coherent vision for the UN beyond somewhat more elegant, eloquent and more lengthily argued expositions of reform than those of press releases. That said, it is fair to raise the question whether the US, or its representatives, have any coherent vision. The performance of the US Congress has, on the whole, been lamentable, chauvinist and shortsighted to the extent of making credible the oft-repeated story that fewer than half its members possess passports. Under the sway of globalization, and the hubris of world political power, US concepts of reform seem often to give the public expression of straying rarely beyond the quests for greater efficiency through cost-cutting. The persistent and thoughtful advocates in the US – and these latterly have included Albright – in favor of a role for the UN and, as part of that, paying outstanding arrears in assessed contributions, have fought a coherent, patient and much-abused battle. Nevertheless and despite the paradox of the US role of being the UN's most important benefactor and delinquent, any lasting reforms, particularly where the financial sector is involved, will mean having to offer some concessions to some of the US demands. This applies particularly where the regular and peace-keeping budgets of the UN are concerned.

It has become self-evident that the problems of the UN in handling its finances have been around since before it came formally into existence and were inherited in both spirit and fact from the League of Nations. The travails of the League arose, from the financial point of view, as a result of disagreement about which organ within the institution should have the control and direction over finances and which should have the majority voting say. The problem was never solved and Boutros-Ghali in his broadside aimed largely at the US for not paying its dues invoked its

memory as an omen for disaster. The Dumbarton Oaks conversations were
in many ways as focused on the administration and running of what
became eventually known as the United Nations as they were on setting up
the mechanisms to prevent the recurrence of world wars.

But the worry was always there about whether the organization
had enough money, whether it was using it wisely, whether it was thrifty
and efficient enough and whether member nations were getting value for
money. The answer to each of these was probably in the negative and each
answer depended on the perspective of the questioner. But there were constant themes. Broadly, the UN has never had sufficient money to carry out
fully what it wanted to do properly. Sometimes this was due to poor planning and sometimes because it could never quite anticipate where
demands might be made. The questioning of the wisdom of its expenditure
and targets was uncommonly justified because the missions which the UN
had to undertake were vastly varied and more often than not subject to
tight political scrutiny and control.

These last aspects have been apparent from the beginning, manifesting
themselves most crudely in the rivalries between the US and the Soviet
Union during the Cold War. But they spilled over into the process of former colonial powers coming to terms with reduced international standing,
even if the UN, in particular the Security Council, left them with some of
the trappings of former influence, in the constant tensions between the
developed industrial world and the developing countries. The strains then
appeared between the Security Council and the General Assembly. Latterly,
after the end of the Cold War, usually symbolized by the fall of the Berlin
Wall in 1989, there have been new tensions and new pressures for reform.
But in the balance of power within the UN, it will not have been lost on
the vast majority of the UN's 185 members that it was this *European* event
which was taken as the ending of a historical era and the beginning of
what is regarded as a new one.

At every twist and turn during these five decades there have been persistent and unglamorous voices asking whether the UN's political, economic and social performances could have been better if its finances had
been in better shape. In some ways, the UN was its own worst enemy in
the presentation of its financial running. The threnody of crisis became
such a familiar theme that it was often not taken seriously. The UN
seemed ever able to muddle through periods of difficulty which would
have caused any bank manager to withdraw from his client further bank-
ing facilities and send in the debt collectors, or any chief executive of a
business to indulge in massive restructuring of his corporation with all the
losses in jobs and departments that this would entail. In the latest round of

reform, some of these parallels with the world outside have been taken on board.

The UN also did itself no favors through not making clear that the costs of running the core of the administration and peace-keeping operations are minimal. They amount, probably, to less than one-fifth of $12 billion or so of expenditures committed in any one year in the name, ultimately, of the United Nations. The vast amounts of these monies are spent by semi-autonomous organs and specialized agencies with a measure of financial independence from the mother organization, which has increased over the years. The UN and its Secretariat are perhaps culpable of failures in running and keeping bureaucratic control over these entities, which have often been in direct competition rather than co-operation. At the same time, those managing the budgets and supervising expenditures have not had the formal links to give them authority to control the expenditures of these agencies. But blame for the mishandling of their finances should have lain more fairly with their immediate chief executives and governing boards.

The chronic political feature, which is more often than not reflected in the overall finances, is that the UN has reacted to rather than anticipated global developments. In part, this is an inevitable feature of its make-up of membership from outside, and, inside, how this membership is divided between and reflected in the organization's structure. The UN beast is not an outdated beast of a distant era, but it is slow moving and rarely adventurous in its reactions. This is mirrored specifically in its two key budgets – the regular budget and peace-keeping budgets and operations. The former has changed fundamentally little in its shape and running from first elaboration to its final execution. By contrast, and perhaps inevitably, the peace-keeping budgets have had a more exciting and tempestuous life, by historical terms almost bringing the UN to financial collapse in the 1960s in the Congo, to being the fall-back fund on which the regular budget drew when in deficit and faced by foreclosure.

Perhaps the crucial test of the UN's mettle both politically and financially came during Boutros-Ghali's tenure of office. In his first assessment of the new historical climate, *An Agenda for Peace*, he recognized that, with the ending of the Cold War, a moment had arrived when the UN might be capable of transcending its role of being in terms of activities just the sum of its members' views. It stood on the brink of being able to initiate, especially in peace-keeping terms, operations in which the UN, in particular through the five permanent members of the UN Security Council, performed actions that determined outcomes, rather than followed them.

In this context one aspect, in particular, which Boutros-Ghali rightly emphasized is preventive diplomacy. It is argued that by accumulating better intelligence on potential crisis zones, pre-stocking arms and making theoretical calculations about the costing of peace-keeping missions, much expenditure in the long term could be saved. The idea has superficial attraction when measured against wars and interventions which, seen with the gift of hindsight, appear as candidates for having been avoidable. The costs of the actual war and its aftermath are then totted up, and a figure for notional savings reached. There are, however, problems. For the establishment of the sort of mechanisms and provisions mentioned already as aids for preventive diplomacy are expensive and immediately unattractive to would-be fund providers because of their imprecision. Furthermore, there have been many cases where game plans and preconditions for war and crises have been drawn up with the prediction that an explosion was imminent. Frequently, despite all the models, the explosion has not occurred and the money for the prediction wasted. There is furthermore the practical consideration that states are notably unwilling to provide information that they are either on the brink of explosion, disintegration or war!

But what happened in practice was typical of UN aspirations and realities. The peace-keeping operations were grossly miscalculated in their size, objectives and nature. Peace-keeping, in its broadest senses from enforcement to returning countries to democratic rule through the supervision of social affairs and elections and picking up the pieces in the aftermath of civil wars, began to slip out of control. The political tasks taken on were too complicated for the narrower remits of UN mandates. Financially, they threatened the organization with ruin once again and resulted in member states, especially the US, being unwilling (or unable, as in the case of Russia) to meet their commitments.

The arguments about the extent to which the UN was empowered in the Charter to enforce as well as keep peace added further expensive complications and some disillusionment with the UN's ability to carry out the function which is its most publicly visible and acknowledged – along with looking after children and refugees. This led directly into the issue of whether it was able to execute the more social and developmental aspects of peace-keeping, which had become the feature of the intra-state or civil wars in which it was being forced to intervene. The issue here is less the political rights and wrongs of intervention but whether the UN had sufficient resources and funds to cope.

By all accounts, the answer is that it probably does not. Its member states do not help. The UN may be universal in membership and its dues almost obligatory, but the payments for all its activities are run almost along the lines of a voluntary body. By its own nature as a forum for international debate and planning and the nature of its composition, it reacts to outside events. In spite of the theories of preventive diplomacy and the investment in development projects it has proved itself to be almost incapable of heading off crises. The most notable example of this has occurred in the field of humanitarian aid in response to the series of intra-state wars, whose origins and outbreaks existed long before the end of the Cold War, but which have proliferated since. The reaction of UN agencies to these disasters and their performance in the field have been consistently, and often unfairly, compared with those of the NGOs. Boutros-Ghali rightly spotted on taking up his position as head of the UN that there was an opportunity for the UN to play an important new role. His aims may have been over-ambitious, but it was, more than anything else, the bureaucracy and politics within and towards the UN that let him down. The mishandling of the financial side and the structure within which it had to operate were contributory factors, but not the ones which caused a crisis in the finances and management. Boutros-Ghali set about, perhaps too tentatively and in a personal style, which alienated support, starting to streamline the UN vehicle to produce a new model. It was never far enough down the production line to ensure that the fuel would be supplied in sufficient quantities or regularly enough to make it work.

In the latter context, it has been shown that there have been many proposed solutions, or rather, half-solutions, for ensuring that money flows on a more regular basis. These have ranged from suggestions of structural deep-seated reform to marginal tinkering. Many suggestions were once original and worth following up. The majority would have the merit of being of a short-term or once-off nature. Indeed that may have been their virtue because they would probably suffer from being dragged into the institutionalizing process of the UN.

At the same time, there has been little difficulty in raising objections to each and every one of these suggestions. Often invoked are conservative principles that breaking away from the methods of raising money hitherto employed, would be injuring the basic thesis that membership of the UN is universal and the responsibility evenly and equally shared. For, the argument runs, its financing must remain universal, if weighted, to fulfill the requirement of the capacity to pay. But with that principle fractured, there is a growing sense that the universality argument has become weakened, as has the whole approach and understanding of sovereignty. At the same time, there would be greater opportunities for the irresponsible or adversely politically minded to exploit these new departures on the basis that others could pay. But it is more than likely that the thesis of universality with its most open expression in collective security and less obviously through member states' obligations to the UN budgets will have to be maintained along with the tenet that money can be allocated only for known and assessed purposes. Against this sort of background, unqualified people are taken on to fulfill the nationalities' quota or are trained, at some expense, for a position for which they are probably unsuited. This probably affects the larger powers and at the higher end of the seniority scales. Here the positions have become awarded and redistributed in a reshuffle on the basis of allocations to major powers. More recent assessments, in part under the current ongoing pressure for UN reform, have begun to erode this principle of the necessity of greater universality of representation in favor of fairer distribution. The fact is that there is probably no practical and clearly defined solution.

The spreading structure of the UN makes it almost inevitable that inefficiency of up to, say, 20 per cent is to be expected. Although not in the center of the UN's finances, the alleged irregularities made public in July 1998 about the UNHCR,[2] suggested a similar figure of an unwritten allowance for inefficiency. This can best be tackled on the basis of attempting to contain and control the potential damage and sterner use of the existing investigative bodies. Clearly one approach has to be through restructuring the bureaucracy from the very highest levels. There are distinct limits as to how much can be learned from similar exercises in multinational companies or local government by the UN. But it can certainly be applied as long as the fact that as an organization the UN is *sui generis*. One lesson in particular from the world outside would be to rely less on internal expertise for the analysis and delivery of solutions to problems and more to buying in specialist knowledge and resources. This would not only be practical but also be in keeping with the acknowledged change that the UN's future role is first to be more open to outside influences and second to remain the clearing house facility and debating center for the world's problems.

At the same time, the complaint that some of these *ad hoc* proposals smack of gimmickry pales beside the argument that the state of the UN's finances are so parlous that every new approach must be explored. Some suggestions may indeed suffer from the weakness of being difficult to enforce, but in spheres outside the UN ideas such as these have been aired and tried. Indeed, the overruling aspect of broaching the troublesome topic of UN finances is that, while the General Assembly (and some members of the UN Security Council) may oppose any apparent weakening of their collective strength, it is reluctant to embrace with enthusiasm any suggestions which might slip beyond their immediate influence. This is despite the fact that numerous committees have been set up on different levels both by the General Assembly and through drawing on groups of high-powered experts from outside in the past. There is a perverse sense that, even if some measures suggested were adopted and helped ease the UN's perpetual financial crisis, the General Assembly and the Security Council might derive some tactical pleasure out of having the UN in a weak financial position. This conclusion is nowhere made explicit, but it is a logically implicit conclusion, which could be drawn from the years of apparently unchangeable crisis.

It reflects an overall lack of collective imagination on the part of the UN's members and a lack in political will to make changes possible in the ways of raising money and changes in the bureaucracy of organizing the UN's finances. In one of the most prominent aspects of its operations – peace-keeping in the Yugoslavia-that-was – it has shown itself to be badly organized and under-funded with the result that peace operations have had to be ceded to NATO. There, as elsewhere, if there had been some investment ahead in shared intelligence, preventive action might have proved to be cheaper than later, under-informed intervention. This could also be supplemented by sharing information with regional organizations of social and economic as well as military concern. In the event of a rapidly developing situation, the availability of a 10 000-man volunteer force – whether this should be a standing force or one on stand-by is not just a semantic difference, but one involving expenditure – and would buy time until the arrival of the national units and, in the end, cost less. Some estimates have put the cost at about $300 million just to set it up. It would have to be paid for through a system outside that of assessments. It remains a questionable option.

But these are minutiæ compared with the tasks which the UN is supposed to be able to undertake. In this context, a sense of history has to be retained. The origins of the current crisis lie in the mid-1980s and were caused essentially by the US attitude, fired by the Heritage Foundation's writings and the thoughts of the administration of President Reagan. It was Cold War time. The US was keen to confront the Soviet Union politically in a direct fashion with the aim of forcing at least global co-operation out of it. The UN was perceived as aspiring to international authority which could be presented to American audiences by Congress as infringing American sovereignty. At the same time, it cannot be overlooked that how money was spent went out of control, and the US, as the major contributor, felt this went strongly.

In turn, this meant that there was a return to looking at the criteria for assessed contributions to the UN budgets, such as the percentage of total taxation, and of total GNP; and consideration of a cap on what can be afforded to the UN. Account had to be taken of inflation, and so forth. US contributions had been at their peak in 1982 and were down by the late 1980s if calculated properly and not by using the crude figures of percentage contributions as is most dramatically illustrated in the earlier years. In the 1980s, moreover, some perceptions of the US were right. The role of the major contributors needed to be downplayed. The whole budgetary process led to various responses: the Kassebaum amendment of August 1985; and consideration was given to a strategy whereby the US should withhold 20 per cent of its contribution until the budgetary procedure was suitably weighted like the IMF and World Bank. There have been echoes of these tactics and governmental and congressional views more than a decade later.

A new bout of reform was heralded when the C-18 was established in February 1986 and reported the following August with the proposal that accountants should be more in charge and that the larger contributions of the main countries should be better reflected in budgetary decisions. Today's attempts at reform have a similar ring about them and the move towards more result-oriented budgets reflects the influence of business measures. The important difference is that the ultimate failure of that attempt in the 1980s left its mark and made the efforts this time more sustained and those behind them more determined to succeed.

Furthermore, developments in the global economy and the operations of transnational companies have forced greater receptivity on the UN of its reduced global role in some senses and the greater acceptability of these business-related and efficiency-oriented approaches in others. But the reform attack and crisis of the late 1980s threw up the difficulty of how to relate general US policy towards the UN to finance. Yet any issue of policy was running ahead of the difficulties caused by those supposed to be paying the bills.

Until 1993–4, the regular budget experienced a measure of success in having its arrears paid off. It is unfair to blame Clinton entirely in his first and second terms as president as the acuteness of the current cycle of crisis has appeared in a relatively short period of time. But there are real problems in the present Congress through passing the bill of reducing to 25 per cent US payments on peace-keeping assessments and the accumulation of US shortfalls, so that in January 1996, the US was paying merely the equivalent of 14 per cent of the UN budgets and not the higher percentage which has always been touted around. When previous crises have occurred, as was the case in 1986–8, high-level, serious committees were set up to examine the workings of the UN, but these working groups did not come out with far-reaching changes. They did not confront properly the key relationship with Washington. They also suffered from an inadequate mandate from the General Assembly. The recommendations of the C-18 could, however, have provided the basis for reform of administrative and budgetary procedures, but were not fully enacted particularly where the member states rather than the Secretariat were involved.

At the same time, they did not confront the possibility that the slipping away of other active parts of the UN, particularly in the areas of providing aid and expertise for development, might well take place unless the fundamental and unglamorous aspect of the UN coming closer to paying its way than it did in the past became a reality. This had never become more apparent than during the period of the mid-1990s when the opposing views of the UN Secretariat and the Clinton administration reached – for reasons ranging from difficulties with the Republican-dominated Congress to US military losses in Somalia – a peak. The opportunities for a new phase came with Boutros-Ghali's departure and the succession of Annan. On a more positive note, the fact will have to be faced that, while operations have begun to back away from peace-enforcement towards the trickier areas of post-conflict, social and political administration, some of the slack is being taken up by the contribution that UN peace-keepers make indirectly and directly towards humanitarian aid. Examples of this are to be found in such operations as some of those in former Yugoslavia and in Cyprus and south Lebanon. Perhaps, the soldiers should receive some reward in the form of payment towards peace-keeping operations and reimbursement to contributing countries which goes more easily and unquestioningly to aid organizations, such as UNHCR, UNICEF and WHO.

This decade has brought in – through the disappearance of the clear division between UN and non-UN operations becoming established and accepted, as seen in activities ranging from humanitarian intervention to the enactment of some of the packages promoted by peace-maintenance – a parallel financial blurring, especially in the civilian-military sector. There has been a growing output of literature on this co-operation. Broadly, it advocates that the UN and NGOs and civilian and military teams should acknowledge the virtues and merits of each other, rather than indulging in mutual recrimination and criticism. For the examples of Rwanda, Somalia and Cambodia have shown, if nothing else, that both need each other and both need to learn from and about each other. In financial terms, some measurable part of the financing which goes to ostensibly civilian operations should be available not just in the field but also in the budgets for the 'peace-keepers'. These would often not be able to deliver their goods – sometimes and reluctantly they admit this – without military protection.

In addition, in this area alone, some considerable savings could be made and duplication avoided if the UN Secretariat and humanitarian agencies and NGOs came closer together in recognizing the usefulness of each other's work. This kind of recognition could take the formal shape of co-ordination in administration, and therefore costs. It would be helped if greater awareness were developed on the NGOs' side that their work has political and cultural repercussions which they have been hesitant to accept before.

Further reorganizations were enacted by Boutros-Ghali in the opening months of 1992, but an impression was left that they were done for the sake of change, not thought through and often caused a breakdown in channels of command in authority, which affected the financial and peace-keeping divisions in particular. They increased the feeling that he was iso-lating much vital decision-making to his level and delegating too little. Above all, and this may well be the crucial factor, the UN political leader-ship seemed to have slipped behind the changes which were taking place in global politics. It had always, as has been observed, tended to be an organization reacting to circumstances around it. But this gap between the perceptions of the UN's ability to cope and its actual performance was wider than before. Consciously, or unconsciously, this slipped irretrievably into a conflict between UN – New York and Washington and its most patent symptom was disagreement over the arcane and apparently impos-sible running of the bureaucracy and finances. For the UN to recover its balance it would have to redefine its concept of its place in the world in such a way as to win some measure of approval from the US – and then to be seen to be doing something active and reformative about its proposals.

Annan would seem to have started by trying to confront his inheritance from Boutros-Ghali and has given indications that he has the standing of an institution to sustain against US demands and that he understands that the UN is more popular amongst Americans than Congress would like to have others believe. As time has passed, and particularly after his triumph at the beginning of 1998 with the Iraqi government over the UN inspection teams, Annan has appeared to sound more confident about reforms and what the Americans should do with them. The Iraqi crisis might turn out to have been a turning point in his relationship with the US. After Annan had negotiated an agreement with President Saddam Hussein in February 1998 over weapons inspections, he spoke, on his return to New York, of the merits of diplomacy backed by force – the UN with the massive build-up of US-led military force in the Gulf. This success earned Annan higher standing in Washington. Unfortunately this has rarely translated itself into the payment of arrears, especially since the US has traditionally regarded an independent-minded secretary-general with suspicion. In any case, the bombing by the US and Britain of Iraq in December 1998 and credible charges that UN inspection teams had been aiding US intelligence dissipated the rise in Annan's prestige.

What is probably required is yet another round of examinations of the organization and the cultural attitudes which it has striven to create over the first half century of its existence. These are connected with large words such as universality, governance and interdependence. The task of reform must be to relate these abstractions which have a bearing on every facet of the UN's activities from acting as a global debating chamber to enacting political and military decisions and to carrying out the wide variety of other activities which range from telecommunication and health to humanitarian aid and trade. Annan's ideas have not produced a revolution in thoughts and ways as to how things could be changed. At best Annan has produced a stopgap extended report on slight changes which back up thoughts already in train. Annan appears to recognize that the UN is a vital organization in more ways than one but that it is also only one of the world's political players. This is seen in no other area more than in humanitarian intervention and multidimensional interventions and building up sustained growth. Perhaps recognizing this and emphasizing that the moment has arrived to make the UN's finances more central to the stability and healthy workings of the organization might lend it more authority. But this has yet to be apparent from the first year and more of the enactment of his proposals. And as time passes, the budgetary bills still have to be paid.

One purpose of arguments aimed at improving the finances and financial flow of the UN is not to press for it to become overtly rich. It could never become that, and it would be dangerous and irresponsible if it took that path. For the organization would be the nightmare of a multinational corporation's chief financial officer – a corporation with no cash reserves, virtually no authority to raise capital or to write off bad debts and having as its most influential customer a chronic debtor. But the UN's 50th anniversary provoked some constructive and useful suggestions about how its operations and direction can be better guided in the future. Reform of the UN applies as much to its means and monies as it does to its actions. The two run together, and the latter will operate effectively and with credibility only on unpredictable occasions unless it has firmer foundations in its finances. Reorganization should not become an alternative to action. And the decisive factor is that the means to enable the UN to pay its way, be efficient and fulfill its roles and have sufficient cash without appearing profligate will depend on political, not financial, decisions.

For the coming years, Annan has set out his reform stall and obtained broad support from the General Assembly. In strictly financial terms there has been little of note. The budget has declined in size. There is to be money diverted from savings into development. There is to be a revolving credit fund. Furthermore, the budgets are to be more results-oriented. This approach has remained something of a mystery although it has been billed as improving efficiency. A decision on its implementation was initially deferred. An informal document[3] in illustrative lecture form listed as topics and challenges:

- changes in management behavior;
- shifting the managerial focus from rules-bound input control to results orientation;
- quarterly monitoring of results;
- focus on results not inputs;
- improving strategic management for achieving objectives and delegating maximum authority; and
- responsibility and full management of human and financial resources.

It exhorted support for top-down budgets, market-type mechanisms and commercial financial management. Almost every page displayed viewer-friendly pictograms including on several pages a person scratching his head with a question mark above it. It contained the improbable statement that: 'All national reforms have been tailored to the needs and characteristics of each country.' Only a discussion paper maybe, but it tends to typify the impression of reform that add up to small and unrevolutionary beer. For two larger factors seem to be missing. One is some clear and coherent idea on where he thinks the UN, in particular both the secretariat and the whole system, is heading. On the financial level, there were for 1998 a tedious repetition of falling cash flow, an unremarkable rise in the number of countries paying their contributions in time. There was a sense of an opportunity lost.

Andrew Natsios has succinctly put his finger on a major problem for the UN. He wrote:

'Perhaps the most closely held secret of the UN is that its country members, for widely divergent reasons, want the institution to remain weak. The great powers wish to avoid complications in the formulation of their foreign policy introduced by an institution that is at least partially managed by developing countries with bitter memories of their colonial past and unstable or unreliable political systems. The great powers have regarded the UN as an instrument to promote their foreign policy objectives; they have, to a limited degree, succeeded in using it for this purpose, especially when their objectives have had broader international appeal.[4]

This was true for support of the US in the Gulf War, where the unity of the five permanent members of the Security Council was paramount. It has become increasingly less the case in the years following. The US, at odds with a unilateralist Congress, has become increasingly disdainful in its relations with the UN. This has shown itself most clearly in its financial relationship.

The UN has to be wary where the US is concerned for it is dealing with a single superpower, which happens also to be the supreme provider of funds. The UN has searched delicately for what would be politically acceptable in the complicated row between the Executive and the legislative sides and Congress. It has accepted that, for the foreseeable future, Congress might be controlled by political forces at odds with the White House over the running and financing of the UN. On this issue, much will depend on how much personal attention President Clinton pays to UN issues. It has been occasional and opportunistic at best and forgotten in the maw of mounting problems at home and abroad. The right-wing comments and criticisms may seem often ludicrous and playing more to a gallery than reality, but they have to be taken into account. The key will be to get the US to love the UN through something like a five-year deal – not an open-ended arrangement – under which it gives a commitment to pay its dues in full and in exchange for UN reform. They have had since the beginning of 1997 a new secretary-general working on this task and the US jury is still out.

The difficulty with making any constructive proposals for a five-year plan is that American critics will interpret such a move as interference in the internal affairs of the US. If previous presidential contests are any guide, the UN easily becomes an emotive target for irrational discussion and criticism – if it is taken seriously at all. But it would be interesting to see what would happen if Annan suggested as a means of wooing the US into constructive involvement the enactment of some of these more attainable proposals over a five-year period:

- the lowering of US rates of assessments for both regular and peace-keeping budgets;
- the reduction of direct costs of UN-linked operations (this is already happening in peace-keeping and, on an even larger scale, in humanitarian intervention and in the specialized agencies);
- the unification of peace-keeping budgets into a flexible annualized budget;

- the closer, independent auditing of budgets and other financial and project exercises to satisfy the more intrusive of the national demands of the US Congress;
- the strengthening of the OIOS to monitor wastage in high-risk and cost-significant areas such as peace-keeping operations, humanitarian activities, procurement and newly-established UN bodies;
- reinforcing the JIU which operates system-wide as an inspection, evaluation and investigation body, looking at the efficiency of services and the use of resources;
- the greater encouragement of voluntary contributions and their integration into the financial system;
- more emphasis on developing the UN regionally;
- and an expansion of the UN Security Council, to include more than just Japan and Germany.

None of these points are new. These implied concessions to US sensitivities would offend other members, who could argue with strength against concessions being made to the chronically largest delinquent. But such suggestions might strike a chord with the US, as many of these ideas have been proposed by the US already. But were the US to be drawn into paying its way, the UN would be reinforced as much as by the political support as by the greater financial stability that it might inject.

It might help to make Aesop's fable irrelevant. The point about the shepherd who cried wolf too often was that these cries were not taken seriously by his neighbors and he lost his flock as a result. This time the UN has yet another, and perhaps seriously last chance, to prove that from an administrative and financial point of view it is worth helping to help itself so that the cry of wolf, if it does have to be made again, will be more muted and taken as a credible and deserving cry for help.

The tasks the UN has to face are much larger than its regular and peace-keeping budgets. The reforms undertaken by Annan are only part of the way in which the organization can equip itself to cope with the demands of globalization, particularly where it affects economies and information. The greater varieties of social challenges are transnational on a great scale than before. Drugs, disease and the effects of weather and the environment result in threats to the security of governments and regions and their people in a way, which requires multilateral approaches on an unprecedented scale. The UN has tended to react to the changes around it and, often, very slowly. It may be the structure and nature of its membership but, in its struggle on one level to stay in useful existence, the UN has measured its concepts of what its reforms should be more against what it has survived and achieved than by the changes needed to take on the challenges out-side. Changes in the way the budgets are run and the administrative and political rigmarole around them alone are not necessarily going to succeed in improving the UN's standing and respect outside. Some changes in atti-tude have come about. The running of the Secretariat has been improved by introducing something that resembles more closely a cabinet. The cen-tral bureaucracy has been slimmed. There is more recognition of the roles of business and of NGOs. But there remains the divide between the North and South. This spills over into the financial area through the discussion on contributions to the regular and peace-keeping budgets where ten coun-tries pay more than three-quarters of the contributions, feel that there are some not paying enough and who are resented by the majority of less prosperous countries. And unchanged now for nearly 20 years is the unseemly position of the arrears of contributors – with the US supremely in the van and apparently undecided as to whether it wants a more business-like UN or merely one with limited powers. An acceptance by the US of a plan of changes over a set period of time would give the UN time to put more substance into the first round of reform which Annan started. It might give the heart of the UN's financial organization more order and authority to play a central part in the challenges which are already upon it. That way it could be part of these changes, not, as it has always tended to be its wont, reacting to them tentatively and slowly.

Notes

INTRODUCTION (PAGES 1–4)

1. J. David Singer, *Financing International Organization. The United Nations Budget Process* (The Hague: Martinus Nijhoff, 1961), p. vii.
2. Klaus Hüfner, *Die Vereinte Nationen und ihre Sonderorganisationen 1971–1995* (Bonn: UNO-Verlag, 1997), Teil 3A: Vereinte Nationen – Friedensoperationen – Spezialorgane, p. 20.

CHAPTER 1   THE BUSINESS OF MAKING ENDS MEET (PAGES 5–24)

1. Working paper doc. WGFS/4.
2. Confidential memorandum.
3. Confidential memorandum, with a reference to a meeting with Trygve Lie on 6 May 1947.
4. Boutros Boutros-Ghali, *An Agenda for Peace. Preventive Diplomacy, Peacemaking and Peace-keeping* (New York: United Nations, 1992), UN doc. A/47/277 – S/24111, 17 June 1992, para. 3.
5. The thirty-fifth annual Ditchley Foundation Lecture given by Annan, press release SG/SM/6613 on 26 June 1998. An edited version appeared in the *International Herald Tribune*, 27–28 June 1998.
6 . See Tapio Kanninen, *Leadership and Reform: The Secretary-General and the UN Financial Crisis of the Late 1980s*, (The Hague: Kluwer Law International, 1995).
7. The budgets have been calculated on a biennial (two-year) basis since 1974–5. For the sake of convenience, the size of annual budgets is reached by dividing the biennial figures in half.
8. Boutros-Ghali, 1992, paras 60–5.
9. Boutros Boutros Ghali, *Supplement to an Agenda for Peace* (New York: United Nations, 1995), doc. A/50/60, S/1995/1, 25 January 1995, paras 86–8.
10. Boutros-Ghali, 1992, paras 23–33.
11. A useful and comprehensive guide is Cindy Collins and Thomas G. Weiss, *An Overview and Assessment of 1989–1996 Peace Operations Publications* (Providence, RI: The Thomas J. Watson Jr. Institute for International Studies, 1997), Occasional Paper #28.
12. The UN web sites and Global Policy Forum in New York (on: www.globalpolicy.org) contain an extensive array of information. The most comprehensive, detailed statistical and analytical work has been done by Klaus

Hüfner, *Die Vereinten Nationen und ihre Sonderorganisationen* in Teil 1 (Bonn: UNO-Verlag, 1991), Teil 2 (1992), and, in particular, *Finanzierungung des Systems der Vereinten Nationen 1971–1995*, Teil 3 A and B (1997). For the early days: J. David Singer, *Financing International Organization: The United Nations Budget Process* (The Hague: Martinus Nijhoff, 1961); John Stoessinger and Associates, *Financing the United Nations System* (Washington DC: The Brookings Institution, 1964); and Ernest W. Lefever, *Crisis in the Congo: A United Nations Force in Action* (Washington DC: Brookings Institution, 1965); Mahdi Elmandjra, *The United Nations System. An Analysis* (London: Faber and Faber, 1973); and David W. Wainhouse, *International Peacekeeping at the Crossroads. National Support – Experiences and Prospects* (Baltimore: The Johns Hopkins University Press, 1973). See also: Siegfried Schumm, *Budgeting in Organizations of the United Nations System. Some Comparisons.* (Geneva: UN, 1989); Susan R. Mills, *The Financing of the United Nations Peacekeeping Operations. The Need for a Sound Financial Basis* (Washington: International Peace Academy, 1989), Occasional Paper Number 3; William J. Durch and Barry M. Blechman, *Keeping the Peace: The United Nations in the Emerging World Order* (Washington DC: The Henry L. Stimson Center, 1992); Volcker/Ogata report. *Financing an Effective United Nations – A Report of the Independent Advisory Group on U.N. Financing* (New York: Ford Foundation, 1993); Anthony McDermott, *United Nations Financing Problems and the New Generation of Peacekeeping and Peace Enforcement* (Providence RI: The Thomas J. Watson Jr. Institute for International Studies, 1994), Occasional Paper #16; Tapio Kanninen, *Leadership and Reform. The Secretary-general and the UN Financial Crisis of the Late 1980s* (The Hague: Kluwer Law International, 1995); Harlan Cleveland, Hazel Henderson and Inge Kaul, eds, *The United Nations: Policy and Financing Alternatives* (Kidlington, UK: Elsevier, 1995); Simon Broadbent, 'Financing the United Nations: International Taxation Based on Capacity to Pay', *National Institute Economic Review*, London, No. 157, July 1996, pp. 77–89; Yves Beigbeder, *The Internal Management of United Nations Organizations. The Long Quest for Reform* (Basingstoke, UK: Macmillan, 1997); publications from the UNA-USA Association, particularly by Jeffrey Laurenti; from the Congressional Research Service, The Library of Congress (Washington) particularly by Marjorie Anne Browne; and from the United States General Accounting Office, notably *United Nations. Financial Issues and U.S. Arrears* (Washington DC: GAO/NSIAD-98-201BR, June 1998).

13. Pelt's account of the stages through which a budget has to pass goes some way to explain why the figures of annual and biennial budgets differ. Reductions are debated and figures adjusted on occasions *after* the budget period. Furthermore assessed contributions may be confused with actual expenditures. The 1946 budget appropriations are often estimated at \$19.39 million – including by the officially audited accounts at the time.

14. *Yearbook of the United Nations 1946–47* (Lake Success, New York: Department of Public Information, United Nations, 1947), p. 95.

15. *Setting the Record Straight: Some Facts About the United Nations.* DPI/1753/Rev.13 (New York: UN Department of Public Information, August 1997).

16. Erskine Childers in the foreword (p.x) to Phyllis Bennis, *Calling the Shots. How Washington Dominates Today's UN* (New York: Olive Branch Press, 1996).
17. *Setting the Record Straight.*
18. Peace-keeping budgets are notoriously difficult to annualize as the dates of the mandates of individual missions (and their budgets) vary. See also Chapter 5.

CHAPTER 2　CHANGES IN PROBLEMS AND PRINCIPLES (PAGES 25–39)

1. Jeffrey Laurenti, *Losing America's Vote at the United Nations. Prospects and Consequences of the Application of Article 19.* (New York: UNA-USA Analysis, 29 June 1998) p. 3. On page 10, note 1, he writes:

   Between its founding in 1919 and its collapse in 1941, the League did succeed in collecting 91 percent of its assessments. However, on average it only collected 76 percent of assessments in the budget year when they were needed to cover expenditure. In contrast to the period since World War II, in which states have viewed membership in the United Nations as an essential attribute of full sovereignty and participation in the world community, a number of states wavered in their commitment to membership in the League, at times withdrawing to protest unfavorable decisions and later rejoining. Nazi Germany pulled out permanently in 1934, however, commencing an ominous downward slide for the organization.

2. Boutros-Ghali, *Supplement*, paras 89–96.
3. Article 17 of the Charter reads:

   1. The General Assembly shall consider and approve the budget of the Organization.
   2. The expenses of the Organization shall be borne by the Members as apportioned by the General Assembly.
   3. The General Assembly shall consider and approve any financial and budgetary arrangements with specialized agencies referred to in Article 57 and shall examine the administrative budgets of such specialized agencies with a view to making recommendations to the agencies concerned.

   The links with the specialized agencies are to referred in Article 57, which reads:

   1. The various specialized agencies, established by intergovernmental agreement and having wide international responsibilities, as defined in their basic instruments, in economic, social, cultural, educational, health and related fields, shall be brought into relationship with the United Nations in accordance with the provisions of Article 63.
   2. Such agencies thus brought into relationship with the United Nations are hereinafter referred to as specialized agencies.

Article 63 brings the main links of the UN's financial system together (see chart on page 16) and reads:

1. The Economic and Social Council may enter into agreements with any of the agencies referred to in Article 57, defining the terms on which the agency concerned shall be brought into relationship with the United Nations. Such agreements shall be subject to approval by the General Assembly.
2. It may coordinate the activities of the specialized agencies through consultation with and recommendations to such agencies and through recommendations to the General Assembly and to the Members of the United Nations.

4.   Boutros Boutros-Ghali, *Egypt's Road to Jerusalem: a Diplomat's Story of the Struggle for Peace in the Middle East* (New York: Random House, 1997). This gives an often amusing and wry account of his career before becoming UN secretary-general. His descriptions of African national politics would surely have excluded him from being the African regional candidate for the UN position had they been published at the time!
5.   The possibility arose in the summer of 1998 of the US losing its General Assembly voting rights from 1 January 1999 if its arrears exceeded $1.28 billion on 31 December 1998. A UNA-USA publication dated May 1998 pointed out that member states were usually informed of their position under Article 19 and many made just sufficient contributions to prevent a loss of their vote when the Assembly session resumed to wrap up business the following spring. Voting rights are restored when enough dues are paid to cross the two-year threshold. In October 1998, the US Congress passed a bill providing sufficient money for the UN to avert the loss of voting rights.
6.   Jeffrey Laurenti, *Losing America's...*, p. 3.
7.   In articles 53, 77 and 107 of the UN Charter. Article 53.2 reads: 'The term enemy state as used in paragraph 1 of this Article applies to any state which during the Second World War has been an enemy of any signatory of the present Charter'.

CHAPTER 3   THE WAYS FROM THE BEGINNING
(PAGES 40–54)

1.   See note 3, Chapter 2.
2.   The UN system here excludes the Bretton Woods institutions, comprising IBRD (or World Bank), IFC, IDA, MIGA, IMF and IFAD.
3.   After a prolonged debate, the US assessment was reduced by 10 per cent to 39.89 per cent.
4.   *Yearbook of the United Nations 1946–47* (Lake Success, New York: Department of Public Information, UN, 1947), pp. 217–18.
5.   Stoessinger, *Financing...* p. 66.
6.   Over the 1995–7 period, the US percentage assessment remained steady at 25. Others varied: Japan 13.95 (1995) and 15.435 (1996); Germany: 8.94

and 9.0425; France: 6.32 and 6.4075; Britain 5.27 and 5.315; Italy 4.79 and 5.1975; Russia: 5.68 and 4.45; and China 0.72 and 0.735. UN General Assembly Resolution A/RES/49/19B, 23 December 1994.

7.   As a mark of displeasure at the US attitude towards Boutros-Ghali's non-reappointment as secretary-general, and at its inability to pay off its arrears, the US was voted off the ACABQ on 8 November 1996 for the first time. The announcement was greeted with applause!

8.   General Assembly. Resolution 2360B (XXII).

9.   Singer, *Financing International* ... p. xvi.

10. In addition, for the budgets assessed payments due are often confused with actual expenditures and payments (which may be in arrears and owed to budgets of a previous year). Gross sums are also often affected by being offset against credits accumulated through the Tax Equalization Fund or the WCF (and, for a while, assets left over from the League of Nations).

11. Hüfner, *Die Vereinten Nationen* ... Teil 3A, Tabelle 1.3–3, p. 105.

12. Kofi Annan, *Renewing the United Nations: A Programme for Reform* (New York: United Nations, 1977), para. 221.

13. H. G. Nicholas, 'The UN in Crisis' in *International Affairs* (RIIA, London,), vol.41, no.3, July 1965, p. 441.

14. Mahdi Elmandjra, *The United Nations System* ... p. 233.

15. Elmandjra, pp. 235–6.

16. *Financial Times*, 29 July 1998.

17. Jeffrey Laurenti, *Considerations on the Financing of an International Criminal Court* (New York: UNA-USA, June 1998), p. 2.

18. Data compiled by Klaus Hüfner for Global Policy Forum.

19. General Assembly doc. A/53/647, 6 November 1998.

20. Elmandjra, pp. 228–9.

21. General Assembly doc. A/51/505/Corr.1, 6 December 1996. A footnote records that: 'The 1997 assessment will be decided by the General Assembly at its fifty-first session'.

CHAPTER 4   THE REGULAR BUDGET – AN UNCERTAIN CAPACITY TO PAY (PAGES 55–75)

1.   For calculations, it is important to differentiate between the assessed rates of payment and actual payments. Furthermore, in terms of arrears, there are both current arrears and those for previous years. The UN Charter contains no effective mechanism to penalize a failure to pay. Article 19 states:

A Member of the United Nations which is in arrears in the payment of its financial contributions to the Organization shall have no vote in the General Assembly if the amount equals or exceeds the amount of the contributions due from it for the preceding two full years. The General Assembly may, nevertheless, permit such a Member to vote if it is satisfied that the failure to pay is due to conditions beyond the control of the Member.

It has rarely been invoked. The Soviet bloc and several Arab countries refused to contribute to the support of the UN Emergency Force (UNEF) in the 1950s. The Soviet Union and France took the same position over the UN Operation in the Congo ONUC in the 1960s. Devices, financial and procedural, were found to preclude a crisis.

2. *Yearbook of the United Nations 1946–47*, p. 217. Italics added for emphasis.
3. J. David Singer, *Financing International Organization: The United Nations Budget Process*, (The Hague: Martinus Nijhoff, 1961), p. 2.
4. John G. Stoessinger, *Financing the United Nations System*, (Washington DC: The Brookings Institution, 1964), pp. 37–8.
5. Stoessinger, *Financing...* pp. 41–2.
6. Singer, *Financing International...* p. 3.
7. The figures for 1970 are recorded in Mahdi Elmandjra, *The United Nations System. An Analysis* (London: Faber and Faber, 1973), p. 224; and for 1970, 1980, 1990 and 1996 in Hüfner Teil 3A, Abbildungen 1.2–1–4, pp. 66–7.
8. Extrapolated from *Scale of Assessments for the Apportionment of the Expenses of the United Nations*. General Assembly doc. A/52/745, 31 December 1997.
9. Letter to *The Economist*, 31 January–6 February 1998, p. 4.
10. In the view of the UN (See, for example, Secretariat document ST/ADM/SER.B/509 of 15 April 1997, p. 18): 'Through accession of the German Democratic Republic to the Federal Republic of Germany with effect from 3 October, the two German States united to form one sovereign State. As from the date of unification, the Federal Republic of Germany acts in the United Nations under the designation "Germany". On 3 October 1990, total contributions outstanding amounted to $15,854,000 for the former German Democratic Republic. There were no contributions outstanding for the Federal Republic of Germany. The Government of Germany wishes to point out that it does not recognize any legal obligation to pay the debts of the former German Democratic Republic. However, it has made voluntary contributions totaling $3,664,000 and will make additional voluntary contributions of appropriate amounts in due course.'
11. Simon Broadbent in 'Financing the United Nations: International Taxation Based on Capacity to Pay' in the *National Institute Economic Review*, London, No. 157, July 1996, pp. 77–89, has written a sophisticated analysis of this system. An earlier outstanding account was written by Susan R. Mills, see Chapter 1, note 12.
12. Article 18, under the heading 'Voting' reads in part: 'Decisions of the General Assembly on important questions shall be made by a two-thirds majority of the members present and voting. These questions shall include ... budgetary questions.'
13. Erskine Childers with Brian Urquhart, *Renewing the United Nations System* (Uppsala: Dag Hammarskjöld Foundation, 1994) pp. 142–3.
14. Global Policy Forum (see chapter 1, note 12) is the source for the size of annual budgets within the biennial budgets.
15. The cumulative arrears of South Africa was a unique case, caused by its suspension from the UN General Assembly between September 1974 and June 1994 because of its government's *apartheid* policies. At the end of 1994, the arrears to the regular budget had reached $57.4 million and $40.2 million for peace-keeping operations. The General Assembly that year decided 'to consider, as an exceptional measure, that the arrears of

South Africa that have accrued to date were due to conditions beyond its control, and accordingly, that the question of applicability of Article 19 of the Charter ... related to the loss of voting rights in the General Assembly in this respect will not arise.' (Quoted in *National Taxpayers, International Organizations. Sharing the Burden of Financing the United Nations* [New York: United Nations Association of the United States, 1995] p. 15.) On 15 December 1995, the General Assembly adopted, without a vote, resolution 50/83 that, under the terms of Article 17, South Africa's burden of arrears would be borne by member states. It decided that 'the present resolution shall under no circumstances constitute a precedent'.

16. *Report of the Group of High-Level Intergovernmental Experts to Review the Efficiency of the Administrative and Financial Functioning of the United Nations.* General Assembly Official Record, 41st session, supp. 49, A/41/49. For a detailed account of these developments, see Rosemary Righter, *Utopia Lost. The United Nations and World Order*, (New York: The Twentieth Century Fund Press, 1995), pp. 231–5. The Group of 18 was established by General Assembly Resolution 40/237, 18 December 1985.

17. General Assembly res. 41/213, 21 December 1986.

18. In the later half of the 1990s there was a near balance between expenditures on the regular budget and those on the peace-keeping accounts, as restraints were imposed. The figures for the latter are notoriously difficult to record exactly. The dates of the original mandates are decided by events not fiscal years and the renewal periods are not always identical. Expenditures in past years may be, as a result, readjusted considerably – but not the trends.

19. On the financial side, the establishment of the RCF was deferred, as was the enactment of a results-based budgeting system, until practical details had been worked out.

20. See Chapter 2, note 3 for the relevant Charter articles 17, 57 and 63 related to ECOSOC's theoretical authority.

21. The exact status of MIGA and the WTO (formerly GATT) is not relevant here.

22. Schumm's studies comparing budgeting in organizations of the UN system and the ACC's *Budgeting Methods* doc. ACC/1995/FB/R.49, 28 December 1995 are essential reading.

23. UN document A/51/505, 18 October 1996 (but taking into account corrigendum A/51/505/Corr.1, 6 December 1996). The figures for 1997 are provisional and the assessments subject to General Assembly approval. The agencies involved are ILO, FAO, UNESCO, ICAO, WHO, UPU, ITU, WMO, IMO, WIPO, UNIDO and IAEA. Doc. A/53/647 of 6 November 1998 recorded approved regular budgets of $3.15 billion (1997), $3.25 billion (1998) and $3.26 billion (1999) – with assessed contributions for the same years of $ 2.98 billion, $ 2.88 billion and $ 2.88 billion.

24. J. David Singer, *Financing International* ... p. 153, drawing on General Assembly and official records.

25. *Financing an Effective United Nations. A Report of the Independent Advisory Group on U.N. Financing.* The Ford Foundation. New York. February 1993.

26. Mahdi Elmandjra, *The United Nations System: An Analysis*, (London: Faber and Faber, 1973), p. 215.

CHAPTER 5   FINDING AND FUNDING THE PATHS TO PEACE
(PAGES 76–93)

1.   Unless otherwise stated or explained, 'peace-keeping', which has suffered
     from a plethora of reinterpretations over the years, is used her to
     cover broadly any intervention by military or civilian personnel with a
     mandate from the UN. The context will, it is hoped, provide sufficient
     guidance.
2.   In theory, the member states which have not been reimbursed for supply-
     ing troops and *matériel*, could object. They were owed over $1 billion at
     the end of 1997.
3.   *The Multinational Force in Beirut, 1982–84*, Anthony McDermott and
     Kjell Skjelsbæk, eds, (Florida International University Press, Miami,
     FL, 1991).
4.   Edwin M. Smith and Thomas G. Weiss, 'UN Task-Sharing: Toward or
     Away from Global Governance?' in Thomas G. Weiss, ed., *Beyond UN
     Subcontracting. Task-Sharing with Regional Security Arrangements and
     Service-Providing NGOs* (Basingstoke: Macmillan Press, 1998), p. 254.
5.   Boutros Boutros-Ghali in *The Blue Helmets. A Review of United Nations
     Peace-keeping*. 3rd ed. (United Nations Department of Public Information,
     New York, 1996) p. 3.
6.   There has been a growing literature on this concept. See Jarat Chopra,
     'The Space of Peace-Maintenance', *Political Geography*, vol. 15, no. 3/4,
     1996, pp. 335–57. Chopra edited 'Special Issue on Peace-Maintenance
     Operations' of *Global Governance*, vol. 4 no.1 January–March 1998,
     published as *The Politics of Peace-Maintenance* (Boulder, CO: Lynne
     Rienner Publishers, 1998) and wrote *Peace-Maintenance: The Evolution of
     International Political Authority* (London: Routledge, 1998).
7.   Table compiled by Michael Renner for Global Policy Forum. For the
     period 1947–56: $57 million; 1961–63 annual average of $126 million;
     and an annual average of $37.5 million 1964–73. Thereafter annual fig-
     ures: $131 million (1974), $153 million (1975–7), $202 million (1978),
     $186 million (1979), $141 million (1980–85). His calculations from 1982
     onwards do not tally exactly with UN figures.
8.   *United Nations. Financial Issues and U.S. Arrears* (Washington: UN
     General Accounting Office, June 1998) GAO/NSIAD-98-201BR,
     pp. 13–18. The report notes that the UN obtains 98 per cent of its operat-
     ing funds from regular and peace-keeping assessments, and two per cent
     from international criminal tribunals assessments.
9.   The General Assembly on the recommendation of the Fifth Committee
     (A/9428) adopted the relevant resolution involving four levels of appor-
     tionments (for UNEF), doc. 3101 (XXVIII) on 11 December 1973.
10. Through General Assembly Resolution 1089(XI), December 21 1956.
     John G. Stoessinger has further details on UNEF I and ONUC in
     Financing the United Nations System (Washington DC: The Brookings
     Institution, 1964) pp. 106–21.
11. The analysis and information provided by Peter Gizewski and Geoffrey
     Pearson in 'The Burgeoning Cost of UN Peace-keeping: Who Pays and

Who Benefits?, *Aurora Papers 21*, (Canadian Centre for Global Security/ Centre Canadien pour la Securité Mondiale, Ottawa: November 1993) has been especially useful.

12. General Assembly resolution 1089 (XI) of 21 December 1956.
13. For the details of the disputes over UNEF I and ONUC, see also John. G. Stoessinger, *The United Nations and the Superpowers: United States- Soviet Interaction at the United Nations* (New York: Random House, 1966), pp. 90–113.
14. Stoessinger, *Financing* ... p. 140.
15. Paul LaRose-Edwards, *United Nations Internal Impediments to Peace- keeping Rapid Reaction*, (International Human Rights, Democracy & Conflict Resolution, Kanata, Ottawa, 2 April 1995) pp. 21–2.
16. *An Agenda for Peace*, para. 23.
17. Boutros-Ghali, *An Agenda for Peace*, para. 43.
18. Independent Working Group on the Future of the United Nations, *The United Nations in Its Second Half-Century* (New York: Ford Foundation, 1995).
19. GAO. *United Nations* ... pp. 31–5 and 56–7.
20. Peter Gizewski and Geoffrey Pearson, 'The Burgeoning Cost ... p. 13.

CHAPTER 6   WASHINGTON: THE UN'S DEAR DONOR AND DELINQUENT (PAGES 94–116)

1. Robert A. Divine, *Second Chance: The Triumph of Internationalism in America during World War II* (New York: Atheneum, 1967), pp. 47–8.
2. A detailed account of the debate about contributions is given by Singer, pp. 122–35 (and Stoessinger, *Financing the* ... pp. 82–90). See also *Foreign Relations of the United States 1946*. Vol I: General, The United Nations (Washington DC: US Government Printing Office, 1972) pp. 460–99, which ends with a secret paper from the US delegation in New York recom- mending to Congress the acceptance of the 39.89 per cent contribution level. A table (pp. 18–25) in John P. Renninger with Daniel Donaghue, Peter Geib, Herman Perez and Wouter Van Nispen tot Sevenaer, *Assessing the United Nations Scale of Assessments: Is It Fair? Is It Equitable?* (New York: United Nations Institute for Training and Research, 1982), Policy and Efficacy Studies No. 9, shows that, in the UN scales of assessments, the US share was 39.89 per cent (1946–49), 39.79 per cent (1950), 38.92 per cent (1951), 36.90 per cent (1952), 35.12 per cent (1953), 33.33 per cent (1954–57), 32.51 per cent (1958–61), 32.02 per cent (1962–64), 31.91 per cent (1965–67), 31.57 per cent (1968–70), 31.52 per cent (1971–73) and from 1974 25 per cent. Source: doc. A/34/11.
3. Pew Research Center (formerly Times-Mirror Center) cited by the UN Department of Public Information in February 1998, doc. DPI/1963.
4. John L. Washburn, 'United Nations Relations with the United States. The UN Must Look Out for itself', *Global Governance*, vol. 2 no.1, January–April 1996, pp. 81–96, here pp. 82–3.

5. Stoessinger, *Financing...* pp. 65 ff. He qualifies these figures as not representing arrears or defaults in 1962. But they do indicate fully the size of the US share.
6. Stoessinger, *Financing...* p. 75.
7. William J. Durch, ed., *UN Peacekeeping, American Politics, and the Uncivil Wars of the 1990s* (Basingstoke, UK: Macmillan, 1997), p. 10.
8. Rosemary Righter, *Utopia Lost. The United Nations and World Order* (New York: The Twentieth Century Fund Press, 1995), p. 211.
9. Righter, *Utopia...* p. 212. In real, as opposed to nominal, terms zero-growth budgets and lower started to occur in 1982–83 and thereafter in 1988–89, 1990–91 and 1996-97, see Hüfner, Teil 3A, Tabelle 1.3–6, p. 107.
10. Robert W. Gregg, *About Face? The United States and the United Nations* (Boulder, CO: Lynne Rienner, 1993) points out that Congressman Gerald Solomon was the author of the original House version. That version was dropped and essentially it was the language proposed by Nancy Kassebaum which became law, p. 90, note 22.
11. Javier Pérez de Cuéllar, *Pilgrimage for Peace. A Secretary-General's Memoir* (Basingstoke, UK: Macmillan, 1997) pp. 8–9.
12. Pérez de Cuéllar, *Pilgrimage...* p. 12.
13. See Benjamin Rivlin, 'Boutros-Ghali's Ordeal. Leading the United Nations in an Age of Uncertainty', in Dimitris Bourantonis and Marios Evriviades, eds, *A United Nations for the Twenty-First Century. Peace, Security and Development* (The Hague: Kluwer, 1996) for Boutros-Ghali's difficult relations with the US, pp. 127–47. This passage draws in part on this.
14. For an account and analysis of PDD-25 see Durch, ed., *UN Peacekeeping...* pp. 51–9.
15. Bourantonis, *A United Nations...* p. 141.
16. The author is grateful to Sam Daws for drawing his attention to the best analysis of invoking Article 19 in Bruno Simma, ed., *The Charter of the United Nations: A Commentary* (Oxford: Oxford University Press: 1994), pp. 327–39.
17. *U.N. Peacekeeping. Status of Long-standing Operations and U.S.: Interests in Supporting Them.* (Washington DC: US General Accounting Office, April 1997). GAO/NSIAD-97-59 wrote: 'Section 404(b)(2) of the Foreign Relations Authorization Act of 1994-95 (P.L. 103-236) prohibits the use of funds appropriated after fiscal year 1995 for the payment of U.S. assessed contributions for U.N. peacekeeping operations in an amount greater than 25 percent of the total of all assessed contributions for an operation.' p. 1, note 1.
18. *Washington Weekly Report*, XXIII-18, 19, 13 June 1997, pp. 4–7.
19. Congress had already passed legislation to that effect earlier. This change would push the burden of negotiation onto the Clinton administration.
20. This had been lost, as a snub to the US, in a race with France and New Zealand in the autumn of 1996. It failed again to win a seat in 1998.
21. Not to be forgotten in the list of conditions was the mundane aspect of the US cutting aid to nations whose UN diplomats did not pay New York parking tickets!
22. *U.S. Foreign Policy Agenda*, USIA Electronic Journal, vol. 2. no. 2, May 1997.

23. *U.S. Foreign Policy...* ibid.
24. *The Wall Street Journal*, 17 November 1997.
25. Marjorie Ann Browne, CRS Report for Congress, *United Nations Peacekeeping: Historical Overview and Current Issues* (Washington DC: The Library of Congress, January 31 1990) p. 13 and pp. 69–70.
26. Browne, *United Nations Peacekeeping Operations, 1988-1993: Background Information* (Washington DC: The Library of Congress, February 28, 1994) pp. 4–8.
27. *U.N. Peacekeeping. Status*, p. 56.
28. This is at the 25 per cent ceiling imposed by Congress from October 1 1996. It is also at odds with the 31 per cent share at which the UN assesses the US.
29. *U.N. Peacekeeping...* p. 5.
30. *U.N. Peacekeeping...* p. 28.
31. This was already the case under Boutros-Ghali. See *UN 21 Better Service. Better Value. Better Management.* Progress of the Efficiency Board to the Secretary-General (New York: UN, September 1996). It was continued under Annan in *Strengthening of the United Nations System. Review of the Efficiency of the Administrative and Financial Functioning of the United Nations.* Doc. A/51/873, 21 April 1997.
32. *United Nations. Limitations in Leading Missions Requiring Force to Restore Peace.* (Washington DC: US General Accounting Office, Washington, March 1997). GAO/NSIAD-97–34, p. 56.
33. *United Nations. Limitations...* p. 3–4.
34. *United Nations. Limitations...* p. 21.
35. Gregg, *About Face...* p. 19.
36. In the original text of the speech of Bill Richardson, the US ambassador to the UN, to the General Assembly's Fifth Committee (Administration and Budget) on 20 October he was to have said: 'I would be remiss if I didn't point out the failure to revise the scales of assessments for UN member states could begin the process of America's disengagement from the United Nations'. *International Documents Review* (Teaneck, NJ) vol. 8, no.37, 27 October 1997, p. 1. It was toned down indicating that Washington considered a reduction in its budget assessments a central reform issue. It was 'of critical importance not only to the future of the United Nations but also to US engagement'.

CHAPTER 7   A GALLIMAUFRY OF MONEY-RAISING DEVICES (PAGES 117–131)

1. The *Diplomatic World Bulletin* reported that:

   By Ted Turner standards it was a pittance, but Microsoft co-founder William H. Gates, currently rated the richest person in America if not the world, has donated through his charitable foundation $1.7 million for UN population control and economic development programs. Nafis Sadik, head of the Population Fund, called it 'a very wise investment for the future' and observed that it was 'deeply gratifying' to see industry playing a part in development.

vol. 29, no. 2, May 1998, p. 7.

2. *Choices. The Human Development Magazine* (New York: UNDP Division of Public Affairs), January 1998, p. 12.

3. Arthur N. Holcombe, chairman, *Strengthening the United Nations. Commission to Study the Organization of Peace* (New York: Harper & Brothers, 1957) p. 52–3. Italics in text. This was the commission's tenth report. The first was published in November 1940.

4. *Renewing the United Nations: A Programme for Reform* (New York: United Nations, 1997), paras 8–9.

5. Arthur N. Holcombe, *Strengthening...* p. 51. Italics in the text.

6. Boutros-Ghali, *An Agenda for Peace,* paras 71–2.

7. 'The Continuing Financial problems of the United Nations: Assessing Reform Proposals', in Paul Taylor, Sam Daws, Ute Adamczick-Gerteis, eds, *Documents on Reform of the United Nations* (Aldershot, UK: Dartmouth, 1997), pp. 201–26.

8. *Financing an Effective United Nations – A Report of the Independent Advisory Group on U.N. Financing,* (New York: Ford Foundation, 1993).

9. Private observation to the author.

10. *Financing an Effective...* p. 23. The bold type is in the original text.

11. Robert E. Riggs and Jack C. Plano, *The United Nations. International Organization and World Politics. 2nd. ed.* (Belmont CA: Wadsworth, 1994), pp. 40–1.

12. Erskine Childers with Brian Urquhart, *Renewing the United Nations System,* (Uppsala: Dag Hammarskjöld Foundation, 1994), pp.154–6. The italics are the two authors'. One promising idea in terms of the sums that would be generated was that of a fractional levy on all transational movement of currencies. The concept of a tax on currency speculation has gained some notoriety as the eponymous Tobin Tax. It was first put forward – it is sometimes called a Foreign Exchange Transactions Levy – by Nobel Laureate Professor James Tobin in 1972 as a way of discouraging speculation in short-term foreign-exchange dealings. In 1978 he suggested a 0.5 per cent tax on such transactions dealings. With the equivalent of around $1 trillion traded every day, this would represent the sum of $1.5 trillion dollars per year.

13. Another comprehensive list came in Overseas Development Institute Briefing Paper 1996 (1) February, where it includes among 'Twenty Recent Suggestions for Global Revenue': a tax on all or some international transactions (the 'Tobin Tax'). Variants include a tax on bond turnover, or on derivatives; a general surcharge on international trade; taxes on specified traded commodities like fuel; a tax on the international arms trade; surcharges on post and telecommunications revenues; an international lottery; a surcharge on domestic taxation (usually expressed as a progressive share of income tax); dedication of some parts of national or local taxes, e.g. on luxuries (or surcharges on them); parking charges for satellites placed in geostationary orbit; royalties on minerals mined in international waters; charges for exploration in or exploration of Antarctica; charges for fishing in international waters; charges for the use of the electromagnetic spectrum; a tax or charge

on international flights (or alternatively, on flights in congested sectors).
A variant is a tax on aviation kerosene; a tax or charge on international ship-
ping; pollution charges (e.g. for dumping at sea); a tax on traded pollution
permits; a voluntary local tax paid to a central global agency; a new issue of
Special Drawing Rights, distributed to the poorer developing countries (or
used for peacekeeping or other global public goods); and a sale of part of
the IMF gold stock. All these proposals, to differing degrees, would involve
fairly formidable supranational institution-building to be enforced.

14. Muchkund Dubey, 'Financing the United Nations' in the *Indian Journal of International Law*, vol. 35, 1995, pp. 161–4.

15. See *Documents on Reform ...* p. 224.

16. Ingvar Carlsson, 'The United Nations: The Imperative for Reform', in *Pacifica Review*, vol. 7, no. 2, 1995, p. 13.

17. *New and Innovative Ideas for Generating Funds for Globally Agreed Commitments and Priorities*, Docs. Nos A/52/203 – E/1997/85, 23 June 1997.

18. *New and ...* para. 3.

19. Drawn from a paper summarizing proposals and ideas advanced during discussions of the High-Level Open-ended Working Group on the Financial
Situation of the UN, doc. WGFS/16, 8 June 1995.

20. This sum was, at the time, higher than all Germany's voluntary and assessed
contributions to the UN in the previous 20 years of its membership, see
Klaus Hüfner *UN Basis Info*, December 1994, p. 4. In September 1998,
it was worth $5.7 billion.

CHAPTER 8   REASSESSING THE BUDGETS
(PAGES 132–149)

1. Statement from the Secretary-General to Razali Ismail, President of the
General Assembly, dated 16 July 1997, submitting the report, *Renewing the United Nations: A Programme for Reform.*

2. The establishment of a UN international criminal court for which states
were invited to sign up at the end of a conference in Rome in July 1998
raised the prospect of additional assessed payments with all its uncertainties. The court's annual base costs, when 'at rest', have been put at $10
million. These could rise to $60–80 million in dealing with a major case. In
1998, member states were paying just over $100 million for the *ad hoc*
tribunals established for former Yugoslavia and Rwanda. These costs were
assessed by the General Assembly separately from the regular budget.
Jeffrey Laurenti, *Considerations on the Financing of an International Criminal Court* (New York: United Nations Association of the United
States of America, 1998), p. 1.

3. That of the US, which has always been the most heavily assessed member
state, was initially set at 39.98 per cent. It has been put higher. The US in
1945 was estimated to have accounted for around 40 per cent of the global
GNP – one measure of national income. Based on a three-year average GNP
for 1993–5, the US share of world GNP stood at 26.25 per cent, according
to the UNA-USA Fact Sheet of 1997. This was used to counter those advocating the lowering of the US assessment rate to 20 per cent.

4. For an instructive view of these problems and some measured suggestions for solutions, see Simon Duke, 'The UN Finance Crisis: a History and Analysis', *International Relations*, vol. 11, no. 2, 1992, pp. 127–50.

5. The ACC's *Budgeting Methods*, doc. ACC/1995/FB/R.49 28 December 1995, provides not only an extensive comparative study of the budgeting methods organization of the UN system but also details of incentive and penalty schemes. See also *Collection of Contributions: Incentives and Penalty Schemes*, ACC/1994/FB/R.22, 13 July 1994.

6. It is summarized with admirable succinctness by Yves Beigbeder, 'The Continuing Financial Problems of the United Nations: Assessing Reform Proposals' in Paul Taylor *et al.*, *Documents on Reform of the United Nations* on pp. 206–7.

7. Mitchell L. Moss, in the *International Herald Tribune*, 18 April 1997 noted that about 16 000 people with combined salaries of $850 million annually were employed locally and that UN conferences produced $27 million in visitor spending a year.

8. This passage draws on Duke p. 138.

9. UNDP 1996/1997 *Annual Report*, p. 24.

10. Thomas G. Weiss, *Military-Civilian Interactions: Intervening in Humanitarian Crises* (Lanham, MD: Rowman & Littlefield, 1998). He looks in detail at the case histories of operations in northern Iraq, Somalia, Bosnia, Rwanda and Haiti. His costings of these interactions make plain how difficult it will be to apportion costs systematically and fairly.

11. *Supplement to an Agenda for Peace: Position Paper of the Secretary-General on the Occasion of the Fiftieth Anniversary of the United Nations*, doc. A/50/60, S/1995/1, 3 January 1995.

12. Boutros-Ghali, *An Agenda* ... para. 48.

13. Once this fund had reached its target level, the proceeds from the investment of its principal would be used to finance the initial costs of authorized peace-keeping operations, other conflict resolution and related activities (*An Agenda*, para 70). Many of such proposals were left unapproved, or repeated in subsequent General Assembly sessions, along with exhortations to member states to meet their financial obligations on time.

14. Ibid, paras 71–3. At the 47th Session, the General Assembly established a Peacekeeping Reserve Fund of $150 million as a cash-flow mechanism to ensure the rapid response off the organization to the needs of peace-keeping operations. The shares of the fund were to be calculated on the basis of the ad hoc apportionment set out in General Assembly Resolution 45/247 21 December 1990 (Beigbeder, p. 221 in Paul Taylor *et al.*, *Documents on Reform* ...).

15. *Financing an Effective United Nations*, pp. 16 ff.

16. The figures give a picture only at a particular time of the year. Japan had nothing outstanding from 1997, and Germany owed under $5 million.

CHAPTER 9   THE DISCOMFORT OF THE RUN-IN WITH
REFORM (PAGES 150–169)

1. Erskine Childers with Brian Urquhart, *Renewing the United Nations System* (Uppsala: Dag Hammarskjöld Foundation, 1994), p. 142. He wrote: 'In the

last forty years there have been major reforms in the main UN Secretariat alone at roughly eight-year intervals (1953–1956; 1964–1966; 1974–77; 1985–1986; 1992–)', p. 34. See pp. 34 ff. for their discussion of reform. For the finance and management initiatives, they list 1955, 1961, 1964, 1965, 1968, 1970, 1975, 1980, 1983, 1985–7 and 1992. They date their eleventh as starting in 1992. To this should be added the current program announced in July 1997.

2. David Usborne, *The Independent* (London), 7 February 1996.
3. *UN Chronicle*, p. 83. no. 3, 1996.
4. *Financial Times*, 1 May 1996.
5. Proposed Programme Budget for the Biennium 1996–1997. Report of the Secretary-General. A/C.5/50/57/Add.1. 28 August 1996.
6. *UN Chronicle*, p. 82. no. 3, 1996.
7. Barbara Crossette, *International Herald Tribune*, 8 July 1996.
8. *The Independent*, 11 November 1996.
9. Tony Jackson, 'Battle of the Bulge', *Financial Times*, 30 June 1997, p. 10.
10. See General Assembly document A/51/421 27 September 1996, on p. 4.
11. Ibid., pp. 8 ff.
12. Yves Beigbeder, *The Internal Management of United Nations Organizations: The Long Quest for Reform,* (Basingstoke, UK: Macmillan Press Ltd, 1997), p. 105.
13. Maurice Bertrand, *The United Nations: Past, Present and Future,* (The Hague: Kluwer Law International, 1997), p. 148.
14. Ibid.
15. Ibid., p. 149.
16. Childers, *Renewing…* p. 187.
17. Norway, for example, was owed about $30 million at end of August 1998.
18. *Strengthening of the United Nations System. Programme Budget for the Biennium 1996-1997. Letter dated 17 March from the Secretary-General addressed to the President of the General Assembly.* Document A/51/829, pp. 2–3.
19. Ibid., pp. 8–9. The emphasized passages are in the original text. Press release GA/9539/Rev. 1 of 18 December 1998 recorded the General Assembly adopting a budget of $2.55 billion for 2000–2001 (while putting the 1998–1999 budget at $2.53 billion).
20. *Strengthening of the United Nations System. Review of the Efficiency of the Administrative and Financial Functioning of the United Nations. Letter dated 21 April 1997 from the Secretary General to the President of the General Assembly.* A/51/873, pp. 51.
21. Reported in *UN 21: Better Service, Better Value, Better Management. Progress Report of the Efficiency Board to the Secretary-General.* New York, September 1996.
22. *International Herald Tribune*, 14–15 December 1996.
23. Kofi A. Annan, 'The Secretary-General and the UN Budget', in *The Challenging Role of the UN Secretary General: making 'the most impossible job in the world' possible.* Benjamin Rivlin and Leon Gordenker eds, (Westport, Connecticut: Praeger, 1993), p. 107.

CHAPTER 10   AND BACK INTO THE NEW ERA
(PAGES 170–185)

1.   Press release SG/2037, ORG/1239 of July 16 1997.
2.   See Chapter 3, note 16.
3.   *Results-based Budgeting*, labeled 'for discussion purposes only' dated 2 April 1998, p. 17.
4.   Andrew S. Natsios, *U.S. Foreign Policy and the Four Horsemen of the Apocalypse. Humanitarian Relief in Complex Emergencies* (Westport CT: Praeger, 1997), pp. 77–8.

Index

Index